Understanding Social Policy

Seventh Edition

Michael Hill

350 Main Street, Malden, MA 02148–5018, USA
108 Cowley Road, Oxford OX4 1JF, UK
550 Swanston Street, Carlton, Victoria 3053, Australia
Kurfürstendamm 57, 10707 Berlin, Germany

The right of Michael Hill to be identified as the Author of this Work has been asserted in accordance with the UK Copyright, Designs, and Patents Act 1988.

First edition published 1980 by Blackwell Publishing and
Martin Robertson & Co. Ltd
Second edition published 1983
Third edition published 1988
Fourth edition published 1993
Fifth edition published 1997
Sixth edition published 2000
Seventh edition published 2003 by Blackwell Publishing Ltd,
a Blackwell Publishing company

Library of Congress Cataloging-in-Publication Data
Hill, Michael J. (Michael James), 1937–
Understanding social policy / Michael Hill.— 7th ed.
p. cm.
Includes bibliographical references and index.
ISBN 1-4051-0057-5 (pbk.)
1. Great Britain—Social policy. 2. Welfare state. 3. Welfare economics. I. Title.
HN390 .H52 2003
361.6′1′0941—dc21

2002014971

ISBN 1-4051-0057-5 (paperback)

A catalogue record for this title is available from the British Library.

Set in 10 on 12 pt Sabon
by SetSystems Ltd, Saffron Walden, Essex
Printed and bound in the United Kingdom
by MPG Books Ltd, Bodmin, Cornwall

For further information on
Blackwell Publishing, visit our website:
http://www.blackwellpublishing.com

Contents

7 Health Policy 155

8 The Personal Social Services 180

9 Education 201

Preface to the Seventh Edition

This book is an introduction to the study of social policy. It is based on the view that those who study this subject need to consider the way in which policy is made and implemented, as well as to learn about the main policies and their limitations. It has been written for people who have had no previous training in the social sciences, with the needs of social workers, nurses, health visitors and other social policy 'practitioners' very much in mind, as well as those of undergraduates.

The preparation of the sixth edition of this book involved a substantial revision to take into account the impact of the election in 1997 of a Labour government led by Tony Blair. This seventh edition, completed a year after the government was re-elected, takes that analysis further. That government claims to be engaged in a radical reform programme led by a philosophy which departs, in a 'third way', from the positions adopted by both the old Left and the new Right. In examining, and setting out the details of, the innovations that are occurring in almost all areas of social policy, this book critically examines that claim. It shows that much that is changing can only be explained in terms of the way in which the government is building on previous policy. It also suggests that some of the boldest claims made by the government, particularly those which concern the new role labour-market participation is expected to play in social welfare, need to be viewed with considerable scepticism.

Another feature of the period of Labour rule since 2002 has been the restless re-examination of organizational arrangements for policy delivery. That too was a characteristic of much of the previous period of Conservative rule. Since the first edition of this book was completed in 1979 it has become much harder to describe the social policy system. Where once there were relatively straightforward hierarchical structures, there are now many alternative arrangements ostensibly to facilitate partnership and collaboration or to allow for customer choice. Yet the top–down control aspirations of central government have not been abandoned, rather the control techniques have become more complex too. In this book efforts have been made to convey to readers the main features of the policy systems, without getting too complicated. This means inevitably that many institutions get only a very brief mention. Some phenomena are ignored since they involve small-scale developments, though crucial enough for those who are involved, and perhaps harbingers of further key initiatives. Difficult judgements have been made here; sometimes simplicity just has to take precedence over comprehensiveness. In the end the concern has been to convey a picture of the system that bears some relationship to what most people who are involved – as practitioners or customers – are experiencing most of the time.

The book gives sharper attention than ever before to some of the issues about how the social policy system affects different people, with particular regard to 'social divisions' in respect of socio-economic status, gender and ethnic origin. This is given special attention in the last part of the last chapter. The penultimate chapter is also a new addition, a brief consideration of UK social policy in comparative perspective.

At this stage in the history of a textbook, it is impossible to acknowledge satisfactorily all the people who have helped to shape the author's approach. However, special thanks are due to Sarah Falkus, at Blackwell Publishing, who played a particularly helpful role in the planning of this edition, consulting the market extensively, and Valery Rose for her help with the final preparation of the book.

Thanks are due to John Hudson for his comments on the whole manuscript and to Jamie Harding, Helen Jones and Adrian Sinfield who have offered helpful comments on parts of the draft book. The book remains dedicated to my wife Betty who, when she was a health visitor student, first helped me to identify the gap in the market. As usual, she has helped with the preparation of the book, collecting relevant material and reading the final draft.

M.H.

Chapter 1

What is Social Policy?

- Introduction
- Which policies?
- Conclusions: studying social policy
- Suggestions for further reading

Introduction

This is a book about social policy in the United Kingdom (UK). Social policy is defined as 'actions aimed at promoting social well-being' (Alcock in Alcock et al., 1998, p. 7). Other definitions often use 'welfare' as a synonym for 'well-being'. While non-state bodies may be described as having 'policies', a generic expression like 'social policy' is primarily used to define the role of the state in relation to the welfare of its citizens. That is how it is used in this book.

However, this usage raises two key questions:

1 Since the welfare of citizens is affected by their own actions and by the actions of others, what is it about the role of the state in relation to welfare that is different?
2 What are the kinds of actions which have an impact on welfare?

One, perhaps simpler, way to answer the question 'What is social policy?' is to provide a list of the areas of public policy included under that heading. However, the issues identified above cannot be ignored altogether. It is necessary to look a little at the rationale for the policy areas chosen. In doing so, this chapter will also throw some light on some of the main concerns of the study of social policy.

Which Policies?

The policy areas covered in this book are set out in the titles of chapters 5–10. The chapters (5, 7 and 8) on social security, health and the personal social services deal with policy areas that everyone seems to include within their definition of social policy. Chapter 6, which looks at employment policy, examines a topic on which actual government expenditure is very low by comparison with the other areas of social policy. Consideration is given there to some very important issues for the study of social policy, about the role of government management of the economy and intervention in the labour market, with implications not only for other areas of social policy but for social welfare in general. Issues about the impact of economic policy and the relevance of economic and commercial considerations arise in chapter 10, which looks at housing policy. Most books and courses on social policy deal with housing, though varying in how far they are concerned with the private sector. There are important questions in relation to housing policy that concern the extent to which a free market can operate in relation to the private sector, and the extent to which housing which is publicly subsidized can be managed as if it were a private business concern. While employment and housing are two policy areas where social and economic issues are particularly mingled together, they are not alone; social issues arise, for example, in relation to many aspects of environment policy and transport policy. While environment policy does not have a specific chapter, some aspects of it are discussed in chapter 7.

A chapter on education policy is included in this book (chapter 9). Often, this is not examined by social policy texts. The fact that it is difficult to find reasons either for including it or for excluding it tells us something about the peculiarly arbitrary process involved in categorizing policies as 'social'. Clearly, the field of education is one in which there is a considerable amount of public expenditure on services that contribute to public welfare. So, is the hallmark of social policy expenditure its contribution to public welfare, and what does this really mean? If education policy is included, why not also include leisure policy or environment policy? In fact, the inclusion of education, and the exclusion of leisure and the environment, are the consequence of a comparatively arbitrary decision based on a conventional view of the limits to social policy which is clearly open to challenge; see Cahill (1994, 2002) and Huby (1998) for such a challenge.

Another omission from this book is a chapter on policies concerned with the prevention of crime, which are obviously important for welfare. The decision not to include that has been influenced by the fact that criminology and criminal justice are topics with a large specialist literature, often given attention in separate courses run alongside, or as specialist options within, social policy courses.

The introduction to this chapter mentioned one of the problems about a straightforward definition of social policy which equates it with state activity to influence public welfare: namely, that it is important not to let this lead to the false assumption that it is *only* state activity which influences or promotes welfare. However, there is another problem. To see policies as having objectives involves confusing the character of the policies with the motives and purposes of the people who advocate, adopt and implement them. Policies proclaimed to be 'social' may advance welfare; but they may also be instruments for securing other objectives, which may be detrimental to people's well-being.

Several influential discussions of social policy have suggested that welfare policies are promulgated not from humanitarian concerns to meet need, but as responses to social unrest. Piven and Cloward, for example, argue about social security policies (Piven and Cloward, 1972, p. xiii): 'The key to an understanding of relief-giving is in the functions it serves for the larger economic and political order, for relief is a secondary and supportive institution.' Other writers have analysed social policy in similar terms. In particular, Marxists have argued that advanced capitalist societies require an infrastructure of welfare policies to help in maintaining order, buying off working-class protest and securing a workforce with acceptable standards of health and education; see, for example, O'Connor (1973) and Gough (1979). Other radical analyses of social policy have shown that social policy may sustain not only class-based patterns of domination, but also patriarchy and racial inequality (F. Williams, 1989).

Clearly, perspectives like these give a very different meaning to 'welfare'. Policies that promote welfare are explained in terms of social control; they are measures to combat disorder and crime, just like policing and penal policies, or measures to legitimize and prop up the capitalist system. It is not necessary to accept totally this interpretation of public policy to agree that there may be circumstances under which social control motives mingle with humanitarian motives in creating what we describe as 'social policies'. Moreover, the more extreme interpretations of the origins of social policies that have been mentioned do not exhaust the range of possibilities. Contemporary studies of both policy making and policy implementation suggest that we need to give attention to some very complex relationships between the mixed goals of those able to influence policies and the varied consequences of their interventions. Outcomes may be the unintended results of policy inputs. Most policy is incremental in character, involving marginal adjustments to what has gone before and being motivated to correct what are seen as undesirable consequences of previous policies. Accordingly, social policy need not be interpreted in terms either of the continual evolution of a welfare state inspired by humanitarian ideals or of a conspiracy to manipulate a powerless proletariat. Yet the rejection of these interpretations need not imply either that individuals with altruistic motives play no part in the evolution of policy, or that manipulative and social-control-motivated actions are not involved in the policy process (see the essays by Clarke and Page in May, Page and Brunsdon (2001) for a further exploration of these issues).

This discussion implies three things for the definition of social policy:

1 the policies that are identified as 'social' should not be interpreted as if they were conceived and implemented with only the welfare of the public in mind;
2 other policies, not conventionally identified as social policies, may make a comparable, or even greater, contribution to welfare;
3 public policy should be seen as a whole in which social policies are significantly interlinked with other policies.

Just because it is convenient to single out some policies for special attention, and just because there are courses on social policy that require the study of a specific and limited range of public policies, we should not fall into the trap of seeing these as the main government contributions to welfare, or the 'general good'. Let us look at the implications of these arguments a little more by examining the implications, for welfare and for social policy, of developments in those important areas that no one defines as social policy: foreign and defence policy, and economic policy.

It is important to recognize that the origins of the modern nation-state lie in the achievement of a monopoly of force within a given territory. The central preoccupations of the government of any insecure nation are with the defence of its boundaries, the recognition of its integrity by other nations, and the maintenance of order within its territories. It is only too easy for British students of public policy to lose sight of the importance of these issues. They are the daily fare of our news bulletins, but we rarely stop to think about their relevance for our own state. English incomprehension over events in Northern Ireland and a propensity to underestimate the intensity of the feelings of some people in Scotland on the issue of devolution stem from a tendency to take the integrity and security of the nation for granted. Yet, without a secure nation-state the scope for development of what is conventionally identified as social policy is severely limited.

These facts have three implications for the study of social policy:

1 Social policy expenditure has to compete with other public expenditure dedicated to the defence of the realm. The case against heavy defence expenditure cannot rest simply on arguments that some of the money would be better spent on social policy; it is necessary to prove that some of that expenditure is

inappropriate or irrelevant, or to face the argument that, without it, no social policy would be secure.

2   The forms of this defence expenditure have a wide range of social effects in creating employment, disrupting family life and so on. Readers may like to think about the type of policy interactions involved by asking themselves what would be the effects on social life and social policy of the reintroduction of a two-year period of compulsory national service. The important effects they should be able to identify will nevertheless be insignificant by comparison with the effects of mobilization for war itself.

3   While social policies do not have much of an impact on relations with other states, it is important not to lose sight of the contribution they make to integration and harmony within the nation. It is this that has led students of social policy to draw attention to the significant impact of war on policy. Thus Titmuss (1958, p. 86) argued: 'The aims and content of social policy, both in peace and in war, are thus determined – at least to a substantial extent – by how far the co-operation of the masses is essential to the successful prosecution of war.'

The development of the role of the UK state in the nineteenth and twentieth centuries is often portrayed as the establishment of 'the welfare state'. To present it in this way is to emphasize social policy developments. However, it is perhaps more important to give attention to the growth of the UK economy over that period, and to the role played by government in relation to that economy. Two apparently conflicting political interpretations of these events lead us to ask some broadly similar questions about the relationship between social policy and economic policy.

To the followers of the 'classical economists', who argued that the economy would make the greatest possible contribution to public welfare if competition were to remain unshackled, the period between the middle of the nineteenth century and early in the twenty-first has been marked by extensive government interference with the economy. Some of this interference has been seen as necessary, where competition has been impossible or illogical. Some of it has been seen as justifiable, because it seeks to ensure competition and prevent monopoly. Much of it has been regarded as stemming from forces eager to interfere with and undermine the market economy, shifting the locus of decision from the market-place to the political arena.

Theorists influenced by Marxism, on the other hand, interpret the same evidence the other way round. They argue that as the industrial economy has grown, so the 'contradictions of capitalism' have increased. Government intervention has been prompted in their view by a desire to save capitalism, not by a desire to undermine it. Regulation has been introduced to prevent the logic of competition from destroying the system. State interventions to protect the working class have been designed, according to this view, to stave off revolution and to help the capitalist system to survive. Late capitalist society, it is argued, experiences a form of 'welfare capitalism' in which those who originally gained so much from competitive industry are still dominant in our society.

Both these views of the relationship between government and the economy stress the extent to which social policy should be seen as dependent on, or even a derivative of, economic policy. The key internal political issues of our age are: who controls our economy, and how the rewards that stem from our industrial achievements are to be distributed. These are the implications for social policy:

1   The main determinants of welfare are economic.
2   The government's role in diverting resources into social policies must be seen to be closely interrelated with – even dependent on – the role it plays in the management of the economy.
3   Social policies will be determined by views about the way the economy does, or should, operate. Specific social policies need, therefore, to be understood in terms of their relationships to economic policies.

Here are some examples of important questions frequently asked about social policy which are essentially about the relationship between social and economic policy:

•   Are social security policies redistributive?
•   How does any redistribution by this mechanism compare with redistribution that occurs through other economic mechanisms – the effects of competition, the impact of unemployment and the results of wage bargaining, for example?
•   How do social policies, particularly social security policies, affect the labour market?
•   What are the effects of public housing on the housing market? How far are market forces in this area more influential than state intervention in determining who lives in what housing?

It is important to take a wide view of social policy development, relating it to economic policy. Social policy expenditure amounts to about two-thirds of all public expenditure. To what extent are there limits to the growth of public expenditure in a mixed economy, and therefore what impact may such limits (or the belief that there are such limits) have on social policy expenditure? Similarly, what is the impact on the economy, and also on the whole political system, of the pattern of employment that has emerged as social policy has become 'big business'? Unlike those stressed above, these are questions about the impact of social policy on economic policy, rather than the other way round. Nevertheless, the key decisions about resources for the social policy sector will be regarded as economic policy decisions.

It has been suggested, then, that, while certain policy areas, (subject to a few difficult boundary problems) are defined as social policy, any proper understanding of the forces that determine outcomes in these areas must rest on considerations of other policies not included within the conventional social policy rubric.

However, the introductory comment on the definition of social policy also indicated that the state is not the only body that may have 'policies', and that social welfare depends on much more than state action. Our welfare depends also on our own actions, our job opportunities, the support we enjoy from families and friends, and on the activities of a range of non-state institutions (churches, charities, community organizations, trade unions and so on). An examination of (state) social policy, as in this book, must have regard to the things the state does to support or interfere with these other sources of social welfare. Much ideological debate about social policy is about what the state should or should not do to influence the activities of individuals as economic actors, to affect the roles played by families or to alter the legal framework within which voluntary organizations operate. While the ideological 'colour' of much of that debate derives from alternative views about the management of the economy, considerations regarding the implications of policies (or their absence) for gender and ethnic divisions in society are also important.

CONCLUSIONS: STUDYING SOCIAL POLICY

Social policy may be studied in a number of ways. We may merely set out to determine the main policies in the areas in which we are interested; for example:

- What is the system of social security?
- What benefits does the health service provide?
- How has the government intervened in the housing market?

These and similar questions need to be answered by those who want to understand social policy. They can also be related to many other points about the way the services are organized and administered. Hence, the simplest approach to the study of social policy is to describe the policies and institutions that together comprise the system of social services.

Many accounts of the system of social policy include comments on the strengths and weaknesses of specific policies. They relate what there is to what, in the authors' views, there ought to be. The study of social policy, as it has developed in the UK, has been concerned to examine the extent to which the welfare state meets people's needs. Often, indeed, students of social policy go further, and explicitly analyse the extent to which it contributes to social equality. In this sense, an academic discipline has been developed with an explicitly political stance. Social policy is seen as concerned with the alleviation of social ills; its objectives are accepted at face value; and it is analysed in terms of its success in achieving them. Many who have written about social policy have done so from the standpoint of Fabian socialism, concerned with incremental social change to create a more equal society. Few challenged this perspective until the 1980s, when Conservative political thinking shifted sharply to the 'right', to express much more directly suspicion of the claims of the state to regulate many aspects of our lives and to portray welfare policy as a threat to economic enterprise.

In this edition, considerable attention will be given to the impact of the Labour government elected in 1997. It will be shown to have developed an approach to social policy that does not involve a return to the Fabian perspective. Many Conservative initiatives from the 1980s have been modified, but not entirely transformed. Is this new Labourism another version of 'new right' thinking, or is a distinctive 'third way' being developed which is taking British social policy into hitherto uncharted territory? (See Powell, 1999, and Glennerster in Seldon, 2001, for discussions of this issue.) It is not appropriate to try to answer this question at this stage, but the discussion of the various new initiatives in social policy will provide some of the data needed to provide an answer, to which we will return in the final chapter.

There has been an extensive debate among social scientists about the extent to which the analysis of society and of social institutions can be 'value-free'. Broadly, there is today a consensus that there are limits to the extent to which those who study and write about society can set aside their own commitments and prejudices. Some go on to argue, however, that value-freedom within the social sciences as a whole may be achieved by the interplay of arguments and evidence, each biased in different ways but contributing to the advancement of unbiased knowledge as a whole. Others are more sceptical about the extent to which a body of systematic unbiased knowledge can be created, and argue that the value problem is ubiquitous. The study of social policy has been particularly conspicuous for the specific political or value commitments of those who write about it.

The strong normative bias in the study of social policy has led at times to a greater preoccupation with criticism of policies than with attempts to discover why they take the forms they do. In practice, if one believes that policies are wrong or ineffective, it is important to understand why this is so, particularly if one's objective is to change them. The view that it is sufficient to point out that policies are 'wrong' is often linked with a view of policy making according to which men and women of good will are believed to be responsible and anxious to rectify the unwitting mistakes made in the past. This approach to the understanding of the policy system was criticized on pp. 3–4.

At this stage, as an author who is arguing that the study of social policy in the UK has been strong on criticism and value-judgement, but weak on analysis, I should make my position clear. Since I believe that students may be aided in drawing their own conclusions if writers make their own value biases explicit, it is particularly important to do this. I should not pretend that my personal motivation in studying social policy is not linked with a commitment to non-revolutionary movement towards social equality. However, I feel strongly that a concern to influence the content of social policy must be supported by an understanding of how social policy is made. In this book, therefore, I am concerned with what social policy is, how it was created and how it was implemented, as well as with its weaknesses and arguments about what it should be. I think it very important to see social policy in its political environment. These consider-ations lead me to be sceptical about 'new Labour', but to have some sympathy for the constraints facing the government as it sets out to tackle social policy issues.

An understanding of the factors that influence the character of social policy must rest on several foundations. Some attention must be given to the social and economic conditions that create the need for social policies. This is a difficult chicken-and-egg issue. One cannot simply look at the kinds of problems found in particular social structures and economic situations and analyse policies as responses to those problems, since policies themselves influence the character of the societies in which they are adopted. For example, government provision of housing may be seen as a response to the inadequacies of the market as a provider of houses, but it also transformed the character of that market. Interactions between policies and society are complex. It is important, therefore, to draw on economics and sociology to help with the understanding of what occurs. It is also necessary to keep in mind the historical dimensions to these issues.

Social policy making must also be seen as a political process. It has already been stressed that social policy cannot be analysed on its own, without reference to other activities of the state. Policies must be under-stood as products of politics, and attention must be given to the policy-creation roles of politicians, civil servants, pressure groups and the electorate. Policies must also be seen as, to a considerable extent, products of other policies. There is a cumulative process to be analysed in which policies create needs for more policies, opportunities for other policies, and new social situations for further political responses. It will be clear that to understand social policy, considerable attention must be given to the findings of political science.

An often-neglected part of the study of policy is the examination of its implementation. The actual impact of any policy on the public will depend on how it is interpreted and put into practice. The implementation process throws light on the strengths and weaknesses of a policy, and experience at the implementation end (by junior officials and the public) is fed back into the policy process to influence future policy changes. An understanding of these issues requires the student of social policy to give some attention to organization theory and to the study of administrative law.

A particular characteristic of a state in which extensive social policies have been adopted is that it tends to be bureaucratic. The organizational complexity of such a state necessarily complicates the implementation process. Recent interventions in UK social policy have involved the design of new approaches to policy delivery which aim to break out of the traditional bureaucratic approach, creating more flexible organizations and new kinds of public/private partnerships (Newman, 2001). A discourse has developed, which we will revisit in chapter 4, about the extent to which there is no longer 'government' directly implementing its policies, but a more complex process of 'governance' in which there are many participants.

The portrait of the study of social policy as presented in the last few paragraphs shows that it is a subject that draws on a number of different academic disciplines. The problem of defining the extent to which it is necessary to delve into these disciplines is like the problem discussed earlier of ascertaining the boundaries between social policy and other kinds of public policy. There is a need to make what we can of an essentially applied subject, hoping that we can gain what is required from other disciplines without going too deeply into them. The boundaries between all the social sciences are unclear. Sometimes, this is a necessary feature of subjects that put some parts of the human experience under the microscope and so must abstract these from other parts. In other cases, it is a result of historical accidents in the development of the disciplines, and if the study of society were to be initiated all over again, it would surely be divided rather differently. The study of social policy particularly, hives off a specific area of social activity in a way that must violate subject boundaries. If it is important to understand a number of practical policies, because of a concern about their effects on society, it is necessary to accept studies that cannot be defined in terms of a discrete intellectual discipline.

In setting out to examine what social policy is, and how it may be studied, some answers have been suggested to the question 'Why study it?' Many who are required to study social policy are, or expect to be, involved in its implementation. The part of a social policy course that is concerned with describing and analysing policies and the institutions responsible for them has a clear face value to the social policy 'practitioner'. Equally, it is important for such a person to understand something of the way in which social policy works, and the internal and external forces that shape policies.

It may also help to understand other agencies to which a 'practitioner' has to relate, particularly as a great deal of policy depends, or is intended to depend, on successful co-operation between organizations. It has been stressed that no policy area is discrete, that policies in one area affect those in others. This is particularly true of social policies, whose impact on the public depends on the way they interrelate. Successful treatment of the sick requires attention to housing and income-maintenance problems; the care of the neglected child depends on co-operation between health service workers, personal social services staff and schoolteachers; the homeless often face income-maintenance problems as well as housing problems; and so on – the examples are legion.

Hence, the most obvious case for studying social policy is a need for the staff of the various social services to understand the system in which they operate, but that is not all. A characteristic of many of the people who are drawn to work in the social services is a strong commitment to those services. Therefore, it is not surprising that the study of social policy has been deeply concerned with the improvement of policies. Many staff care considerably about the inadequacies of the policies they administer. Yet, achieving policy change is never an easy process, particularly if one is a comparatively junior participant in a large organization. To make a contribution towards this end requires not only knowledge of alternatives and commitment to putting them into practice, but also an understanding of how social policy is made and implemented.

These arguments for studying social policy have been addressed to people likely to be employed in delivering benefits and services. I say 'employed'– however, as has been noted, recent changes to social policy have increased the extent to which private and voluntary organizations are involved in the delivery of social policy. As noted on p. 7, they have also made it evident that many social welfare services are not delivered by state agencies, but are left to the slender resources of families, neighbourhoods and communities. Hence this is a book for all concerned citizens who want to influence social policy. Its underlying justification is that participation in policy making, for a group of services of considerable importance to us all, must rest on understanding: understanding of what the policies are, of how they are made and implemented, and of the implications of the many prevailing suggestions on how to change those policies.

SUGGESTIONS FOR FURTHER READING

A deeper exploration of the rather arid debate regarding the boundaries of this subject is not recommended. However, Cahill's *The New Social Policy* (1994) offers a valuable survey of the ways in which the traditional concerns of social policy analysis might be widened.

A good introduction to the key issues about social policy is to investigate the various ideological perspectives on its role in society. George and Wilding's *Welfare and Ideology* (1994) offers an excellent overview of this subject. Lois Bryson's *Welfare and the State* (1992) and Fiona Williams's *Social Policy* (1989) offer introductions to the ideological debate, with a strong emphasis on the need to take into account issues about gender, class and race. Issues about the relationship between social problems and social policy are explored in May, Page and Brunsdon (2001). An overview of the whole field of social policy is offered in an edited volume by Alcock, Erskine and May (eds), *The Student's Companion to Social Policy* (1998, second edition due 2003). Alcock, Erskine and May have also produced a valuable reference book, *The Blackwell Dictionary of Social Policy* (2002).

The Social Policy Association has a good website with many links to other useful sites at www.york.ac.uk/depts/spsw/spa. There is also a government website that provides a gateway to sites for individual departments, agencies, local authorities and some international organizations at www.ukonline.gov.uk.

Chapter 2

The History of Social Policy

- Introduction
- Developments before the twentieth century
- 1900–39: an emergent welfare state?
- 1940–51: laying the foundations of the UK's modern system of social policy
- 1951–79: consolidation and modification
- 1979–97: the UK welfare state in crisis?
- 1997–2001: back from the crisis?
- Suggestions for further reading

Introduction

This chapter deals with some of the key events in the development of social policy in the United Kingdom (UK), relating them to social, economic and political trends in our society. To understand the character of social policy in the UK today, it is important to have a historical perspective, particularly on the relationship between social and political change.

At one level, the story is simple. The growth of state involvement with the social welfare of its citizens can be related to the development of an industrial society, and its subsequent maturation, or perhaps decline, into what some writers have described as 'post-industrialism'. Alongside this industrial development are political developments associated with the extension of the suffrage, involving citizens more thoroughly in the activities of the state. Accompanying these are changes to social life, particularly family life; and changing views of the respective responsibilities of the individual, the family, voluntary organizations and the state, for remedies to social problems. The result is a package of developments – of the state's role, the character of the economy, the nature of political processes and of ideologies – which those without a dogmatic belief about the motive forces in political development find difficult to disentangle in cause–effect terms.

This version of the story of the development of the state's role in social welfare can be applied to a number of industrialized nations – to the USA, to most of the other countries of western and northern Europe and to Australasia – as much as to the UK; this theme has been widely analysed (Ashford, 1986; Esping-Andersen, 1990; Hill, 1996). However, while these 'broad brush' features of the story must not be forgotten, it is important also to try to single out characteristics of the UK's development that help to explain the particular shape of its own social policies. A proper understanding of this subject requires consideration of the general factors which may apply to a distinct group of nations; the special factors, which are perhaps unique to one nation; and furthermore, a number of factors that do not fall neatly into either of these categories. Included in this last group is, for example, the 'insurance principle' in social security, adopted in a variety of ways by various governments who clearly attempted to learn from each other's experiences (Heclo, 1974; Baldwin, 1990).

Developments before the Twentieth Century

In dealing with the relationship between past events and contemporary policies, it is always difficult to know how far back to go in time. To understand social policies in the UK, some consideration of the history of the Poor Law, with its roots in Elizabethan legislation, is necessary. The Tudor age saw considerable population movements, with changes in agriculture, the growth of towns and some rudimentary developments in manufacturing. The government found it necessary to try to impose a centrally determined framework on what had hitherto been entirely local, and often monastic, charitable initiatives. It placed responsibility for the poor on each parish, with the requirement, under the Acts of Settlement, that the itinerant poor should be returned, if necessary, to their parishes of origin. The parishes were required to levy taxes on property known as 'rates', to provide for the relief of the poor.

The history of the Poor Law between the sixteenth and twentieth centuries was one of attempts to make this work despite social changes. As the UK became industrialized and urbanized, this strictly local system of administration came under strain. Population movements gradually rendered the Acts of Settlement obsolete. The tasks of the Poor Law became more costly and more complex as parishes had to cope with, for example, trade recessions and outbreaks of infectious diseases, each affecting large numbers of people in the new towns and cities.

The most significant nineteenth-century attempt to modernize the Poor Law was the Poor Law Amendment Act of 1834. This set up a national Poor Law Commission to superintend the system, and formed the parishes into groups known as Poor Law unions. This important step towards the development of a national system provoked local opposition and was only a limited success. However, its main contributions to the development of policy were the 'workhouse test' and the doctrine of 'less eligibility'. The aims of these were to curb indiscriminate 'outdoor' relief, i.e. outside institutions. If the poor were not sufficiently desperate to enter the workhouse, they could not be really in need. The system was intended to ensure that those who received help were worse off ('less eligible') than the poorest people in work. In practice, many Poor Law unions did not strictly enforce the workhouse test and, as the years passed, the elderly and the sick were increasingly given outdoor relief. Nevertheless, the elimination of the workhouse – and the abolition of the means test adopted to confine relief giving – became an important preoccupation of twentieth-century critics of the Poor Law. The principle of less eligibility continues to influence decisions about relief today.

While the basic nineteenth-century response to poverty was to try to strengthen older institutions, some of the consequences of urbanization and industrialization posed problems for which entirely new responses were necessary. Measures were taken to curb the hours worked by women and children in factories, and to improve safety and working conditions. This significant development in state intervention in the economy seems to have come about as a result of a mixture of growing humanitarian concern and embryonic working-class pressure. The enforcement of this legislation was put into the hands of a central government inspectorate, the first of a number of such inspectorates to be set up in the nineteenth century and one that operated, according to Roberts (1960), as an important source of pressure for further social reform.

The rapid spread of infection in areas where people were crowded together was – like the exploitation of child labour – not a new phenomenon, but in an increasingly urbanized society it took new forms which were more apparent to political opinion, and more threatening to life and industry; and there were growing numbers of large populous areas devoid of the most elementary arrangements for disposing of waste or supplying pure water. Furthermore, it was only in the nineteenth century that scientific advance identified the main links between insanitary conditions and disease. In a few areas, local government agencies took some steps to tackle this problem, but real progress did not come until central government gave local authorities powers to act effectively, and also required them to take such action.

Here, then, was an important area of government intervention, pushing local authorities to tackle some of the problems of their own areas. The local government system of the time had been given some shape by the Municipal Corporations Act of 1835, but it was not until the end of the century that it acquired a structure that would enable it to take on the range of functions it carries out today. In the nineteenth century, therefore, some reforms required local authorities to take action and to employ professional staff, such as the medical officers of health required by an Act of 1871. Others, however, set up *ad hoc* authorities to take on functions delegated by central government.

The evolution of state education during the nineteenth century provides a good example of a series of *ad hoc* responses. Religious societies had begun to become involved in the provision of cheap basic education for the children of the poor early in the century. By 1833, they had persuaded the government to provide a small grant towards this work. In 1839, the government set up an inspectorate to provide central supervision of the way the increasing state aid was being spent. It was not until 1870, however, that the government moved effectively into the provision of primary education. Motivated, it is widely believed, by a concern about the illiteracy of the growing electorate (the franchise had been considerably widened in 1867), but also undoubtedly by a recognition of a need for a better-educated workforce, Parliament provided that school boards (which set up state-financed schools), could be established where there was a clear educational need and where the voluntary schools were insufficient in number. In 1880, a further Education Act made schooling compulsory for children between the ages of five and ten, and in the 1890s it was established that most elementary education should be free. During the last years of the century, some of the school boards even became involved in secondary education, producing a confused pattern of educational growth that was to prompt government action at the beginning of the twentieth century.

Developments in medicine began, in the late nineteenth century, to render inadequate the traditional Poor Law approach to the care of the sick. Alongside the development of Poor Law hospitals, many voluntary hospitals, assisted by charitable funds that enabled them to provide cheap or free services to the poor, were founded, or grew in strength from their earlier origins. The local authorities were also given powers to establish hospitals to fulfil their duties to contain infectious diseases, and to care for mentally ill people. Medical care outside the hospitals grew in importance in the second half of the century, becoming more than the prerogative of the rich. This was partly a Poor Law development, partly the extension of the services of the voluntary hospitals, and partly an aspect of the growth of insurance against misfortune, widely practised by the more prosperous of the working classes. In all, a mixed package of health care measures was evolving. This complex mixture, dominated by a powerful medical profession firmly established during the nineteenth century, posed problems for subsequent attempts to rationalize the health services, and therefore influenced the shape the National Health Service (NHS) eventually achieved.

The dominant view amongst the governing classes in the last part of the nineteenth century was that state involvement in dealing with social issues and problems should be kept to a minimum. Middle-class concern about the state of the poorer classes, stimulated by worries about their impact upon the better off (the spread of disease, the rise in crime etc.), was particularly channelled into charitable activity. There was a substantial growth of voluntary organizations concerned to rescue children, improve housing conditions, teach the poor how to manage their family lives, and even to offer cash relief. Many middle-class women, still shut out from most opportunities for formal employment, involved themselves in this charitable activity. As a result of this work some of the more prosperous people became more aware of the reality of working-class life. For some this generated a commitment to more radical government action. But this increased awareness of social problems also led to efforts to try to ensure that charitable work was better organized, able to effectively distinguish the 'deserving' from the 'undeserving'.

Nevertheless, by the end of the nineteenth century the factory legislation, and the government intervention in the cause of health and safety, implied important changes in the role of the state. The educational system at the primary (or, as it was known then, the elementary) level had received a crucial injection of public provision. The Poor Law, on the other hand, had been changed but little. A need for new policies in that area was just beginning to become apparent at the end of the century, as social surveys (Booth, 1889; Rowntree, 1901) and journalistic investigations charted the existence of severe problems of poverty caused by factors – in particular sickness and old age – largely outside individual control.

It was stated earlier that the agencies set up during the nineteenth century to implement social policies were often *ad hoc* bodies. While local government was responsible for public health, and for the rudimentary planning, housing and hospital functions required to help to achieve more sanitary urban areas, education was made the responsibility of separately elected school boards. The Poor Law came under yet another kind of authority, the boards of guardians, descendants of the former parish officials. However, legislation late in the century provided a new local government structure much better able to take on a wide range of functions. Local Government Acts in 1888 and 1894 set up a system of local authorities that was to remain almost unchanged until the 1970s. They gave a shape to local government, with a split between the highly urbanized areas and the rest of the country, which dominates local politics to this day. The less urbanized areas acquired a two-tier system of county government, accompanied by lower-tier urban and rural districts. In many urban areas, county boroughs were set up as single all-purpose authorities. London acquired a special two-tier system of its own.

It is convenient, for the presentation of historical accounts, when a specific date can be identified as a watershed. It further adds neatness when that date is the beginning of a century. While there is always an arbitrary aspect to the choice of such dates, particularly in social history, the dividing point between the nineteenth and twentieth centuries seems a particularly significant one. At this time, the large working-class male element added to the electorate in 1885 was just beginning to influence political thinking. The Labour Representation Committee was set up in 1899 to try to elect more working men to Parliament. This body was to turn itself into the Labour Party in 1906. The major political parties, the Conservatives and the Liberals, were increasingly aware of the need to compete for working-class support. For the Conservatives, the formula was an interesting blend of imperialism and social reform (Semmel, 1961). The Liberals had a radical wing, temporarily disadvantaged by the conflict over home rule for Ireland and the jingoism of the Boer War, but ready to push the party towards acceptance of a package of new social measures.

Late in the nineteenth century, the UK had begun to discover that an advanced industrial nation is vulnerable to alarming economic fluctuations, owing to the uncoordinated nature of much business decision making and the international complications of the trade cycle. New competitors had also emerged as other nations – particularly Germany and the USA – industrialized rapidly. The Empire still looked secure, but the competition for new trading outlets was increasing dramatically. At the same time as doubts were beginning to be felt about the UK's economic vulnerability, working people were increasingly organizing in trade unions to try to secure, or guarantee, their share of the progress. The political price of economic failure was being raised. New initiatives to preserve the unity of the nation were required.

1900–39: an Emergent Welfare State?

The period immediately before World War I was dominated by a series of reforms adopted by the Liberal government after 1906. However, before those reforms are considered, two earlier events require comment. In 1902, the Conservative government passed an important Education Act. This shifted the responsibility for state education from the school boards to the county and county borough councils, and devised a formula for the financial support of the church schools that preserved a measure of voluntary control. The other important feature of this Act was that it legitimized expenditure on secondary and technical schools, and thereby stimulated the growth of this element of state education.

The other significant event was the Boer War. This rather inglorious episode in British imperial history had a considerable significance for social policy. In general, it led to a concern to examine what was wrong with *Great* Britain that she should have been unable to fight effectively against apparently fragile opposition. In particular, politicians, in this age when Britain's imperial success was believed to have been based on racial superiority, sought to examine why so many volunteers to fight had been found to be unfit to do so.

An Interdepartmental Committee on Physical Deterioration was set up. It reported in 1904, urging the establishment of a school medical service and the provision of school meals within the public education system. Both these measures were adopted by the Liberals and implemented soon after they came to power.

Before they lost office, the Conservatives also responded to the growing evidence on the extent of poverty, and the inadequacies of existing measures, by setting up a Royal Commission on the Poor Laws in 1905. The report of this body, which did not appear until 1909, contains a most thorough discussion of social policy at that time. There was both a majority and a minority report, and the latter provided a well-argued critique of the system. However, without waiting for the Royal Commission, the Liberal government decided to promote two pieces of legislation that significantly modified the role of the Poor Law in the provision of social security, the Old Age Pensions Act of 1908 and the National Insurance Act of 1911.

These two measures provide interesting contrasts in approaches to the provision of social security. The old age pension was non-contributory and based on a simple test of means. It was an extension of the outdoor relief given by some boards of guardians, but its means test was a personal and not a family one. The National Insurance (NI) scheme, on the other hand, was contributory but not means-tested. It provided cover against sickness and unemployment for some, initially limited, categories of workers. The contributions were to come jointly from employees, employers and the state. The sickness scheme provided not just cash benefits but also medical treatment from a 'panel' doctor, who was remunerated on a 'capitation basis' depending on the number of patients on his or her panel. The Friendly Societies and insurance companies, who were already involved in the provision of sickness cover for many working people, were allowed to participate as agents for the scheme and providers of additional benefits. The scheme protected only employees themselves, not any members of their families.

The National Insurance Act is most important for introducing the 'insurance principle' into UK social security legislation. A number of European countries had adopted state or municipal insurance schemes during the last years of the nineteenth century. The UK policy makers were particularly aware of German social insurance (Heclo, 1974, p. 81; also J. Harris, 1977). This had been adopted in the conservative society of Bismarck's Germany because it offered a low-cost mechanism to meet some social needs while committing workers, as contributors to their own benefits, to the social and economic *status quo*.

This adoption of the insurance principle had important consequences for the development of social policy. In various measures after 1911, governments extended benefits in ways that undermined the *true* insurance basis of the scheme. However, the contributory principle remained an important political symbol and, from time to time, attempts were made to return the scheme closer to its roots.

The 1911 National Insurance Act had implications for more than social security policy, in two ways. The provision of medical services under the sickness benefit scheme used a model for the state payment of general practitioners (GPs) that has continued in the National Health Service to the present day. Abel-Smith (1976, ch. 2) has pointed out that, before 1911, the doctors were in conflict with the Friendly Societies about the conditions under which they were hired to care for members. Hence they were predisposed to secure contracts under the state scheme which preserved their freedom. This right to operate as independent contractors rather than as salaried servants of the state has been zealously defended by GPs.

It is also important to recognize the National Insurance Act as the kind of response to the problem of unemployment that became dominant in the UK until the 1970s. The early years of the twentieth century saw a number of small experiments in combating unemployment by providing publicly subsidized work. Yet these did not achieve any scale, perhaps because of suspicions of their implications for state involvement in the economy. There was, however, one measure adopted in 1908, the Labour Exchange Act, that came to assume importance. The National Insurance Act gave the newly set-up exchanges the role of administering the system of unemployment benefit. This was the activity with which they came to be most closely identified. The hallmark of the UK response to defects in the working of the labour market became the provision of relief to the unemployed, and not the creation of special work programmes or measures to facilitate movements of workers between jobs (J. Harris, 1972).

The Liberal government could, of course, have developed their social security measures to redistribute incomes without either means tests or contributions. Neither then, nor later, have social security measures involved the wholesale redistribution of resources. However, both of the early schemes required quite large subventions from taxation. It is important, therefore, to bear in mind the significance of the budget that Lloyd George introduced in 1909 to finance both social welfare reforms and increased government expenditure on other matters such as defence, by increasing taxation and making it more redistributive. This seems to have been the first occasion on which a UK government's annual budget was presented, or perceived, as an instrument for the redistribution of income.

The events of 1909–11 have been given comparatively lengthy attention. Key foundations of the UK system of social policy were laid at this time. What was established was essentially an embryonic welfare state for male breadwinners, with a strong influence on what was to come. These developments occurred against a background of a rising volume of political controversy within the UK (emergent political movements on the Left, the women's campaign for votes and the conflict over the future of Ireland). A more dramatic tipping of the balance than actually occurred in the next few years might have been expected. In practice, many of the new social policies of this period and the years to follow did little to disrupt the *status quo*; indeed, many must be seen as designed to preserve it.

In World War I, the UK experienced conscription for the first time, and the mobilization not only of the whole male workforce but also of many women, to assist the war effort. The war economy produced many domestic shortages. Initially, the government was reluctant to impose controls and rationing, but its desire to curb wage rises and industrial unrest forced it to intervene. In general then, the role of the state advanced considerably during the war. Civil servants learnt to carry out, and members of the public came to expect, government policies in areas of life never before influenced by state action. This was the general impact of war on public policy. Its specific impact on social policy was more limited. The imposition of controls on private rents in 1915 was a rare, but significant, example of social policy innovation in this period.

However, during and at the end of the war, the government made many promises for a better future. Even before the war ended, an Education Act was passed which recognized the case for state support for free education up to the age of fourteen. At the end of the war Lloyd George promised 'homes fit for heroes', and one of the first pieces of post-war legislation was a Housing Act that provided government subsidies to local authorities to build houses 'for the working classes'. This Act, known as the Addison Act after its sponsor, the Minister of Health, while not the first legislation to allow local authority house building, was the first to subsidize it. It effectively initiated a programme of council-house building that continued, albeit subject to regular modification as governments changed the subsidy arrangements, until the late 1970s. After the Addison Act, both of the minority Labour governments, in power in 1924 and in 1929–31, extended the local authority house-building programme by means of further subsidies. In the 1930s, there was a shift in housing policy, with the government encouraging local authorities to put their emphasis, in house provision, on clearing the slums. The strict rent control, introduced in the war to protect private tenants, was partly lifted during the inter-war period. However, with this, as with council-house building, no real attempt was made – until the 1980s – to turn back the clock on processes that were ultimately to transform totally the character of the UK's housing market.

The evolution of relief policies for the unemployed in the inter-war years is an interesting story. Unemployment was a recurrent problem throughout this period. Immediately after the war, the government mismanaged the discharge of servicemen back into civilian life, and unemployment rose rapidly. Then the economy picked up and the problem abated, but this proved to be a temporary respite and, by 1921, registered unemployment was over two million. It remained over a million throughout the inter-war period, falling back a bit in the middle 1920s but then rising steeply in 1930. By 1931, it was over two million again, and it did not fall below two million until 1936.

The 1911 National Insurance Act provided unemployment benefit only for workers in a limited number of trades, which were not liable to extensive or prolonged unemployment. It also contained strict rules to protect the insurance fund. Benefits were dependent on past contributions, and the duration of weekly payments to individuals was limited. The scheme was not designed to provide widespread relief in a period of mass unemployment. Gilbert, in his detailed study of social policy in this period, has shown that politicians were alarmed by the reports they received of unrest and agitation among the ranks of the unemployed (Gilbert, 1970). They were particularly conscious of the expectation by ex-soldiers that they would receive generous treatment from the government. Hence the government faced a dilemma. They resolved it by breaching the strict insurance principles and extending the scope of the unemployment benefit scheme.

It would be inappropriate here to set out all the convolutions in public policy on relief for the unemployed in this period. What a whole succession of ministers and official committees had to try to resolve was the conflict between the demand for economy in government expenditure and the rising cost of an insurance benefit scheme no longer strictly restrained by insurance rules. Broadly, the compromise reached provided extended but not unlimited insurance benefits, the operation of strict and quite unrealistic tests to ensure that people were 'genuinely seeking work' (a measure particularly aimed at unemployed females) (Deacon, 1976), the use of additional means-tested benefits known then as 'doles', and acceptance that the Poor Law authorities would give extensive 'outdoor' relief to the unemployed. Eventually rationalization came, in 1934, when a unified national means-test scheme for benefits additional to insurance benefits was devised, to be administered by the Unemployment Assistance Board (UAB). The UAB provided a model that enabled central government to take over the functions of the Poor Law agencies. It transferred responsibility for means-tested benefits for the unemployed to this national organization in 1934, added similar benefits for elderly people to its responsibilities in 1940, and most other means-tested cash aid in 1941. By 1948, when it was finally killed, the Poor Law was all but dead already.

Alongside efforts to deal with the way the National Insurance system dealt with unemployment there was also legislation in 1925 to develop a contributory pension scheme for working men to run alongside the non-contributory one.

The demise of the Poor Law was also assisted by another piece of legislation in this period: the Local Government Act of 1929. This handed over responsibility for the Poor Law from the boards of guardians to the local authorities. As far as the administration of relief was concerned this made little difference; the public assistance committees of the local authorities could be regarded as broadly the guardians under another name. However, the handover of powers brought the institutions that had evolved from the old workhouses into the hands of authorities that could more effectively bring them up to date. This was particularly important for the hospitals, since now a unified public service could be provided. This was a step towards a National Health Service, though in practice few authorities did much to modernize their facilities. Instead, the transformation of the hospital service awaited the special arrangements that were made to co-ordinate their activities with those of the voluntary hospitals during World War II.

While little attempt was made to alter the character of the patchwork of health services available in the inter-war period, all the parties that were to be involved in their transformation in the 1940s were beginning to examine the weaknesses of the existing provision and to formulate alternatives. In view of the importance of medical acquiescence in the system eventually adopted, it was probably necessary for many doctors to become aware of the need for change.

Education services similarly went through a phase of detailed examination of their weaknesses and future potential during the inter-war period. Here, however, the roles given to the local authorities by the Acts of 1902 and 1918 left scope for innovation where money allowed. The teaching profession grew in strength at this time, developing a formal system of training to replace the nineteenth-century pupil-teacher system. Education beyond the primary stage grew in various ways, and this part of the system was ready for rationalization by the end of the 1930s.

The period between the 1914–18 War and 1939 is often thought of as one of failure in UK politics, of failure to cope with the rise of Hitler and Mussolini abroad, and failure to deal with unemployment at home. It was, however, also a period when complete adult suffrage was achieved, and in which a political consensus was generated that enabled the Labour Party to establish itself alongside the older parties, so that an element of working-class power developed without turning into a revolutionary force. The key Conservative politicians of that age, Baldwin and Chamberlain, were very much men of the 'consensus', eager to promote cautious innovation in social policy. The Labour leader, Ramsay MacDonald, however, was equally eager to occupy the middle ground. Some historians of the period regard this consensus politics as another of the failures of this age, urging that the compromises by the Labour Party prevented radical change from occurring. Its significance, though, for social policies, was that it created a platform for changes to occur in the 1940s, changes that secured wide-spread social and political acceptance.

1940–51: Laying the Foundations of the UK's Modern System of Social Policy

The government was much more ready to mobilize all the nation's resources in World War II than it had been in World War I. Regulation and rationing were not adopted reluctantly but as measures essential to the war effort. Politically, at least after Churchill replaced Chamberlain as Prime Minister in 1940, the nation was more united. The Labour Party regained its self-confidence, shattered by having been deserted by its leaders – who formed a National Government and then heavily defeated Labour in a general election in 1931. It joined the coalition government. Although Churchill sometimes appeared to be unhappy about it, planning for the peace was widely accepted as a legitimate political task during the war. Before looking at the two most important examples of planning for peace – the Beveridge Report and the Butler Education Act of 1944 – it is important to note a number of ways in which peacetime policy changes were foreshadowed by *ad hoc* wartime measures. In the last section, reference was made to the way in which the UAB, which was renamed the Assistance Board in 1940, took over various functions from the public assistance committees in the early part of the war. Mention was also made of the integration of the hospital services during the war, under the Emergency Hospital Scheme. The evacuation of children called for the development of special services, foreshadowing developments in child care practice after the war. Rents were again strictly controlled, and empty houses were requisitioned. Price controls and food rationing, together with the full employment that followed from the enormous state investment in the war effort, also made important contributions to welfare. The wartime state had many of the characteristics of the 'welfare state', which is popularly regarded as having been created after the war.

The Beveridge Report was the report of a committee, chaired by one of the architects of the 1911 Insurance Act, on *Social Insurance and Allied Services* (Beveridge, 1942). This recommended the adoption of a contributory social security system that improved on the existing system by protecting all citizens against poverty at times of sickness or unemployment, and in old age. The new system should, it was argued, include family allowances, maternity benefits and provision for widows. The contribution principles should be insurance ones, involving the employee, the employer and the state as before, but the coverage of the scheme should be universal and therefore involve a national pooling of risks. In the arrangements for dependants and widows, there were certain assumptions built into the scheme – about the male breadwinner and his relationship to the family unit – which have left a difficult legacy for attempts to balance the interests of men and women in our own age.

Beveridge argued that other social policies were necessary to underpin his insurance scheme. Support for children would be necessary through a universal 'family allowance' scheme. A system of means-tested assistance would be necessary as a 'safety net' for the minority whose needs were not adequately covered by the scheme. The maintenance of full employment would be essential to enable social insurance to work properly. A universal health service should take over the provision for medical care in the old insurance scheme and effectively underpin the new one. Additionally Beveridge's perspective was that the state contribution to social security should only involve the setting of a basic structure of minimum protection, leaving individuals to make voluntary additional contributions of their own through savings and private pensions schemes. In this sense the Beveridge design differed from the more comprehensive 'Bismarckian' approach adopted by some of the continental European countries, the latter involving proportional contributions towards graduated income-replacement benefits, making supplementary private additions largely unnecessary.

Beveridge's insurance scheme was broadly put into legislation. Family allowances were provided for second and subsequent children in each family, by one of the last measures of the coalition government. Most of the rest was enacted by the post-war Labour government, though there was a crucial departure from the insurance principle in that the qualifying period for a full pension was very short. This deviation from Beveridge's plan made the scheme expensive for general taxation, and probably tended to prevent the adoption of benefit levels sufficient to provide subsistence incomes to those with no other resources, and to inhibit subsequent increases to keep abreast with the cost of living.

The Education Act passed in 1944 and often identified by the name of the minister responsible, R. A. Butler, provided the framework for the education system until 1988. The Butler Act provided for universal free state secondary education, but did not specify the form it should take or rule on whether there should be selective schools.

At the end of the war, the coalition broke up. In the ensuing general election, both parties promised substantial social policy reforms, but the electorate swung strongly towards the Labour Party, rejecting the old war-leader Churchill in favour of Labour's clearer commitment to a vision of the 'welfare state'. The social security reforms embodied by the Labour Party in the National Insurance Act of 1946 and the National Assistance Act of 1948 have already been mentioned. With the adoption of these measures came the abolition of the Poor Law, its income-maintenance responsibilities going to the National Assistance Board and its responsibilities for residential care and other welfare services going to local authority welfare departments.

In 1948, the creation of the National Health Service provided another crucial innovation in social policy. GPs and hospital services were provided free for everyone, in a complex structure designed to unify the hospital sector, while leaving GPs as independent contractors, and other community services in the control of the local authorities. This structure was achieved after hard bargaining between the minister, Aneurin Bevan, and the doctors, who were deeply suspicious of state medicine (Eckstein, 1960; Pater, 1981). The scheme was funded out of general taxation, though an element of payment for the health service remained in the insurance contribution, creating a confusing illusion that this was what paid for the service. The notion of a totally free service did not last for long. Very soon, Chancellors of the Exchequer, exploiting concern that demand for services was much greater than expected, secured first small payments for spectacles and dental treatment, and then prescription charges, as ways of raising revenue.

Among these widely publicized social policy reforms came another measure, with much less impact on the general public but nevertheless with important implications: the Children Act of 1948. The origins of this reform of the services for deprived children seem to have been in a child care scandal – the O'Neill case – which led to the setting up of the Curtis Committee to investigate contemporary practice (Packman, 1975, ch. 1). The Children Act consolidated the existing child care legislation, and created departments in which professional social work practice would develop in child care and, in due course, in work with families.

The Labour government of 1945–51 did not alter the system of su__
ing local authority housing developed in the inter-war period, but it did,
by the Housing Act of 1949, substantially extend the subsidies available.
The Act formally removed the limitation confining local authority provision
to housing for the 'working classes'. The government's concern throughout
the late 1940s was to stimulate building to make up the deficiencies in
housing stock arising from bomb damage and the wartime standstill in
house building. However, post-war shortages of materials made it difficult
to accelerate new building. The Labour government laid its emphasis on
local authority housing rather than on private building for sale. It also
involved itself, as no government ever had before, in an attempt to secure
effective land-use planning and to curb land speculation. The Town and
Country Planning Act of 1947 provided a grand design for this purpose,
though one of limited success, which was subsequently dismantled by the
Conservatives. Another crucial planning innovation, with major implications for the provision of public housing, was the New Towns Act of 1946.
This provided jobs and houses in new communities for people from
overcrowded cities and run-down industrial areas.

Government involvement in the planning of the use of national
resources, which had been one of the necessities of wartime, was continued
by the Labour government as a matter of principle. This, in itself, was
important in enlarging the involvement of government with many aspects
of life in Britain. The continuation of the wartime system of food subsidies
and the slow phasing out of rationing protected poor people from the full
rigour of market forces. There was a commitment to the maintenance of
full employment, with the Keynesian doctrine (Keynes, 1936) that budgetary management could achieve this now a matter of economic orthodoxy.
In the 1940s, such economic management was slightly inflationary, but this
was broadly seen as a reasonable price to pay for full employment and
economic growth. In retrospect, it is difficult to judge the extent to which
the success of this policy – and, despite all the worries it caused at the time,
it was a success by comparison with the economic management disasters of
either the 1920s and 1930s or the 1970s and 1980s – was due to good
management, and the extent to which it was due to external and internal
economic factors outside government control, in particular to the post-war
recovery and the stimulus provided by the continuing military activity of
the 'cold war' (Cairncross, 1985).

The 1940s were, in both war and peace, crucial years for the building of
the system of social policy the UK has today. The substantial social reform
programme of the 1945–51 Labour government meant that they were the
main architects. However, it has been shown that few of the innovations
of this period were without precedent in the policies of earlier years, and
that much of the crucial thinking about the form these new institutions

should take had been done in the inter-war period. Continuity is also evident in the behaviour of the two major political parties. The Butler Education Act and the Family Allowances Act were both measures of the Conservative-dominated wartime coalition. Preliminary work had also been done during the war on the ideas for the social security scheme, and plans had begun to be drafted for a health service.

The post-war social policy settlement was essentially a continuation of the process of creating a wage-earners' welfare state. Policies for women and children treated them as essentially the 'dependants' of male workers. Little attention was paid to the enormous contributions women had made to the formal economy during the Second World War. The assumption was that they would largely withdraw from the labour force once the war was over. The 1940s may be seen as a period in which men, but not women, acquired limited 'social rights' to accompany their political rights acquired earlier in the century.

1951–79: Consolidation and Modification

The Conservatives did comparatively little, on returning to power in 1951, to dismantle the 'welfare state'. The Labour Party policies that they did contest, and partly reverse, were its nationalization policies, not its social welfare ones. Otherwise, they shifted the house-building emphasis from public to private building but by no means eliminated a substantial public element from their enlarged building programme; they were marginally more ready to increase health service charges; and they were, perhaps, rather slow to raise social security benefits. In the later 1950s, they encouraged education services to flourish; and some local authorities began to innovate in this policy area in ways that, in due course, came to be regarded as radical and politically contentious. In retrospect it is particularly important to note that all the political parties saw social services as state services, to be provided through bureaucracies hierarchically responsible to central government.

The Labour Party increasingly saw itself as the protector of the 1940s settlement, making commitments to improve social services in its election manifestos. It had two opportunities to put its promises into practice, first in 1964–70 and then in 1974–9. On both occasions its achievements were limited by economic difficulties.

The period 1951–79 was one of full employment and steady economic growth, punctuated by difficulties in controlling inflation and balance-of-payments problems, particularly at the very end of the period. Domestic standards of living rose rapidly, the political dilemma for those politicians who wanted to improve social services was the conflict between expectations of increased private consumption and the need for taxation to support state services.

However, it is misleading to see this period as some sort of stable 'golden age'. Many changes were occurring, whose significance for social policy did not become really evident until later in the twentieth century. The UK's role in the world was changing fast. The colonial countries of the British Empire gained their independence, but the government continued to behave as if the UK was a world power. This implied tardiness in recognizing the way UK economic interests were changing. The UK was slow to pay attention to the emergent European Economic Community, eventually joining it in 1973. Even after that it often seemed to be a reluctant member of the 'club'.

Economic change over this period had implications for social policy, particularly because of its impact upon the composition of the labour force. Industrial employment shrank dramatically, but service employment (both private and public) grew in its place. Existing regional inequalities were exacerbated by this development, given the former dominance of industry in the north of England, Wales and Scotland. But perhaps even more important was the way in which women were drawn into the new services. There was a tendency on the part of governments to see women simply as a new flexible element in the labour force, often working part-time and more poorly paid than men. But issues about the rights of women in employment were gradually put on the political agenda. Anti-discrimination legislation in 1970 and 1975 gave particular attention to pay inequalities. This development highlights the extent to which, as indicated above, the welfare state had been designed for a 'male breadwinner' society. It will be noted at various places later in this book that this is still 'unfinished business'.

The withdrawal from Empire was also accompanied by substantial migration from some of the former colonies, notably the islands of the Caribbean and the Indian subcontinent. Migrants were initially accepted as entrants to the 'mother' country, contributing to the labour force in the fully employed 1950s and 1960s. Then governments bowed to racist movements, imposing steadily increasing limits upon this migration from 1962 onwards. The long-term consequence is that the UK has now an ethnically diverse society (around 6 per cent of the population are non-white though most of these were born in the UK); but racism (both individual and institutional) has inhibited effective recognition of the need to combat discrimination in public services, including social services.

Equally slow was the recognition that all was not well with the relationship between Britain and its very first colony, Ireland. The south of Ireland acquired independence in 1922 and left the Commonwealth in 1949. But migrants continued to come to the UK in large numbers, many of them entering jobs at the bottom of the market and suffering largely unrecognized discrimination. But it was in the part of Ireland remaining within the UK, Northern Ireland, that the 1922 settlement began to collapse in the 1960s. After 1922 Northern Ireland had a devolved system of government dominated by the Protestant majority. As far as social policy was concerned it adopted British legislation, though sometimes slowly and reluctantly. Arguing that devolution made many aspects of life in Northern Ireland none of its business, the UK government simply turned a blind eye to the systematic discrimination against Roman Catholic people there. Gradually in the late 1960s a peaceful civil rights movement, attacking gerrymandering and discrimination against Catholics, began to be noticed by UK governments. From the initial efforts of the civil rights movement to draw attention to their grievances, and the efforts of the Northern Ireland government to obstruct them the situation escalated. Violence developed on both sides and the British army was sent to try to keep the peace. The army's primary concern at the outset was to protect the Catholics from the Protestant backlash. But as the situation escalated, and the activities of the pro-nationalist Irish Republican Army and its various offshoots grew more violent, it came to be seen as an army of occupation to protect the Union. In 1972, despairing of an effective response by the Protestant politicians who dominated the Belfast government, the UK government imposed direct rule. The Belfast Parliament was suspended and UK ministers became responsible for public policy in Northern Ireland. A search began for a new political settlement for Northern Ireland which was to continue for the next 30 years (and may not yet have ended, see chapter 3, pp. 58–9).

Broadly the period 1951–79 can be divided as followed:

1 **1951–64** was a period of comparatively little social policy innovation; it may be regarded as a time of consolidation or stagnation, according to one's political viewpoint.
2 **1964–74** was a period of fairly intense policy change stimulated by both political parties, in which considerable difficulties were experienced in translating aspirations into practice.
3 **1974–9** was a period in which rapid inflation, rising unemployment and government by the Labour Party without a parliamentary majority administered a severe shock to the political and social system, and to all who believed that there was still a need for developments in social policy.

Bearing these points in mind, this section will look at developments in each of the main policy areas over that period (in the order they are examined in the chapters later in the book).

Social security policy

Towards the end of the 1950s, the two parties began to produce competing plans to impose an earnings-related pension scheme on top of the inadequate flat-rate system. After a number of limited developments (see Ellis, 1989), the Labour government enacted in 1975 a mixed scheme involving both public and private pensions, with many of the better paid and more secure groups of workers able to 'contract out' into private schemes so long as they were at least as good as the State Earnings Related Pensions scheme (SERPS). An important feature of this legislation was provision for the recognition, for pension qualification purposes, of time spent out of the formal labour force in caring roles; an attempt to make social security more 'woman friendly'.

In the early 1960s, a number of academic studies were published showing that the 'welfare state' had by no means abolished poverty (Cole and Utting, 1962; Lynes, 1962; Abel-Smith and Townsend, 1965). This helped to stimulate a reappraisal of social security. The Labour government of 1964–70 therefore made a number of changes to social security. Some of the changes raised some people's incomes, and there were a number of increases in benefit rates. However, inflation was increasing, and public resources were, as ever, limited and in great demand for a wide range of policy objectives. In 1965 earnings-related supplements to sickness and unemployment benefits and a redundancy payments scheme were introduced. In 1966 'national assistance' was replaced by 'supplementary benefits'. This reform was designed to remove the stigma of assistance by making rights to these means-tested benefits much clearer, particularly for pensioners.

One particular focus of attention in the debate about poverty was family poverty and, particularly, the problems faced by the low-wage earner. The principle, adopted in 1834, that wages should not be subsidized had been carried forward in social security legislation, but the margin between the income of those in work and those out of work sometimes made the principle of 'less eligibility' appear under threat. The Child Poverty Action Group (CPAG), a pressure group set up in the 1960s, urged governments to deal with this problem by increasing family allowances. In the 1970s, the Conservatives floated an alternative approach, a form of negative income tax called 'tax credits', and implemented a means-tested benefit for poor wage earners, 'family income supplement'. Labour, on return to power in 1974, decided to press on with the development of a new family allowance scheme called 'child benefit', designed to replace the older allowance, extend it to the first child in each family, and offset it against the abolition of tax allowances; see McCarthy (1986) for a discussion of these developments. However, it did not abolish family income supplement.

Employment policy

Early in this chapter it was pointed out that, at the beginning of the twentieth century, British governments adopted an approach to the relief of unemployment that largely ruled out the creation of specific employment opportunities. That continued in the period of very low unemployment in the 1950s and 1960s. Then, in the early 1970s, interest was awakened in the UK in the case for the development of 'active labour market policies' of the kind adopted in Sweden. These involved such methods as assisting labour mobility, expanding training when unemployment increased, and creating special work projects for the unemployed. Their appeal was that they were believed to alleviate unemployment, in a largely fully employed economy, without creating inflation. Their adoption in the UK occurred at a time of rising unemployment. Accordingly, instead of serving the economic function for which they were originally advocated, they were modified to serve the political function of reducing the number of unemployed while minimizing intervention in the economy as a whole. There was a particular concentration on measures for young people, particularly involving a succession of training schemes.

Health policy

In the 1950s, the principal government concern about the health service was with difficulties in controlling costs. No substantial changes resulted from this preoccupation. The relationship of the doctors to the government was, and remains, a sensitive area. A great deal of attention was given to their terms of service and remuneration.

The Mental Health Act of 1959 altered the procedures for the compulsory admission and retention of the mentally ill in hospital, abolishing the old 'certification' procedure. The treatment of mental illness was advancing considerably at that time, and probably contributed more than the legislative change to reducing both the use of compulsory procedures and the incidence of long stays in hospital. A further Mental Health Act in 1983 continued the liberalization of the treatment of mentally ill people.

In the 1960s, as part of the wholesale review of the institutions of central and local government, proposals were introduced for the reorganization of the National Health Service. Eventually the change was effected by the Conservatives in 1974. This change created a new structure, with the former local authority community health services integrated with the rest of the service. Lay participation in the running of the service was reduced; in its place, community health councils were created to represent the public. The new structure – with its three tiers of regions, areas and districts – became regarded as over-elaborate almost as soon as it was created.

Personal social services

The development of the personal social services between the 1940s and the 1970s is a story of steady consolidation and one important structural change. At the end of the 1940s, local authorities organized these services within two or three departments. Children's services were the responsibility of one department, required by statute. Children's departments built up a body of social work expertise, and gradually extended their activities, from work dealing with acute child care problems into work designed to prevent child neglect and abuse and into work with delinquent children. Two Children and Young Persons Acts, in 1963 and 1969, legitimized and encouraged these changes in emphasis.

The other local authority welfare services, or personal social services, were organized by welfare departments and by health departments (or by departments that combined these two functions). A social work career was developed in connection with this work, but not so effectively as was the case in the children's departments. A government report in 1959 made recommendations that influenced developments in the training of social work staff of this kind. However, the activities of these departments were growing in other ways, too. Their legacy from the Poor Law was a stock of homes for the elderly and disabled that were ex-workhouses. A central task, therefore, was to phase out these institutions, replacing them by smaller, more welcoming, civilized homes, and also to seek to develop ways of caring for people within the community. Developments in day care, the home-help service and other domiciliary services were the currency of growth in these departments.

The important structural change for all these local authority services was an Act passed in 1970, on the recommendations of the Seebohm Committee (HMSO, 1968), which created integrated 'social services departments' in local authorities in England and Wales. In Scotland, the Social Work (Scotland) Act of 1968 had already created integrated 'social work departments'. The structural change in England and Wales was accompanied by a change in central government organization, whereby the Home Office's responsibility for children's services was passed over to the Department of Health and Social Security, which was already responsible for other welfare services. These changes represent an example of the statutory creation of a 'platform for growth'.

Education

In the period 1951–64, there was a considerable amount of innovation in education policy. This was, however, very much localized and piecemeal within the general structure laid down by the Butler Act of 1944. That Act had laid the foundation for the creation of a sound secondary education system. Initially the orthodox view was that such a system should be selective, with children routed at the age of '11-plus' into grammar or secondary modern schools (and in some areas technical schools) according to their aptitudes and abilities. As time passed, an alternative, non-selective, comprehensive model began to be championed. Various local authorities began to introduce comprehensive schools in the 1950s, motivated some-times by political and educational ideology but sometimes, particularly in rural areas, by a recognition that such schools were a more realistic response to local needs. Then in the 1960s political 'battle lines' began to be drawn up, with Labour in favour of comprehensive education and the Conservatives against it. Labour legislation requiring local authorities to introduce comprehensivization schemes, enacted in 1976, was repealed by the Conservatives in 1980.

The resources available to state education were substantially increased in this period. In many respects, this was a necessary response to the child population 'bulge' created by the 'baby boom' of the immediate post-war years. This, in itself, created a need for new schools and teachers, and therefore provided a platform for educational innovation. Clearly, govern-ments were ready to encourage innovative thinking. Advisory committees were created to look at various educational issues. The crucial policy changes influenced by this committee activity were the rapid expansion of higher education in the 1960s, the raising of the school-leaving age to sixteen in 1972 (after delays in implementing a change first announced in 1964), and a distinct shift away from streaming and selectivity at all stages before the teenage years. It was the change in the amount of public money spent on education, however, that was most important.

Housing

The period 1951–64 was a boom period for house building, both private and public. It was during this time that two kinds of tenure began to dominate in Britain: owner-occupation and local authority tenancy. Politicians of both parties became, by the late 1960s, increasingly concerned to stimulate owner-occupation. Tax relief was used to assist borrowing. The decline in the size of the privately rented sector was rapid and, towards the later part of this period, it was accelerated by slum clearance. In 1957, the government, believing that the private rental market could be revived if rent controls were removed, passed a Rent Act that allowed some decontrol. The main impact of this measure was that many landlords used the freedom to evict, which was allowed under decontrol, to sell previously let properties for owner-occupation. In the 1960s, the Labour government legislated to restore security of tenure and to allow rent levels to rise only to levels that fell short of market prices.

When Labour returned to power in 1964, they were also committed to reversing the emphasis on building for owner-occupation within the building boom, but at the same time they wanted to produce even more houses per annum. By the end of the 1970s, the additions to the housing stock had been so considerable that arguments were increasingly heard that the UK had enough houses. What complicated this debate was the question of whether there were enough houses of the right kind in the right places. Certainly some of the earlier building activity may have been misplaced effort. In particular, many local authorities produced poor-quality industrially built high-rise flats which were difficult to let (Dunleavy, 1981).

When they returned to power in 1970, the Conservatives decided that public expenditure on local authority housing needed to be curbed. Their Housing Finance Act of 1972 set out to adapt the 'fair rent' principle, which Labour had applied to private rents in the 1960s, to the local authority sector. They linked this with a national rent rebate scheme, rationalizing the variety of local schemes that had been set up over the previous decade, to offset the costs to poorer tenants. This Act was designed to reduce the general subsidy to council tenants; it was linked to changes in the system of national subsidies to local authorities, designated to phase out indiscriminate help of this kind in due course. Labour opposed this measure and limited its impact during their term of office in 1974–9.

1979–97: the UK Welfare State in Crisis?

The last section has described policy developments in a period in which the Conservatives and Labour alternated in power. When the Conservatives secured power in 1979, they were to retain it until 1997.

Before looking at the measures developed during this period of Conservative rule it is important to consider the extent to which a crisis for social policy had been gradually developing over the preceding period. It has been suggested that between 1951 and 1979, levels of controversy over social policies were, arguably, not particularly high. Conservative ideologists had had much to say about the case for bringing market conditions more effectively to bear on the distribution of social services, but only in the housing field had Conservative governments taken steps that represented major responses to this viewpoint. Labour disappointed many of its supporters, who closely identified the party with the advancement of the welfare state. A succession of economic crises limited the money available for new social policies. Yet both parties considerably advanced public expenditure, particularly on social policies, to the point where some economists argued that this kind of expenditure had become an inflationary force, limiting the scope for new wealth-creating private investment. This is a view politicians began to take very seriously by the 1970s. The most staggering growth was in public employment and in social security transfer payments, two forms of growth that politicians find very difficult to limit.

Hence, while it is tempting to attribute the change in the climate for social policy in the UK to the election of the Conservative government led by a right-wing leader (Margaret Thatcher), the changes had been gradually emerging before that date, and those changes were rooted as much in economics as in ideology. It was a Labour minister, Anthony Crosland, speaking in 1975, who warned local government that, as far as public spending increases were concerned, the 'party is over'.

In the 1950s, Keynesian economic management techniques, involving manipulation of levels of government expenditure and taxation, were employed to try to retain full employment without inflation. This generated a cyclical pattern of economic (and government expenditure) growth regularly punctuated by curbs to prevent rapid inflation. In the 1960s, despite an increasing commitment to economic planning, the cyclical pattern worsened. Inflation increased, balance-of-payments crises forced strong restraints to be applied to public expenditure and private incomes on a number of occasions, and, at the depressed point of the cycle, quite marked increases in unemployment occurred. In the mid-1970s the UK faced a more severe crisis, in which very high inflation, a balance-of-payments problem and continuing high unemployment occurred all at the same time. Measures to cope with the first two by traditional means worsened the third.

Different schools of economists preached different solutions to these problems. On the Right, the 'monetarist' school of thought became increasingly influential, arguing that governments must control the money supply and let economic forces bring the system under control (Friedman, 1962, 1977). This viewpoint had some influence over policies in the 1970s, but politicians were reluctant to let bankruptcies and redundancies occur on a sufficient scale to test the monetarist hypothesis properly. More influential, and more in conformity with Keynesian orthodoxy, were those economists who argued that income restraint was necessary to bring unemployment and inflation into balance, and to prevent the UK's balance of payments becoming unmanageable as rising wages led us to import goods we could ill afford, while making it more difficult to sell things. In their view, what was happening was that wage bargaining was no longer restrained by the social and political forces that hitherto limited rises to figures that would not disrupt the economy. Incomes policies were seen as crucial to solving these problems, yet over and over again governments found that political pressures made these very difficult to sustain for any length of time. The whole picture was, however, complicated by changes in the pattern of trade in the world and, particularly, by rises in prices of primary commodities, especially oil.

After 1979, the 'monetarist' theory was more boldly put into practice by the new Conservative government. It treated the money supply, and particularly the public sector borrowing rate, as the key phenomena to keep under control. It was prepared to let unemployment rise rapidly in the cause of the war against inflation. It abandoned income policies in the private sector, seeking only to keep pay increases to public employees tightly under control. Initially, it found the removal of pay controls and its own taxation adjustments produced severely inflationary effects. It was subsequently successful in bringing inflation under control, but achieved that at the expense of a rapid increase in unemployment. Numbers registered as out of work rose from just over a million in 1979 to over three million in 1983.

Later in the 1980s, the government abandoned any rigorous attempt to keep the money supply under control, concentrating attention instead on the foreign exchange value of the pound. However, it continued its tight control of public borrowing. By the 1990s, with the economy depressed and the 1992 election approaching, even the latter monetarist nostrum was abandoned by the Conservatives.

After 1979 the Conservatives, particularly in the period in which Margaret Thatcher was dominant, were undoubtedly hostile to state social policy. This hostility was rooted in a commitment to privatization, the curbing of public services, and attacking trade unions. The government was untroubled by the evidence that such an approach was generating increased poverty. Paradoxically, while the Conservatives were committed to public expenditure restraint, they found social policy expenditure very difficult to curb. Public sector housing expenditure did experience severe cuts. Education expenditure remained more or less static in real terms. The trends in spending on health and personal social services are more difficult to interpret. The figures indicate growth in real terms but needs and specific health care costs have also risen so that there has been some decline in volume. Nevertheless, social policy expenditure as a whole grew, driven upwards by the considerable growth in its major component, the social security budget; see Glennerster and Hills (1998) for a detailed analysis of these trends.

The Thatcher government was particularly hostile to local government and concerned to curb any likelihood that it could drive up public expenditure as a whole in contradiction of the aims of national government. This concern was obviously influenced by the tendency for Labour to control local government in the major urban areas, and for some of the local Labour leaderships to regard themselves as having a mandate to establish 'local socialism' (Gyford, 1985).

In the period before 1979 local government had, not surprisingly in the light of central government's expectations of it in areas like education, personal social services and housing, become an increasing spender. In the period up to the middle 1970s, central government steadily increased its grant contributions to local expenditure. It also struggled, rather fruitlessly, to find ways of wholly or partly replacing the system of local taxation, the 'rates' assessed on property. In the later years of the 1974–9 Labour government, the central contribution to local expenditure began to be cut. After 1979, the Thatcher government continued this process much more zealously, developing a formula which deliberately penalized those authorities they deemed to be over-spenders. Then, in addition, they decided they must limit local authorities' powers to go on increasing local rates. They developed legislation that enabled them to 'rate cap' authorities that they deemed to be high spenders. Finally, they decided to abolish rates and replace them by a poll tax known as the 'community charge'. This measure proved to be enormously unpopular, and contributed to Margaret Thatcher's political downfall (Butler et al., 1994). Her successor as Prime Minister, John Major, rushed legislation through Parliament to try to remove the stigma of the poll tax. He sharply increased the central subsidy to local finance and enacted a modified version of the old domestic rating system known as the 'council tax'.

Let us now move on to look at the key measures adopted by the government between 1979 and 1997, sector by sector.

Social security

Early in the 1980s, the Conservatives set out to make piecemeal adjustments to the social security system. They reduced the value of contributory benefits by altering the procedure for inflation-related increases, and by extending the taxation of benefits. They eliminated earnings-related additions to sickness and unemployment benefits. They then shifted the responsibility for provision for sickness absence for the first 28 weeks from the insurance (NI) scheme to a statutory sick pay scheme to be run by employers. They attempted also to rationalize the burgeoning social assistance scheme, 'supplementary benefit', by developing a stronger rule-based structure, and introduced a housing benefit scheme.

However, in 1983 they decided that a more radical reform of social security was necessary. Social security was an element in public expenditure that they were finding very difficult to control, not surprisingly in the face of an ageing population, rapidly rising unemployment and government measures designed to shift the subsidy of housing on to the social security finances. The 1986 Social Security Act extended the scope for contracting out from the SERPS pension arrangement (see p. 31), allowing schemes which did not necessarily compete favourably with the state scheme and also reducing the benefits available under SERPS. This encouraged a rapid growth of private pension plans, including some that were poorly protected. The collapse of some of these led, in the early 1990s, to further regulatory legislation.

The 1986 legislation also replaced supplementary benefits by 'income support', and family income supplement by 'family credit'. These two schemes operated with simpler rule structures than had supplementary benefits. Housing benefit was altered to bring it in line with these other two benefits. Some anomalies that had arisen as a result of the previous piecemeal evolution of means-tested benefits were eliminated. The maternity grant and the death grant, two universal benefits initiated in the 1940s but not properly updated in line with inflation, were abolished, to be replaced by means-test related benefits for the very poor. The system of single payments – available to help people who are on supplementary benefits and who have specific needs – was replaced by a much more limited system, known as the 'social fund', under which all that most people could be given were loans.

Alongside these major structural changes, the Conservatives substantially weakened the benefits designed to protect the unemployed, making support for under-18-year-olds conditional on their undergoing training, and sharply reducing the amount of help available to other young unemployed people. Penalties for refusing to undergo training and for leaving jobs were made very severe. This was an issue to which they returned with further legislation in 1995, to rename unemployment benefit 'job seeker's allowance', to emphasize the behaviour required, and to make the allowance means-tested for all after the first six months. At about the same time, the Conservatives changed invalidity benefit to incapacity benefit, aiming to force all but the severely handicapped, below pension age, to become job seekers.

Another feature of Conservative social security policy in the 1990s was efforts to reduce state support for single parent families. A complex piece of legislation designed to secure increased contributions from 'absent' parents (normally fathers), the Child Support Act of 1991, immediately ran into implementation difficulties and was revised in 1995.

In many respects, the Beveridge design for social security had been undermined before 1979 by failures to update insurance benefits adequately, by rising unemployment and by the need to provide means-tested benefits for the growing number of single-parent families. The policy changes of the 1980s continued that process, ensuring that means-tested benefits were of key importance for the relief of poverty.

Health

The Conservative government sought to increase its control over the NHS by means of various management changes. Failure to curb rising costs led them then, towards the end of the 1980s, to explore more radical options. Their 'right wing' urged them to privatize the system. While being unprepared to go this far, the government, in the National Health Service and Community Care Act of 1990, encouraged hospitals to become quasi-independent 'National Health Service Trusts' and general medical practices to become 'fundholders'. Both of these measures were designed to bring about increases in efficiency, accompanied by general arrangements for a managerial split between 'purchasers' and 'providers'. The overall aim was to create an 'internal market' within the NHS in which hospitals were in competition with each other. All hospitals and community health services changed to trust status. The establishment of a system of GPs as fundholders was more limited. These developments made desirable another alteration in the structure of the health service, eliminating 'regions' (except as administrative outposts of the centre) and amalgamating the authorities that managed the family practitioner services with the district health authorities in 1996.

Personal social services

Reference was made earlier (pp. 33–4) to the way in which the Seebohm reforms of the personal social services created a 'platform for growth'. This growth was still occurring in the early 1980s but was then checked by the constraints on local government spending. With that check came renewed questioning about the balance between services provided by the social services departments and the many forms of family, neighbourhood and commercially purchased care that they supplemented. Within social work, the quest continued for the best way to organize a service that could be responsive to community need. Outside social work, doubts were increasingly raised about the adequacies of that profession, particularly in the face of a growing number of child abuse 'scandals'. Child protection legislation was consolidated and updated in the Children Act of 1989.

A related problem, exacerbated by the ageing of the population, concerned the balance between domiciliary and residential care for handicapped adults. This is a complex issue, because it is not merely about forms of care but also about who should bear the costs of care. In the 1980s, a strange piece of government carelessness brought the whole issue to a head. The social security minister relaxed the rules under which means-tested benefits could be used to subsidize private residential care. The result was an explosive growth of this sector, making demands on the social security budget that were difficult to control. The Conservative government's eventual response to this problem was to try to develop a version of the health service's purchaser/provider split in which local authorities would be purchasers and the various forms of residential and domiciliary care would be provided by a range of organizations in which private and voluntary enterprises would be dominant. The 1990 Act, which developed similar ideas for the NHS, authorized this and was brought into full force in April 1993. The measure highlighted issues at the boundary of the health and personal social services systems.

Education

By the mid-1970s, the 'bulge' (see p. 34) had nearly worked its way through the education system, and this, together with disillusion with innovation in education, brought to an end the role of the education service as an expenditure growth-leader among the public services. Controversy grew about some of the bolder experiments in egalitarian education, and it was increasingly alleged that basic education was being neglected. Some people put some of the responsibility for the growing youth unemployment on educational inadequacies, giving sustenance to the Department of Employment's bid to control low-level post-school education. Once the Conservatives came to power in 1979, the unrest began to be translated into policy. The completion of the comprehensivization programme was arrested, and new opportunities were created for state-financed places at private schools. The 1980 Education Act, which extended parental choice of schools, was justified as a measure to create pressures for the raising of academic standards. But it had the effect of undermining comprehensive education in some areas, where it increased the tendency towards social segregation particularly when linked later with measures, described in the

next paragraph, which enabled some schools to opt out of local government control.

The 1988 Education Act largely replaced the 1944 Act as the framework
law for state education in England and Wales. This Act laid down a
requirement that there should be a 'national curriculum' of 'core' subjects
(English, maths and science) and 'foundation subjects' (see also
pp. 212–13). It required that children be tested regularly, starting at the
age of seven, to assess the extent to which attainment targets had been
achieved, and that information about test outcomes be published. This
legislation also weakened local government control over education by
strengthening the autonomy of individual school managements, and by
enabling schools to apply to become directly funded by central government
(grant maintained schools). Supplemented by further measures, it also
extended central control over higher and further education, and removed
the last vestiges of local authority responsibility for these sectors.

Housing

On returning to power in 1979, the Conservatives – by reducing new
expenditure on public housing, modifying the subsidy formula and encouraging rents to rise – set out to eliminate most subsidies to public housing
other than means-tested benefits (housing benefit) for individual occupiers.
Measures at the end of the 1980s prevented local government subsidy of
council housing and accelerated the rate at which central subsidies were
withdrawn.

Legislation enacted in 1980 to give local authority and housing association tenants a 'right to buy' made extensive inroads into the system of
public housing. An Act passed in 1988 sought further to dismantle the
system of local authority-owned public housing. It aimed to replace it by a
mixture of housing associations, tenants' co-ownership schemes and private
landlords. In practice, the government faced difficulties in implementing
this legislation. Tenants and local authorities were often resistant to change,
and private capital was not particularly eager to move in. However,
subsequently, local authority difficulties in raising capital to enable them to
improve their decaying stock encouraged the exploration of ways of
effecting the voluntary transfer of local authority houses to housing
associations.

In the 1980s, changes to financial markets led to growth in the availability of finance for house buyers. The growth of house prices fed a belief
that there was little risk in mortgage borrowing. Then, at the end of that
decade and in the early 1990s, the combination of a new recession and
government efforts to combat inflation (including a reduction in tax relief

on mortgages) led to a fall in house prices. Many buyers, p₂
who lost jobs, found themselves in 'negative equity' situa
their houses had fallen in value and their mortgage reɪ
difficult to meet. This proved, however, to be only a temp
for the housing market as a whole.

1997–2001: Back from the Crisis?

The author of a textbook giving an account of contemporary policy faces
the obvious dilemma with a preliminary history chapter, that when very
recent events are reached, any account of them will tend to be duplicated
in chapters setting out the up-to-date situation. An account of social policy
today is clearly an account of the shape it has been given by the government
dominant at the time of writing. Only brief comment will therefore be
made here on the actions of the Labour governments led by Tony Blair
from the general election of 1997, through the election of 2001 when
another overwhelming parliamentary majority was won, to the time of
writing (Spring 2002).

The sub-heading for the last section included a question mark after the
word 'crisis'. The motive for that question mark was that, while many have
seen the events leading up to the Thatcher governments and beyond as
constituting a crisis for social policy, I doubt whether the word 'crisis' is
entirely appropriate for what – viewed from a longer perspective – will
surely be seen as a sequence of incremental adjustments. By that token the
sub-heading for this section should perhaps include two question marks –
one because of the repeat of the word 'crisis', the other because of doubts
about whether the UK's social policy system is moving 'back from' that so-
called crisis. The fact is that whilst the rhetoric of the Labour government
has suggested that it is engaged in a dramatic reversal of Conservative
policies, the reality has been a series of marginal changes.

Crucial for that last judgement is the fact that in 1997 the incoming
government committed itself initially to keeping within the spending plans
of its predecessor and has over the longer run been eager to present itself
as not imposing any additional taxation (though in the latter case it has
allegedly found ways to impose covert 'stealth' additions to taxation).
While 'new' Labour clearly approaches issues about social policy expenditure without a 'Thatcherite ideological enthusiasm for cuts, the government
nevertheless believes that pressures, needs and demands for increased social
spending must continue to take second place to what are seen as overriding
economic considerations. In the Blair government's first period of office
(1997–2001) some flexibility for additional spending emerged because of
the overall health of the economy, raising income and employment levels

and thus increasing the tax yield. There is of course room for doubting its claims to much of the credit for that. Since the 2001 election it has committed itself to a substantial growth in expenditure on the health service, and some on education. When it made those commitments it was widely predicted that towards the end of its term of office its aspirations to improve services and its commitment to holding tax levels would be on a collision course. This seems to have been confirmed by the Chancellor in his 2002 budget, in which he has increased social insurance contributions, justifying this in terms of the need for much greater expenditure on the NHS.

Hence, the Labour record since 1997 consists of a wide range of institutional changes but an absence of expensive innovations. Most important here has been devolution: the creation of a Scottish Parliament with a substantial measure of policy-making autonomy, a Welsh Assembly with limited administrative autonomy, and an Assembly for Northern Ireland which is, at the time of writing, just managing to survive (see chapter 3, pp. 58–9, for more discussion of the implications of these measures).

Within those parts of the administrative system which have *not* been devolved (all in England, much in Wales, and social security throughout the UK), while there has been much detailed change, Labour has not really reversed the new institutional directions for social policy established by Thatcher and Major: the commissioner/provider split, a reduced role for local government, greater participation of private providers. The government is much more sympathetic to mixed public/private institutions to deal with social policy issues than was any earlier Labour government.

As far as the relationship between central and local government in England is concerned there has been some easing of central–local conflict (not least because the government and most of the major urban authorities are under the control of the same party). Some central controls have been eased, or more likely are being given more subtle forms – for example, the replacement of compulsory competitive tendering by a requirement to achieve 'best value' in public contracts. However, the centre shows no willingness to reduce its intervention in local affairs.

Social security and employment

In the field of social security the Blair government proclaimed 'we will be the party of welfare reform' but the combination of the commitment to a stable public expenditure programme and the tendency of social security costs to rise regardless of policy change has limited their room for manoeuvre. They see the solution of that dilemma in increased employment; the stimulation of labour-market participation by single parents and the disabled as well as the unemployed is central to their social security policy strategy. A strong emphasis on training is present in what the government proclaimed in 1997 to be one of its most important social policy initiatives: its 'welfare to work' programme for young people under 25. Unemployment fell substantially between 1997 and 2001 but at the time of writing it shows signs of rising again. Other key policy innovations involved transforming the family credit into a tax credit (back to the 1970 Conservative agenda!) and devising a similar credit for disabled people and for low-income pensioners. A greater integration of tax and social security is likely to be one of the government's long-term achievements.

Despite continuing evidence of problems with private pension schemes the government is unwilling to take on the cost burden that would follow from improvement of the National Insurance pension and a return to the strong version of SERPS enacted in 1975. It has adopted instead a new public/private-partnership approach to this topic involving what are called 'stakeholder pensions' and a new residual pension scheme for very low earners.

Health

Various changes to the organization of the National Health Service have been noted earlier in this chapter. The government is changing the system yet again. The system of trusts remains, but GP fundholding has been abolished. Commissioning of secondary health care is becoming the responsibility of Primary Care Trusts, within which GPs are represented. The change of terminology from 'purchasing' to 'commissioning' means that the largely unrealized 'internal market' ideal has been abandoned.

The substantial increase in health expenditure, noted above, is accompanied by a plethora of initiatives designed to increase control over the NHS.

Education

The arrival of the Labour government in 1997 did not reverse the general thrust of the education policy measures enacted by their Conservative predecessors. In some respects, indeed, the Blair governments have been even more vehement about the need for central control over a relevant education system. In relation to higher education the government added to the cut in the resources available to students a requirement for all but the poorest to pay fees. Under pressure from the new Scottish Parliament, which abolished fees for Scottish students, the government is currently thinking again about this issue.

Reshaping the field

Finally, it is appropriate to comment briefly on changes to the overall institutional arrangements for public social policy. After the 2001 election, social security and employment policies were brought together under a new Department of Work and Pensions. That department then proceeded to structure its activities to make a distinction between social security policies before and after pension age, linking the administration of the former with policies to assist people to get work. At the same time the development of tax credits has involved a shift of operational responsibility for many social security policies onto the Inland Revenue – tax credits and child benefit – a department closely linked to the Treasury.

Training policies remain linked with education, but are now much more explicitly separated from other employment services. At the same time a further change seems to be beginning to fragment personal social services, with adult services becoming increasingly linked to health policy. Social services for children are divided between mainstream child care services under the supervision of the education system, and those for children 'at risk', which may be called 'child protection' services, still under the Department of Health at national level in England but sometimes cut loose at local level from their links to adult social services. Hence the conventional ways in which the social policy world has been structured – as reflected in the chapter headings in much of this book – are shifting.

Conclusion

Overall, the new 'watchword' is pragmatism, what matters is what works best. At the same time the tendency to tinker with organizational arrangements in the hope that a much better service can be achieved without any significant change in public expenditure is being manifested as much by this government as by any of its predecessors at the end of the last century.

SUGGESTIONS FOR FURTHER READING

Derek Fraser's *The Evolution of the British Welfare State* (2002) is a good but general historical textbook. Pat Thane's *Foundations of the Welfare*

State (1996) deals with the period from 1870 onward. The inter-war period is well covered by Gilbert (1970). A number of books deal specifically with the 1945–51 Labour government. Among these Morgan's *Labour in Power, 1945–51* (1984) and Hennessy's *Never Again: Britain, 1945–51* (1992) are recommended.

Four books which deal specifically with social policy history since 1945 are the author's own *The Welfare State in Britain* (Hill, 1993), Rodney Lowe's *The Welfare State in Britain since 1945* (1999), Howard Glennerster's *British Social Policy since 1945* (1995) and Timmins's *The Five Giants: A Biography of the Welfare State* (1996).

The impact of the Thatcher and Major governments on social policy has provoked various accounts, the best overall sources are a collection edited by Savage, Atkinson and Robins (1994), for the Thatcher period, and Dorey's edited volume *The Major Premiership* (1999).

Recommended sources on the ongoing story of the Blair government are a collection edited by Martin Powell (1999) and an edited book by Savage and Atkinson (2001). Powell brought out another collection in 2002, *Evaluating New Labour's Welfare Reforms*.

Chapter 3
The Making of Social Policy

- Introduction
- The representative government model
- The central government system
- Devolution
- Local government
- The United Kingdom in Europe
- The voice of the people?
- Influences on policy making
- Ministerial power: the role of officials and the influence of outside groups and policy communities
- Suggestions for further reading

Introduction

This chapter deals with the social policy-making system, introducing the key institutions involved in the process in the United Kingdom (UK); chapter 4 looks at the implementation of social policy. The two chapters must be considered together; dividing the policy processes between 'making' and 'implementation' is, in various respects, difficult. It is difficult to identify a dividing line at which making can be said to be completed and implementation to start. There is also a considerable amount of feedback from implementation which influences further policy making, and many policies are so skeletal that their real impact depends on the way they are interpreted at the implementation stage. In fact it is more appropriate to describe policy making as comprising both *policy formation* and implementation.

The starting point in this chapter is the ideal to which the system of government in the United Kingdom is presumed to correspond, in which policy formation is seen as the responsibility of our elected representatives, who answer to the people at elections for their stewardship of the public interest. This chapter first looks at the features of the system that correspond to this model, and at the institutions that are reputedly responsible for the policy-making process. Since 1998 the system has become more complicated because of devolution of some governmental powers to Scotland, Wales and Northern Ireland. The implications of this are considered before the chapter goes on to aspects of the role of local government and of the place of the UK within the European Union (EU).

The discussion then turns to the various ways in which the model of representative government is modified, or perhaps even undermined, in practice. It considers how the people's will is translated into political action. It looks at the part played by pressure groups in the system, and examines the case that has been made for regarding democracy as significantly undermined by 'political elites'. The relationship between government and the UK Parliament is scrutinized, together with its parallels in the devolved governments and in local government. Attention is given to the role played by the machinery of government, by the civil service and by local government officers in the policy-formation process, and some general points are made about what we mean by that 'process'. These later issues lead naturally into the examination of the implementation process in the next chapter.

The Representative Government Model

When the systems of government in the UK, the USA, most of Western Europe and much of the Commonwealth are claimed to be democratic, that proposition rests on a view that a form of representation of the people prevails in their governmental systems. Clearly, these systems do not involve direct democracy since, in complex societies, large numbers of decisions are taken by small numbers of representatives. Some countries seek to involve the people more directly, from time to time, by the use of plebiscites and referenda. The latter device has been used a little in the UK. It was used in connection with the devolution measures and the government has promised to use it before the UK joins the European monetary system (Euro).

There is a further sense in which representative government is indirect. A distinction is often made between representatives and delegates. Delegates are regarded as mandated by those who elect them to support specific policies and to return to explain their subsequent decisions. British politicians have persistently rejected the view that they should be regarded as delegates, arguing instead that their duty is to make judgements for themselves in terms of their understanding of their constituents' best interests, while recognizing that they may, of course, be rejected at the next election if they become seriously out of touch with the people they represent. In this sense, they claim to be concerned with the interests of all their constituents, and not just those who voted for them. This doctrine was first expounded by Edmund Burke in the late eighteenth century. Today, of course, the importance of political parties makes it difficult for elected representatives to claim to represent all their constituents; but equally this makes it difficult for them to assume delegate roles. The presence in Parliament, and in the local councils, of party groups exerts an influence in favour of party programmes and away from a direct relationship between member and constituency. The modern modification of representative democracy is therefore to see the public as being allowed to choose from time to time between two or more broad political programmes, and being able to reject a party that has failed to carry out its promises (Schumpeter, 1950). However, political parties and others also use a variety of polling techniques to test the movement of opinion.

According to the theory on which this model of democracy is based, social policies may be expected to be determined by the commitments of the political parties, and proposals for policy changes will be set out in election manifestos. The growth of the welfare state can be clearly related to the growth of democracy, with the people choosing to see their society change in this way. There are, however, weaknesses in this view of the policy-making process, which are explored later in this chapter. First, there is a need to identify more explicitly the institutions of government to which such an analysis must relate. Those who have previously taken courses on the constitution of the UK may wish to skip the next section.

The Central Government System

The curious feature of the constitution is that the UK has democratized institutions that were created in an undemocratic age. Most countries have systems of government that are relatively modern creations, either designed after cataclysmic political events which required the setting up of entirely new institutions, or set up to meet the needs of newly created or newly independent states. The governments of France and Germany, for example, fall into the first of these categories, and those of the USA and the Commonwealth countries into the second. The British pride themselves on having developed a system of government that has been a model for the rest of the world. The truth is that, while certainly many constitutional ideas have been borrowed from the UK, our system contains features that no one designing a system of government today would conceivably want to adopt.

In the later section on devolution it will be suggested that what happened in 1998 has further confused the whole character of the government of the UK. First, however, there is a need to look at the institutions that govern the UK as a whole, bearing in mind that some of their powers have been devolved to Scotland (and to a lesser extent to Wales and Northern Ireland) but not to any separate governing body for England.

The monarchy and the House of Lords are two peculiar features of the government of the UK. Formally, the monarch has little influence on the policy-making process. The House of Lords, on the other hand, still has extensive power to scrutinize legislation, but its capacity to obstruct the will of the government has been undermined by successive Acts since 1911. It is now a curious mixture of appointed life members (peers) with a limited number of hereditary peers who have been allowed to remain. At the time of writing, the government is planning to legislate to add an elected element. It is not proposed to complicate further the discussion in this chapter by going into the issues about the residual rights and responsibilities of the monarch and the Lords.

The main legislative body, the House of Commons, is elected from over 600 constituencies (an exact number has not been quoted as regular constituency boundary changes alter it), each of which returns the candidate who gains a simple majority of votes at each election. After a general election, the monarch has the formal responsibility to ask the leader of the majority party to form a government. On most occasions, the monarch's duty is clear, but situations in which there is no party with a clear majority may complicate the task. Broadly, the expectation is that the monarch will not have to take a decision that will then prove to be a violation of the democratic process, because it will be the responsibility of whoever agrees to form a government in these circumstances to prove that he or she has adequate parliamentary support. In other words, the position of a minority government can be made untenable if all the other parties combine against it. There are, however, ambiguities in such a situation, as the lives of minority governments may be perpetuated more by a reluctance to force them to resign than by any positive commitment to their support.

The newly appointed Prime Minister will form a government, giving a hundred or more governmental offices to his or her supporters. Again, the normal assumption is that these will be members of his or her own party, but exceptionally a coalition may be formed in which government offices go to other parties. All those given office will normally be, or will be expected to become, members of either the Commons or the Lords. Most will be members of the Commons (known as 'Members of Parliament' or 'MPs'). The choice of members of the government rests significantly on the preferences of the Prime Minister. However, he or she cannot disregard interests and factions within his or her own party, and will obviously give some attention to the competence of those appointed.

The most important Prime Ministerial appointments will be those of the members of the Cabinet. The normal practice is to appoint a Cabinet of fifteen to twenty-five members. It will include the heads of the main departments of government, together with some members who do not have departmental responsibilities, who may be given political or co-ordinating roles. The Cabinet, chaired by the Prime Minister, is the key decision-making body within the government. Traditionally, new policy departures of any significance and new legislation need Cabinet approval, but there have been suggestions that the current Prime Minister, Tony Blair, has been ignoring that tradition. Conflicts of interests between departments are generally also fought out in the Cabinet or its committees. Each Cabinet sets up a number of committees to do more detailed work. Some of these will draw on the help of non-Cabinet ministers.

The main government departments to which attention must be given in the discussion of social policy in England (the different situation in the other component countries of the UK is outlined later) are the Treasury, the Department of Health, the Department for Work and Pensions, the Department for Local Government and the Regions, and the Department for Education and Skills. To these may be added the Department for Environment, Food and Rural Affairs inasmuch as it has responsibility for issues which affect both health in general and other aspects of welfare in the countryside. Two other departments, the Cabinet Office and the Home Office, also play a small part. Readers must be warned that it has been the practice of governments in recent years to alter the departmental structure from time to time, ostensibly in an effort to find the best possible frame-work for policy co-ordination, but – it may be suggested – with less elevated political motives in mind too. Accordingly, it may be the case that, by the time this book is in your hands, departments may have new names, and policy responsibilities may have been moved from one department to another. For example, in 1995, the Departments for Education and Employment were combined, while, after the 2001 election that department became the Department for Education and Skills and some of its employ-ment responsibilities were combined with social security in a new Depart-ment for Work and Pensions to replace the Department of Social Security. Then, just before this book went to press, a government reshuffle entailed the alteration of the year-old Department for Transport, Local Government and the Regions, with the creation of a separate ministry for transport.

The Prime Minister is technically the First Lord of the Treasury. This archaic title serves to remind us that, while today we regard the Chancellor of the Exchequer as the senior Treasury minister, the Prime Minister is, above all, bound to be involved in major decisions on expenditure, taxation and the management of the economy. In fact the relationship between the Prime Minister and the Chancellor of the Exchequer seems, from all the accounts provided by insiders and by informed journalists, to be enormously important for the functioning of modern government. Since 1997 in particular the key role played by Gordon Brown the Chancellor has been very evident, as have disagreements between him and Tony Blair (Rawnsley, 2001).

The role of the Treasury in shaping social policy through control over expenditure has secured increasing attention in recent years (see Deakin and Parry, 1998). But in addition the arrival of tax credits as a crucial instrument of social security policy has given a more direct role to the Treasury. Tax credits are administered by the Inland Revenue, an ancient administrative 'agency' which in practice implements policies determined by the Treasury and is in the last analysis answerable to that department.

Each of the departments listed above has its senior minister, the secretary of state, in the Cabinet. Again, the Prime Minister may sometimes choose to have other ministers from specific departments as Cabinet members. Each department head has the support of several junior ministers, known as ministers of state or under-secretaries, who may take on particular responsibilities for specific policy areas.

The role of the minister who is also a Cabinet member involves a quite considerable conflict between the demands of a position as a member of the central policy co-ordination team within the government and responsibility for the protection and advancement of the interests of a department. It is personally difficult for any individual to give wholehearted attention both to departmental issues and to the main political strategy problems arising outside his or her own responsibilities. There is, likewise, a crucial problem for a rational approach to government in which strategic questions may not be best resolved by bargaining between a group of individuals all of whom have conflicting, 'tunnel vision', images dictated by departmental needs and priorities. There is a number of, still competing, ways of trying to resolve this problem. Prime Ministers have developed the Cabinet Office to help them to do this task. The Treasury's overall responsibility for public expenditure has led its members, particularly under powerful and ambitious Chancellors, to try to perform a co-ordinating role (Deakin and Parry, 1998). Members of the Cabinet without departmental responsibilities may also be expected to help in the resolution of this problem. There would seem, however, to be a continuing and inevitable conflict here.

As far as departmental duties are concerned a minister's work will fall into roughly four categories:

1 He or she may be responsible for putting forward new legislation. Clearly, this is something the ambitious politician will want to do. He or she will hope to secure a job that involves the initiation of policies from the party's programme.
2 He or she will have a large amount of day-to-day administration to oversee. Much of this will involve the formulation of new policies that do not require legislation, or the determination of responses to new crises within the department. It is in this kind of work that the distinction between policy formation and implementation becomes so unclear.
3 He or she will have to deal with questions from MPs about the policies and activities of the department. While this may be seen primarily as a defensive kind of action, involving much routine work by civil servants who are required to produce the information required for parliamentary answers, it may also provide opportunities for publicizing new policy initiatives. Indeed, many questions are planted by friendly MPs, from the backbenches on the minister's own side, to enable activities to be advertised.
4 The minister has a wide public-relations role beyond Parliament. This will involve a programme of speeches, meetings and visits relating the department's activities to the world outside.

Several references have already been made to the support of ministers by civil servants. It is self-evident that civil servants have an important role to play in implementing policy. What also needs to be emphasized is that civil servants are heavily involved in forming policy. Each major department has, at its headquarters, a group of a hundred or so civil servants, up to the top position of 'permanent secretary', who are concerned with decisions of a 'policy' kind, many of which require ministerial approval. The theory of representative government clearly requires that they be called the servants of the minister, ostensibly providing information and evidence on policy alternatives but not taking policy decisions.

The British system of government involves more than a network of departments headed by ministers. Responsibility for various specific public services is hived off to a range of special agencies, though, in each case, ultimate responsibility for policy lies with one of the central departments. Students of social policy will come across a number of important examples of bodies of this kind; some with a nation-wide remit, others with local or regional responsibilities. They have grown in numbers and importance in recent years, to such an extent that a 'new public management' (Hood, 1991) system has been seen to emerge in which a formerly single civil service has been replaced by a network of different organizations with different terms of service for their employees. In central government, the 'next steps initiative', started in the 1980s, has led to the delegation of most routine governmental tasks to separate 'agencies'. While most of these remain wholly public in character, some are private organizations working under contract for the government (such as the Stationery Office Ltd, which publishes government documents). In social policy, the most significant of these agencies are those concerned with social security and employment; see chapter 4 for a further discussion of agencies.

The discussion in this section has moved from the consideration of the composition of Parliament, and the nature of the relationship of government to Parliament, to a more detailed account of the organizations concerned with policy formation. There is a need, however, to look a little more at the role of Parliament. It has been shown that about 100 of the more than 600 members elected to Parliament become involved in specific government jobs. What role do the rest play in policy formation?

Primary policy formation involves the promulgation of Acts of Parliament. The overwhelming majority of these are promoted by government, and thus the initial 'Bills' are prepared by civil servants within the departments. Bills then go through four stages in each House (Commons and Lords):

1 a 'first reading', which simply involves the formal presentation of the Bill;
2 'second reading', at which there is likely to be a large-scale debate on the basic principles of the Bill;
3 a 'committee stage', when the legislation is examined in detail (normally by a small 'standing committee' and not by the whole House);
4 a 'report stage' and 'third reading', at which the Bill that emerges from the committee is approved, but may be re-amended to undo some of the actions of the committee.

Clearly, members without ministerial office may participate in all of these stages, and opposition members will take particular care to scrutinize and attack government action. The leading opposition party organizes a 'shadow cabinet' to provide for a considered and specialized response to the activities of the government.

Backbench MPs may be able to promote new policies through 'private members' Bills'. These cannot have direct financial implications for the government, and they have little chance of becoming law without government support. Occasionally, governments assist private members with their Bills, particularly by allowing extra parliamentary time.

In addition to Acts of Parliament, both Houses have to deal with a great deal of what is known as 'subordinate' or 'delegated' legislation. Many Acts allow governments to promote subsequent changes and new regulations. It is important to recognize that many policy changes pass through Parliament in this way. It would be an extravagant use of parliamentary time to require new legislation for all detailed changes of this kind. Controversy arises, however, over the extent of the use of delegated legislation, since some Acts convey wide scope for this kind of ministerial action. To promote subordinate legislation, the government has to publish a 'statutory instrument' which is open to scrutiny by MPs. Some of these require parliamentary approval; others may be annulled if a negative resolution is passed by either House within 40 days of their initial publication. Hence, backbenchers may intervene to prevent subordinate legislation. A joint committee of the Commons and the Lords has been set up to scrutinize statutory instruments, and therefore to facilitate parliamentary review of subordinate legislation. They have, however, a mammoth task and only give detailed attention to a limited number of the statutory instruments that are put before Parliament.

Readers will find good examples of legislation for which statutory instruments are important in most social security measures. For example, they will look in vain in the 1986 Social Security Act for detailed information on the housing benefit scheme or the 'social fund'. This is contained in subsequent regulations. In particular, actual benefit rates are not included in such legislation, but are set out in regulations which are regularly updated and amended.

Reference has already been made to parliamentary questions as providing an opportunity for backbench scrutiny of government actions. Members put down initial questions in advance. Many questions are answered in writing, but those that receive oral answers may result in supplementary questions. In addition to the powers to ask questions, various parliamentary procedures provide scope for MPs to promote short debates on topics that concern them. The main opposition party is extended more specific facilities of this kind, so there are days allocated for debates on topics of its own choice.

One peculiar characteristic of the British Parliament that distinguishes it from many legislatures in other countries, and particularly from the US Congress, is the slight use made of specialized committees. The standing committees that consider Bills are in no way specialized; they consider new legislation in rotation regardless of subject and do not do any separate investigative work.

There is also, however, a system of rather more specialized select committees. Perhaps the most important of these is the Public Accounts Committee, concerned to look at the way in which public money has been spent. Then, there are select committees on the work of the Parliamentary Commissioner for Administration (the 'Ombudsman'), on Statutory Instruments and on European legislation. In 1979, a system of committees was set up to concern themselves with the work of specific (or in some cases two specific) government departments. In the field of social policy, the social services committee has conducted a number of influential investigations of issues. Ad hoc committees may also be set up to investigate specific subjects. However, such is the power of the executive in our system that it is doubtful whether these committees can do other than play a rather superior pressure-group role. They investigate specific topics, with the aid of specialist advisers, and have issued some influential reports, but they have no role with regard to legislation.

This account of the institutions of British central government has shown that elected representatives have a wide range of parliamentary duties. If they belong to the party that wins power they may well take on a government office of some kind. If they do not achieve office, they are still in a special relationship to government in which, while some advantages may accrue from being a member of the ruling party and having many colleagues and friends in office, there will also be disadvantages in that party allegiance implies a duty to support the government. Some of the scope for the criticism of policy that comes to opposition members is denied to government supporters. On the other hand, opposition, in a Parliament organized strictly on party lines, implies a situation in which it is very difficult to secure majority support for your own ideas.

Devolution

It has been noted that in 1998 there was devolution of government powers to Scotland, Wales and Northern Ireland. Devolution to Scotland was substantial. The main characteristics of the devolution settlement embodied in the Scotland Act 1998 are:

- A Scottish Parliament is elected by a voting system known as the 'additional member' system of proportional representation.
- The Scottish Parliament has a fixed term of four years, with provisions for exceptional dissolution and re-election.
- A Scottish Executive is headed by a First Minister appointed by the Queen following its election by the Scottish Parliament. The First Minister then has powers to select other ministers.
- The functions of the Scottish Parliament are defined in terms of those powers not specifically noted in the Act as 'reserved'. But there is a clause that declares that the legislation does 'not affect the power of the Parliament of the UK to make laws for Scotland' (section 28, sub-section 7).
- The main reserved powers are: constitutional matters, foreign affairs and the European Union, defence, economic policy, immigration and nationality, most social security policy, employment policy.
- Most of the funding for Scotland comes from a block grant but the Scottish Parliament has power to vary income tax up to 3 per cent of the rate in the UK.
- There is a procedure to ensure that the Scottish Parliament does not overstep its powers, involving a combination of veto powers in the hands of the UK

government with adjudication in some situations by the Judicial Committee of the Privy Council.

Hence, as far as the concerns of this book are concerned all the main areas of social policy other than social security and employment policy are now the responsibility of the Scottish government. However, the retention of control over economic policy and over most of the Scottish budget still gives Westminster a substantial influence over policy making even in the devolved areas of policy.

In Wales devolution is to an 'assembly' and not a 'parliament'. The main features of devolution to Wales under the Government of Wales Act 1998 can be best set out by means of a series of contrasts with the items in the list above for Scotland:

• The Assembly is elected by the same voting system as in Scotland.
• The Assembly also has a fixed term of four years, but there are no provisions for exceptional dissolution.
• The Assembly also elects its 'head', to be known as First Secretary rather than First Minister. The First Secretary has powers to select an executive and the Assembly may set up committees.
• There are no 'legislative functions' of the Assembly but rather the Act sets out a list of policy areas where the Secretary of State for Wales (a UK government appointee) must consider whether to devolve executive powers. They include agriculture, health, local government, social services, transport, planning, culture, the Welsh language and the environment.
• Funding for services in Wales comes from a block grant and there is no power to raise additional or separate taxes.
• The absence of legislative devolution means that comparatively little attention is given to a mechanism to resolve disputes with the UK Parliament, the latter clearly has the last word.

In Northern Ireland the search has been, as before, for a way of restoring partial self-government that would satisfy both Nationalists and Unionists. This involved a complex negotiation process involving Eire as well. There was a need to reach a deal that comprised measures to bring violence to an end and arms under control. Negotiations towards this end that were to come to fruition in 1998 were started before Labour came to power. The crucial agreement was reached on Good Friday 1998. The constitutional aspects of this agreement involve the following:

• an Assembly elected by the single transferable vote system of proportional representation;
• election by the Assembly of a First Minister and a Deputy First Minister by a complex proposal designed to ensure that the two individuals, who hold office jointly, are broadly acceptable to both 'communities';

- the formation of an executive by a procedure designed to ensure that it represents the main 'communities' represented in the Assembly;
- devolution of a specific range of executive (as in Wales, not legislative) powers – principally agriculture, health, social services, economic development and the environment;
- funding by block grant with no devolved taxation powers;
- the establishment of mechanisms to ensure that there is an active relationship between Northern Ireland and Eire, including in particular the setting up of a North–South Ministerial Council and a British–Irish council.

Mechanisms had to be set up under devolution for resolving disagreements between the UK government and the devolved governments; but these are only really important in the Scottish case, as there is no devolved legislative power to the other two countries. The key issues about disagreement resolution are three related features of the settlement already set out above: the fact that the UK still has general powers to legislate for Scotland, the long list of reserve powers about which definitional disputes are likely to arise and the fact that the UK retains veto powers and relies upon an arcane legal body, the Judicial Committee of the Privy Council, to assist with the resolution of disputes. In this situation the UK government seems able to protect its own definition of the limits to devolution, and indeed even pull them in should it want to do so. Where there is a justiciable dispute – which would be about a piece of Scottish legislation (but not the other way round) – then there is no autonomous 'supreme court' able to operate as the guardian of an agreement between the levels of government.

The financial settlement associated with devolution is governed by a formula that already operated prior to devolution. Until 1980 there had been no public effort to rationalize the way money was allocated between the countries. In 1980 a procedure to deal with *increments of additional expenditure* was developed which took into account population size. The new procedure was governed by what became known as the Barnett formula, after the minister who developed it in 1978.

It is argued that Scotland and Northern Ireland are over-subsidized and Wales under-subsidized, relative to England. Yet the Barnett formula – while it may change these relativities over time – was not designed to redress such inequalities. Moreover the evidence for inequalities is complicated, depending upon the stance taken about relative needs in each country. Nevertheless devolution makes much more explicit the issues about transfers between the four countries, fuelling – if the claims mentioned above are to be trusted – a sense of grievance in the two proportionately lower-spending countries.

It has been noted however that only Scotland has tax-varying powers, and even these are limited. But what would happen to the overall financial relationship if those powers were used? The current understanding with regard to the limited powers possessed by Scotland is that there would not be a cut in the contribution from central funds if they were used, but there is no absolute guarantee on this. While there is no doubt that a devolution measure in which the Treasury at Westminster still holds the financial reins can be easily presented as a fairly minimalist measure, it is important not to disregard the complexities inherent in financial devolution.

It is important, when looking at devolution, to give some attention to its impact upon England. There has been a considerable amount of attention recently to the question of English identity. Arguments that the arrangements after devolution are unfair to England may feed into a more atavistic English nationalism. The central issue about the implication of the devolution arrangements for England is that, in respect of a range of domestic policy issues, the legislative body for Scotland has become the Scottish Parliament whilst the legislative body for England is the UK Parliament (in short, 'Westminster'). Hence Scottish members of the UK Parliament can vote about domestic English issues, while most of their own domestic policy issues are reserved for their own Parliament.

This issue has been set out in terms of a contrast between Scotland and England. This is where it is at its starkest, but there are clearly more complex equivalent issues affecting the other two countries of the UK. This issue is often analysed as one about how the UK Parliament operates, leading those who dismiss its importance to argue that this can be handled by conventions about how the Scottish (or Welsh or Irish) MPs behave at Westminster. Committees dealing with legislation solely concerning one of the countries can only be composed of members who come from that country, and so on. But such an approach totally disregards the fact that to a very large extent the Westminster Parliament is subservient to the government of the day. It is generally the case that legislative decisions are made by the government and endorsed by Parliament (using its political majority to secure this).

Hence the issue about the role of the Westminster Parliament as the government of England for matters devolved to the legislature in Scotland would come to a head if there were a UK government with a narrow majority which would not be in power but for its support from Scotland. This may well occur if the electoral support for the ruling Labour Party declines, since Labour tends to have much stronger support in Scotland than in England.

How then could this 'English question' be tackled? Is a convention about the behaviour of MPs sufficient? One step beyond that is to have a law that formally prevents Scottish MPs voting on English legislation etc. But that brings us back up against the scenario portrayed with reference to an election in which the balance of power amongst England's MPs is different from that in the Westminster Parliament as a whole (that did occur in 1974). Surely a ban on voting in such a situation would have to mean the existence of parallel governments dominated by different parties, one for the UK, the other for England.

The simplest alternative scenario involves the election of two governments: one for England and the other for the UK. But this would require that problems about the comparatively fudged distinctions between the rights of the UK Parliament and the rights of the devolved governments would have to be addressed. While quite small parts of the UK (Scotland contains less than 9 per cent of the UK population, Wales just under 5 per cent and Northern Ireland just under 3 per cent) have devolution there is perhaps a case for a relatively ambiguous settlement. That would become much more contentious with this alternative, sometimes known as 'devolution all round'. There would have to be clearly entrenched rights for each government and a mechanism to resolve disputes which was not simply loaded in favour of UK government dominance. In the divided-rule scenario with one party controlling the UK and another controlling England there would be a very strong clash of 'legitimacies' between the organ speaking for 100 per cent of the population and the organ speaking for 83 per cent.

'Devolution all round' thus implies the development of a form of 'federal' government. The imbalance of numbers between the 'nations' inevitably leads those in search of a federal solution to the problem to look at the case for regionalizing England. England is divided into regions for a variety of administrative purposes. Some efforts are being made to try to ensure that the administrative regions used for one function are the same as those used for another. To this is then added a system of regional consultative arrangements that have the potential to evolve into organs of government, for which direct elections may be held. But it is a big leap from an emergent regional consultative system to the formation of units for a federal system of government. The latter would involve regarding regional divisions as firm and clear cut. Collaboration across regional boundaries could become much more difficult and services (such as health and education) might become radically different on either side of those boundaries. Territorial justice issues would loom much larger. Nevertheless the government seems to be moving towards the exploration of some forms of democratic devolution to English regions.

It is contended therefore that there are elements of 'unfinished business' in respect of the devolution settlement. Inasmuch then as devolution encourages further 'nationalist' forces in any of the constituent nations of the UK, we may see further constitutional changes. In the meantime the presence of separate governments means that policies may diverge. On the one hand that may be seen as a healthy development underlining local autonomy. On the other hand it generates conflicts and anomalies within a hitherto comparatively 'united' kingdom. Hence in social policy there have already been two Scottish initiatives of some importance. One of those has been the rejection by Scotland of the already enacted UK measure to impose fees upon students in higher education. In fact the consequence has been a debate about the withdrawal of fees for all UK students. The other initiative involved the acceptance of the recommendation of the Royal Commission on Long Term Care (1999) that care costs (as distinguished from 'hotel costs') in residential social and nursing care should be met from the public purse. In the rest of the UK only nursing care costs are so met.

Local Government

Local government in England is organized into two distinctive systems. In the metropolitan areas of London, West Midlands, South Yorkshire, Greater Manchester, Merseyside, and Tyne and Wear, there is a long-established one-tier system of metropolitan districts responsible for personal social services, education and housing. After 1996, a number of further one-tier authorities came into operation. These are mostly in urbanized areas, with enlarged districts taking over powers from counties. In some cases – Avon and Cleveland, for example – county authorities disappeared altogether.

In the rest of England, there are county authorities, which are responsible for education and personal social services, but also a lower tier of districts, which include housing among their responsibilities. Planning responsibilities are shared between the two tiers.

There were a number of metropolitan counties, including one covering London. These were abolished in the 1980s and their powers dispersed either to districts or to *ad hoc* authorities. In 1998 the government restored an overriding Greater London Authority, with a directly elected mayor and an elected assembly. This does not have specific implications for social policy; the new authority is only concerned with certain conurbation-wide issues such as transport and the environment.

There is also, in the counties, a third tier of parish councils, with minimal powers. While many of these are old parishes, others are towns that previously had significant powers of their own, some retaining mayors and calling themselves town councils. None of these third-tier authorities have significant social policy responsibilities, so they will not be examined further here.

The local government system of Scotland has been totally restructured; throughout that country, since April 1996 there is a one-tier system of local government. There is a similar but slightly more complicated situation in

Wales, with most powers being in single-tier authorities, known either as counties or as county boroughs, except that there is also a system of community councils resembling the parish councils in England.

Local government in Northern Ireland has been stripped of almost all its significant powers. It had previously been notorious in some areas for the manipulation of electoral boundaries and for the practice of religious discrimination. Health services and personal social services come together under four appointed boards. Education is the responsibility of three separate education and libraries boards. Public housing is the concern of the Northern Ireland Housing Executive.

National legislation defines the powers of local authorities, and may set limits to those powers. It also imposes on local government a range of duties. The relationship between central and local government in Britain is a complex one. Local government is not autonomous, but neither is it merely local administration. Some statutes impose fairly clear tasks for local authorities, but many give powers, and indicate ways in which those powers should be used without undermining the scope for local initiative. Other Acts of Parliament merely grant local authorities powers, which they may choose whether to use. Exceptionally, a local authority may itself promote a 'private' Act to secure powers to undertake new ventures.

The relationship between central and local government involves both partnership and conflict. Central government seeks to impose its will not merely through legislation, but also through the communication of large amounts of guidance. This may be embodied in circulars, regularly sent from central departments to local authorities, or through less formal communications from ministers, administrators and professional advisers. Central intervention will be justified in terms of national political commitments, to ensure that central policies have an impact on all localities. There is an inherent conflict between the demands of local autonomy and the principle of 'territorial justice', requiring that citizens in different geographical areas secure comparable treatment.

The Conservative governments led by Margaret Thatcher and John Major considerably curbed the powers and autonomy of local government. They imposed increased financial controls (see below), partly removed some services from local government (such as parts of the education system), increased the regulation of others and forced authorities to consider contracting out services. Labour, in power, is continuing that process, albeit with a slightly less dogmatic perspective on privatization (Department of the Environment, Transport and the Regions, 1998).

The 1999 Local Government Act established a system requiring local authorities to demonstrate that they are achieving 'best value' in the services they provide. The 1998 White Paper described 'best value' as follows:

Best value will be a duty to deliver services to clear standards – covering both cost and quality – by the most effective, economic and efficient means available. In carrying out this duty local authorities will be accountable to local people and have a responsibility to central government in its role as representative of the broader national interest. Local authorities will set those standards – covering both cost and quality – for all the services for which they are responsible. But in those areas such as education and social services where the Government has key responsibilities and commitments, the Government itself will set national standards.   (Ibid., para. 7.2)

The 1999 Local Government Act imposes this duty on all local authorities except parish councils. Local authorities are required to establish the following for all their services:

• specific objectives and performance measures;
• a programme of fundamental performance reviews;
• local performance plans.

Efforts to secure 'best value' are therefore required to be very much in the public domain. But in addition to general public scrutiny the government has set up a system of auditing and inspection in which the responsible government departments are assisted by the Audit Commission. Hence there is a system of reporting back to central government, which has given itself powers to intervene if the evidence suggests what it regards as below-standard services. In the field of education the government took powers in an earlier Education Act (1998) to replace all or parts of failing local education authorities with alternatives, which might be voluntary organizations, private companies or even other local authorities. It has already used these powers. The 1999 Local Government Act means that such actions can occur in any area of local government.

Policy making in local government is the responsibility of elected members, known as councillors. These represent districts, or wards, within each authority in much the same way as MPs represent constituencies. Today, a great deal of local politics is arranged along party lines, and most councillors represent the political parties that are also found at Westminster. The politicization of local government has intensified the conflict between central and local government. This was particularly sharp in the early 1980s between radical Labour authorities and the central Conservative administration.

Until 2000 the work of councillors was organized into committees. Each councillor sat on a number of these. Most business was transacted in the committees, so that the meetings of the full councils were largely rubber-stamping affairs, affording opportunities for the making of political points. These committee structures were primarily related to the various functional responsibilities of the authority. The Local Government Act of 2000 moves away from this. Instead it requires local authorities to adopt one of the following three forms of government:

1 **A directly elected mayor with a cabinet**
   The local community elects a mayor who, once elected, selects a cabinet from amongst the councillors.
2 **A cabinet with a leader**
   A leader is elected by the council and the cabinet is made up of councillors, either appointed by the leader or elected by the council.
3 **A directly elected mayor and council manager**
   A mayor is directly elected to give a political lead to an office or 'manager' to whom strategic policy and day-to-day decision making is delegated.

In any of these systems there has to be an 'executive' responsible for effective implementation of council policy. Hence the government aims, in a way not attempted before, to influence the way councils organize their political decision-making processes. Their idea is that a mayor or minority of councillors should take executive responsibility for decisions leaving the rest to engage in representative work. A key device to involve councillors is investigatory committees, which, like Parliamentary select committees, examine issues pertinent to the operation of their authority. Most councils have been reluctant to move to the elected-mayor option.

Local authorities have three major sources of income: local taxes, payments for the provision of services, and government grants. The first of these was, until the mid-1980s, a system of 'rates' on property, both domestic and business. Then the government replaced domestic rates by a tax on individuals, the community charge or 'poll tax', and centralized control over business rates. The poll tax was met by a popular reaction that contributed to the end of Margaret Thatcher's career as Prime Minister (Butler et al., 1994). After her fall, her successor sharply increased the central government grant to soften the impact of the poll tax, financing this out of an increase in value added tax (VAT). He then, in 1993, replaced the poll tax by the 'council tax'. The latter is a simplified form of the former domestic rates, with the number of adult occupants of the property partly taken into account.

These changes to local taxation involved a sharp reduction in the independence of local government. Even before the poll tax, the Conservative government had given itself 'capping' powers to prevent local authorities from raising local taxation over centrally prescribed limits. The centralization of the commercial rating system had the effect of bringing three-quarters of local revenue under direct central control; and the panic reaction to reduce the impact of the poll tax, after Margaret Thatcher's fall, had the effect of pushing the centrally controlled proportion up to around 80 per cent of local government revenue (Central Statistical Office, 1995, p. 24). While the Labour government ended 'crude' council tax capping, it retains a 'reserve power to control excessive council tax increases' (Department of the Environment, Transport and the Regions, 1998, para. 5.7, p. 34). It is certainly not increasing the central funds going to local government. It intends to retain the proceeds of the business rate, but may allow authorities the opportunity to levy supplementary rates or to give rebates (ibid., para. 10.8, p. 77).

Central government also maintains control over local authority borrowing. The trend, in recent years, has been away from a system of strict, item by item, controls, to broad limitations on total borrowing. The system is currently a complex combination of these two approaches to control.

Most of the specific detail in this section describes the local government system in England. It is not possible to go into great detail here on the other countries of the UK. The systems in Scotland and Wales are broadly similar but, as indicated above, local government has a much more limited role in Northern Ireland.

The United Kingdom in Europe

There is one part of the political and administrative system that needs to be mentioned, even though its impact on social policy is slight. The UK's membership of the European Union (EU) has had an impact on its constitution and on its policy-making process. There are areas of the law that are now determined by the institutions of the EU, where the role of the UK Parliament is limited to one of administering implementation.

It is mainly economic activity that is subject to this European dominance. The origins of the EU lie in the aspiration to build a supra-national trading area. Other European legislation has followed from that aspiration for several reasons:

1 The presence of different regulatory systems in different countries to deal with production standards, consumer protection, environmental control and terms of employment will have an influence on competition. Countries with lower standards may have competitive advantages over those with higher ones, which the latter will want to be eliminated.
2 Economic co-operation between nations is enhanced if they enjoy broadly similar opportunities for employment and standards of living.
3 The concept of a single market embraces a single labour market, in which workers can move freely across boundaries in search of work. They will want to carry social rights with them if they do so.

Hence, the evolution of the EU has led it to develop 'social policy' alongside economic and environment policy, but that policy has been principally concerned with the rights of employees and with efforts to stimulate employment through investment and training. The principal social policy interventions have consisted of limited efforts to harmonize rules relating to employment and the provision of funds to help to create work and aid training programmes (Gold, 1993; Kleinman, 2002). The European Social Fund – not to be confused with the social fund in social security (see chapter 5) – which sounds like a major social policy instrument, is in fact a vehicle for the subsidization of training (and to a lesser extent work creation). Compared with agricultural support, Social Fund expenditure is low, and countries receiving this money have to add matching contributions to schemes which it supports. There is, additionally, a rather larger Regional Development Fund, which certainly has 'social effects' as it is used to try to stimulate economic development in regions suffering from underdevelopment or economic decline.

Social policy has figured in the arguments about the scope of the role of the EU, in which Conservative governments in the UK have – during the 1980s and 1990s – been advocates of a limited and cautious approach. The UK secured agreement that it need not accept the 'social chapter' in the 'Maastricht Treaty' of 1992. The Labour government reversed that decision in 1997. However, it is important to recognize that the aspirations of that 'chapter' – towards a greater harmonization of social conditions and of social protection legislation – will not be easy to realize. At whatever 'speed' the EU may be moving towards greater unification, social policy is likely to be a weak element. Furthermore the proposals that the EU should be further enlarged, with entrants from Eastern Europe, add a further complication in this respect, since social policy is poorly developed in those nations. The areas where change has occurred, and will continue to occur, concern the elimination of discrimination in the labour market.

The progress of European social policy may be accelerated by the presence in Brussels of a Directorate which aspires to advance European social policy – which sets out goals for policy, encourages social policy experiments (the European poverty programmes) and publishes data on social conditions and social security systems. This Directorate provides a source of pressure on national governments and helps to keep social policy issues on the agenda (Commission of the European Communities, 1993).

However, since the UK is in many respects an under-performer in social policy, by EU standards (see the further discussion of this in chapter 11), with a relative lack of social insurance policies that give citizens clear entitlements (see chapter 5), it is likely, regardless of the party in power, to tend to want to impose a check upon the evolution of Union-wide social policy.

The Voice of the People?

It has already been noted that, in the UK system of government, MPs are elected in individual constituencies on the basis of a procedure in which the candidate with a simple majority is the winner. It is generally the case that the voter has to choose from between two and four candidates, each of whom is the representative of a specific political party, plus sometimes a range of others whom few people take seriously. In this way, electoral choice is peculiarly structured. Voters have to make their decisions on the basis of assessments of particular people, with their own special policy commitments, in relation to the more general political biases and policy commitments of their parties. The parties' intentions are of more importance than individuals' commitments. However, what the parties offer are broad packages of policies, within which voters may like some items while disliking others.

Hence the individual voter's starting point in trying to influence policy through the electoral process is a situation of limited choice in which it is general policy biases, or even more general considerations, often described as 'party images', that must govern his or her selection of an MP. Moreover, his or her vote will be taken together with large numbers of other votes, perhaps motivated by very different policy preferences. Hence, one person's voting choice might be influenced by a party's commitment to raise pensions, which leads him or her to support it despite its commitment to other policies – say increasing educational expenditure – with which he or she disagrees. Others who vote for the same party might be motivated by directly opposite considerations – a strong commitment to education, say, but no concern about pensions.

The above example was chosen to illustrate the basic underlying problem about the use of choices between representatives as a means of settling policy priorities. The reality is that party platforms are considerably more complex, with choices between desirable ends deliberately obscured. No party presents the electorate with explicit choices between widely desired ends; they generally seek to convince it that they can bring a little more of everything that is wanted, probably at less cost. Voters are forced to discriminate between the parties in terms of their general ideologies, value biases and images.

Furthermore, most voters do not really make electoral *choices*. Many vote for the same party every time they vote, and probably give little attention to the personalities or policies of specific candidates. Voters behave in ways which, as far as the collective pattern of choices is concerned, political scientists are to a large extent able to predict from their occupations, social origins and personalities. Only a minority of the electorate changes sides between elections. Indeed, many of the changes that alter the balance in power at Westminster are no more than changes between voting and non-voting, or vice versa. Research findings suggest, moreover, that the people most likely to change their votes – the floating voters – are generally the least informed within the electorate, and are thus not people who can be said to be making careful choices between policies. It is suggested, instead, that political *images* are particularly significant – the personalities of the leaders, their projections of competence and of their capacities to deal with the nation's problems. An important consideration at a general election is the success or failure of the government in power in coping with the economic situation. In this sense, a verdict may be given on its policies, but only in a very general way.

Clearly, therefore, electors are not normally provided with opportunities to make clear choices about social policies, or between social policy options. There are certainly general characteristics of the parties' approaches to social policies that may help people to decide between them; and, at particular elections, those for or against social policy may be particularly clear.

A general characteristic of UK elections in the last 20 years or so has been a high level of controversy over the extent to which taxation can be cut, or increased taxation avoided. After its major defeats in the 1980s the Labour Party became very wary of being seen as the party of high taxation. However, by the 2001 election the biggest parties could be seen to be trying to balance their concerns about tax levels with concerns about the need for more spending on policy areas identified by the public as under-funded. The Labour government was able to present itself as both against taxation increases and in favour of expenditure increases on health and education, because of the budgetary surplus built up as a result of its caution over expenditure in its first term of office. The Conservative opposition on the other hand seemed to undermine its credibility by being in favour of tax cuts while at the same time not wanting to be thought to favour public service deterioration. At the time of writing the Conservatives seem to be trying to extricate themselves from that position. Conversely Labour is recognizing difficulties with its pledge about avoiding tax increases, as tax receipts fall in a period of recession but pressure to improve services (particularly health services) rises.

Beyond the 'macro-politics' like that set out in the last paragraph there is a complex 'micro-politics' of other issues. Many social policies are specific measures to help quite small disadvantaged groups in the population. Policies to assist disabled people, for example, may be viewed as generally desirable and, in that sense, may have electoral appeal; but the number of people they benefit directly or indirectly is a minority in the population. Disabled people may be a relatively 'popular' minority group;

but what about policies to help the long-term unemployed, rehabilitate criminals or provide facilities for vagrant alcoholics, for example? If there were a direct relationship between the pursuit of electoral popularity and the determination of social policies, surely minority causes would receive much less attention than they do now, and unpopular minority causes would receive no attention at all (or even more punitive responses). Opinion polls suggest that a variety of social reforms carried out in Britain – the abolition of capital punishment and the liberalization of the law relating to homosexuality, for example – were enacted in the face of popular opposition.

Other survey evidence suggests, moreover, that while there are strong public commitments to pensions, education and the health service, other social policies which favour those most in need of help from the welfare state, such as the unemployed and single parents, have little popular support (Taylor-Gooby, 1985; Edgell and Duke, 1991).

It is additionally important to add to this examination of the impact of 'the voice of the people' on social policy determination the observation that the UK's 'first past the post' electoral system can convey an ambiguous message. The victors in general elections tend to have much larger majorities at Westminster than the size of their overall vote in the country would seem to justify. Often more electors have voted against the winning party than have voted for it.

The voting for the elections to the Scottish Parliament and to the Welsh Assembly involves members being elected in constituencies using the 'first past the post' system but then additional members are elected from regions on the basis of proportions, with the additional members drawn in order from lists prepared by the parties. This is known as the 'additional member system' (AMS).

In the elections for the new Greater London Assembly in May 2000 the AMS system was again used. But for the election of the Mayor of London the fact that the vote was for a single person posed a choice between 'first past the post' and yet another system. What was chosen was the supplementary vote (SV) one. Under this system each elector has two votes. If one candidate receives over 50 per cent of first-preference votes he or she is declared elected. If no one achieves this, the top two candidates go into a second round of counting in which the second choices of the eliminated candidates are counted.

The system used for the Northern Ireland Assembly election in 1998 was the single transferable vote (STV). This had been used there before for local government and European Parliament elections. Voters express preferences and there is more than one seat per constituency and success for any one requires the achievement of a quota. Once that is attained, surplus votes go to the second-preference candidates and so on until all seats are filled. This system spreads votes a little towards the less extreme candidates, an effort to bridge the wide divisions in Northern Ireland.

For the European Parliament election in Britain in 1999 yet another system was used, entailing single votes for a party list in each region. Seat allocation depended upon the size of the vote for each party in relation to the quota needed for each seat (100 per cent of the total vote divided by the number of seats plus 1, representing the quota necessary for one seat). A much-criticized aspect of this election was that the system allowed voters no chance to express their preferences between different candidates on a party list.

Meanwhile, despite all this innovation the government shows no sign of a willingness to move on suggestions to change the way the UK Parliament is selected.

Of course, the introduction of some kind of proportional representation system does not necessarily solve the general 'political arithmetic' problem outlined above. In the Scottish Parliament and the Welsh Assembly the absence of an overall majority for one party has forced upon the largest group (the Labour Party in both cases) a need to compromise with some of the other parties. In Northern Ireland the whole system (as was noted in the section on devolution above) has been deliberately designed to force compromise between 'nationalist' and 'unionist' parties.

Influences on Policy Making

Pressure groups

Much of the detailed analysis of the role of pressure groups in the policy-making process has been carried out in the USA. There, the political system has several characteristics that particularly facilitate the mobilization of small groups of people to influence decisions. First, power within the system is fragmented – between the President and the two Houses of Congress, between the federal government and the states, and between the state government and local government. Second, in that vast and diverse country, political choices are much more dictated by local interests than they are in the UK. Hence, the relationship between a Congress member and his or her local electorate is much less affected by national party considerations. Third, at federal level, the parties are accordingly much less unified by political ideologies. Political actors are therefore readily influenced by small groups which can effectively threaten to have an electoral impact.

In the UK, pressure groups are probably just as much in evidence as they are in the USA. A number of studies (Finer, 1958; Wootton, 1970;

Jordan and Richardson, 1987) have dispelled the notion that they are of no importance in the system, but there is a need to beware of the assumption that they have as direct an impact on the political system as they do in the USA. Their importance in the politics of that country has led political scientists to propound a modification of the theory of representative government, in which the weakness of the individual voter, discussed in the last section, is seen as compensated by his or her membership of interest groups (Dahl, 1961). Democracy is thus seen as 'pluralist' in character with politicians engaged in continuing processes of compromise with multiple groups. Such a theory is then seen as explaining the deference of politicians to the interests of minorities; and a new and perhaps superior version of democratic theory is presented which has as its hallmark the achievement of a political consensus in which minority interests are protected.

This theory has, however, come under fire in the USA. It has been pointed out that there are biases in the system that make it much easier for some interests to be heard than others, and much easier for modifications to the *status quo* to be vetoed than to be supported (Schattschneider, 1960; Bachrach, 1969).

These general points about the plurality of pressure groups are worthy of our attention since they suggest important questions about the way the UK system operates. The contrasts made above between the political systems on the two sides of the Atlantic suggest that it may be much more difficult for UK pressure groups to identify points at which the political system is particularly open to influence. In individual constituencies, grievances about the established political parties have to be very deeply felt, and widely shared, to upset national electoral swings. Direct interventions in elections motivated by local issues are rare. Politicians have often been able to be singularly insensitive to local issues, and the current three or more party system further distorts the picture. It will be interesting to see how much difference proportional representation in Scotland and Wales makes.

There are similar problems for a national pressure group in persuading political parties that to disregard its case carries electoral dangers. Furthermore, any interest group able to threaten in this way probably has a special relationship with a major political party, and is acknowledged as important in that sense. Many of the most powerful of the UK pressure groups tend to have an established relationship with one or other political party. The trade unions have been the clearest example of this phenomenon. They played a key role in the original establishment of the Labour Party. However, the modern party is trying to distance itself from them. The other side of industry has been an important paymaster for the Conservative Party. At the time of writing, however, business support for the Conservative Party is seriously in decline whilst the Labour Party is gaining increased funds from this source. Clearly so long as the main political divide was one which corresponded to the division of interest between 'labour' and 'capital' its implications for pressure groups were comparatively clear. Now there are perhaps a variety of more covert influences upon policy emanating from pressure groups. To counteract these there has been a move towards a requirement of greater openness about financial contributions to political parties and individual MPs.

It is important to look more closely at the ways in which particular groups enjoy an institutionalized relationship to the political system. In particular, it is necessary to go beyond the examples of close relationships to political parties, to consider whether the positions some groups enjoy in relation to the political system are unrelated to particular party allegiances. Indeed, there are groups whose very power in Britain might be jeopardized if they were seen as identified with specific political parties.

Political elites

The power of some pressure groups can only be explained in terms of what may be called an 'insider' status within the policy-making system. This implies a further deviation from democratic theory, a system within which some individuals and groups have special status. A number of political scientists and sociologists have suggested that societies possess a political 'elite' (see Bottomore, 1966; and, specifically on the UK, Urry and Wakeford, 1973, and Stanworth and Giddens, 1974) – that decision makers are drawn from a narrow spectrum within a society. Traditional Marxist analyses of the social structure suggest that the political system is dominated by representatives of the bourgeoisie, the capitalist class. Modern updates of this theory have pointed out the relevance of patterns of domination based on race and gender as well (F. Williams, 1989).

Modern interpretations of elite theories seek to show either that key policy offices are held by people from a narrow spectrum of social origins, or that a limited number of people, characterized by close links with one another, dominate decision-making roles. For the UK, it has been shown that Cabinet ministers, senior civil servants, members of key advisory bodies and the heads of prestigious organizations tend to be drawn from a relatively narrow social class group, characterized by education at public schools and Oxbridge, and by having had parents in a similarly narrow range of upper middle-class occupations. The picture is, however, not simple, and there is evidence that the backgrounds of top decision makers have changed in recent years to embrace a slightly wider range of social origins. While, certainly, it seems plausible to suggest that, if there are people from similar social or educational backgrounds in a number of key roles, the relationships between those people will facilitate the sharing of ideas and opinions, the processes involved cannot necessarily be explained as simply as this.

What may be more important to explain the power of some of the pressure groups in the UK is the extent to which there are assumptions that some kinds of consultation should occur. Such assumptions rest on several foundations. One of them is that expertise conveys the ability to help with public decision making. This is the technocratic view: that experts' opinions carry a greater weight than other people's. It is the basis on which academics sometimes secure a measure of influence in government. Similarly, some pressure groups secure attention because of their expert knowledge. In the educational and medical fields, such 'heavyweight' pressure groups abound. It has been suggested that there are a number of 'policy networks' or 'policy communities' in the various specialized policy areas, in which regular consultations occur between policy makers and representatives of pressure groups (including groups representing employees, particularly professional ones) who have been granted partial insider roles (Marsh and Rhodes, 1992b; M. J. Smith, 1993).

Another foundation on which pressure groups may secure influence is their association with traditional elite groups. Voluntary organizations believe they benefit by royal sponsorship and by the acquisition of prestigious figures as vice-presidents and supporters. Such sponsorship is not always easily earned. It is clearly helpful to have a cause that readily attracts the sympathy of influential people. It may also be important to behave in ways that are deemed respectable. This is a curious feature of this kind of pressure group activity; to some extent, the power of groups depends on their ability to forswear the more direct weapons in the pressure group armoury, to avoid mounting vociferous opinion-forming campaigns or threatening forms of direct action. The supposition, here, is based on a belief that there is an underlying elitist approach to government in the UK. A fairly narrow range of people are responsible for key decisions; some of these attain such positions through democratic representational procedures, but they co-opt others to their ranks. These other people may be individuals of shared social backgrounds, but the process of co-optation may be more haphazard. Individuals from pressure groups, or at least representing specific interests, secure entry into the ranks of those who exercise power by virtue not only of expertise but also of personal qualities, such as persistence and charm, which enable them to persuade others that they have something to contribute to public decision making. They also generally have to establish that they understand some of the unspoken rules relating to public participation: that they don't embarrass their sponsors by the use of direct tactics or indiscreet communications with the press or unseemly behaviour in committee situations. In so doing, they join that list of people who have been called on over and over again to sit on public committees and advisory bodies.

This argument, then, is that political influence may be secured in the UK without the aid of independent power. The system co-opts others to join its ranks, and pays attention to some citizens much more readily than others. People are rightly cynical about propositions on the power of ideas; they look around for other explanations and ulterior motives. Yet, in the study of social policy, the importance of individuals should not be wholly underestimated. There are examples of people who, through the strength of their commitments and the power of their attention to detail, have secured a place in the policy-making process. In the first half of the twentieth century, William Beveridge was such an individual (J. Harris, 1977). In the 1980s, experienced businessmen were turned to as advisers, and one (Sir Roy Griffiths) had an important influence on the organization of the health service and on community care policy. Since 1997 a new group of insiders seems to be emerging.

A great deal of pressure group activity is, of course, concerned with 'good causes'. Again, a theory of the policy-making process needs to find room for 'good causes' as well as for 'good people'. There are important questions that should not be brushed aside about the place of altruism in policy making. It is not naive to argue that politicians, or if you prefer, some politicians, have commitments to ideals. It is certainly important to recognize that many politicians want to be seen as supporters of 'good causes'. Hence, pressure groups for disabled or elderly people, neglected children and so on will exert influence out of proportion to their naked power. For them, the skilful use of mass media may be important, and key contacts in positions of power will be a great help. In this sense, they aim to be co-opted into 'policy communities'.

No account of social policy making should disregard the potential influence of these 'good causes', however much there may be scope for controversy about their real power in situations where interests are in conflict. Indeed one of the frustrating phenomena many pressure groups of this kind experience is continuing assertions by politicians that they do matter, which is accompanied by minimal concrete action. It is difficult to predict the political circumstances that will favour interests of this kind; but, manifestly, many have secured benefits without the use of any perceptible political 'muscle'. It is perhaps useful here to bear in mind the distinction often made in the study of pressure groups between 'interest' groups and 'cause' groups, though in the tactical struggle for influence each may seek to co-opt the support of the other. Interests seek to be recognized as 'good causes', and causes try to enlist the backing of more powerful 'interests'.

It has been suggested earlier that pressure groups provide a crucial qualification to the notion of a simple relationship between electors and elected. Some writers have suggested that they solve the problem of the powerlessness of the individual in relation to the political machine (Dahl, 1961; Beer, 1965). While there are many circumstances in which that is true, it seems important to acknowledge that the political system contains biases that make it much easier for some groups to secure influence than others. In addition, in the UK, there is the peculiar phenomenon of the exercise of influence by groups that, according to the crude calculations of political arithmetic, do not seem to have a power base at all. A minority who occupy powerful positions in British society are able to make choices based neither on notions of democracy nor on calculations about who has power, but about whom they will listen to or consult.

Ministerial Power: the Role of Officials and the Influence of Outside Groups and Policy Communities

The author (Hill, 1972, 1997a) has developed a typology of government styles to try to elucidate different characteristics of politician/official relationships in different political situations. Three types of political system are identified: 'ideological politics', 'administrative politics' and 'bargaining politics'.

A system of 'ideological politics' relates most clearly to the model of 'representative government'. It is one in which the traditional distinction between politics and administration is most easily made. Political parties compete to win elections by submitting distinct programmes from which the electorate can choose. Politicians instruct administrators to frame policies compatible with their mandates and commitments. The Thatcher governments stood out as examples of this phenomenon.

'Administrative politics' describes a contrasting system in which full-time officials are much more clearly dominant. The 'politics' are organizational rather than public, and many of the key conflicts are between departments. Ministers in central government, while formally possessing the key decision-making powers, in fact find themselves involved primarily in expounding views and defending policies generated within their departments. Politicians of the majority party without ministerial office find themselves frustratingly shut out from a decision-making process into which they are given few insights.

The concept of 'bargaining politics' was derived from examination of accounts of local politics in the USA. Partly as a result of exposure to the US literature and partly because of a desire to adopt a tough-minded approach towards power, social and political scientists have been on the look-out for signs of a similar system in the UK. In such a system political outcomes are seen to depend on inputs of resources of power. Those who hold elected positions are not 'representatives' so much as 'brokers' bringing together coalitions of interests. Their desire for re-election forces them to adopt strategies in which they are highly sensitive to pressure groups. Some reservations about this view have already been suggested, but it was acknowledged that elements of bargaining are by no means absent from the UK scene. Bargaining politics implies a clear role for politicians, which may suggest that officials will occupy subordinate positions. While this is true inasmuch as political futures are at stake, it has been suggested that in the UK deals with quite explicit electoral implications are rare. Bargaining may therefore be more concerned with the maintenance of specific policies or particular organizational arrangements. If this is the case, it may be that officials have more to lose, or have more explicit commitments, than the politicians. Key conflicts concern relationships between departments and the outside world; ministers are expected to support the defence of departmental interests.

UK central government must be noted as a context where conflicts often appear to be of an ideological nature and where the representative model is treated as of some importance. Yet a key theme in discussions of relationships between ministers and their departments has been the extent to which politicians enter with apparent policy commitments, but become socialized into roles determined by the permanent administrators and particularly by the need for 'policy maintenance' within their department. Furthermore, a related theme to the ministerial discovery that cherished policy innovations are not administratively feasible is the recognition that vested interests and pressure groups carry a political 'clout' that had not been realized when policies were planned outside government. Policy-making outcomes may be determined by the interaction of three forces: political input (ideological politics), organizational considerations within departments (administrative politics), and external pressures (bargaining politics). Marsh and Rhodes' *Implementing Thatcherite Policies* (1992a) offers a good account of the way in which ideological politics was muted in practice in the 1980s. Conversely, Campbell and Wilson (1995) show that civil service domination was partly undermined by the tendency of the Thatcher and Major governments to advance civil servants who were prepared to offer them uncritical assistance in the pursuit of ideological goals. This is probably still broadly true of the Blair governments.

Beyond these generalizations, a more detailed study of the factors that influence the way that policy is made needs to take various considerations into account. First, what kinds of policies are involved? This raises the question so far evaded in this book: What is policy? Writers on policy analysis are agreed that a policy is something more than a decision. Friend and his colleagues (Friend, Power and Yewlett, 1974, p. 40) suggest that 'policy is essentially a stance which, once articulated, contributes to the context within which a succession of future decisions will be made'. Jenkins (1978) similarly stresses the notion of interrelated decisions concerned with the selection of goals and the adoption of a course of action. Smith suggests that 'the concept of policy denotes ... deliberate choice of action or inaction, rather than the effects of interrelating forces'. He emphasizes 'inaction' and reminds us that 'attention should not focus exclusively on decisions which produce change, but must also be sensitive to those which resist change and are difficult to observe because they are not represented in the policy-making process by legislative enactment' (B. C. Smith, 1976, p. 13; see also Marsh and Rhodes, 1992b).

Policies are thus not easy to define. It is doubtful whether much can be gained by trying to achieve any greater precision than that suggested in the definitions above. It is more fruitful to look, in a concrete way, at the relevance of policies for the activity of a minister and his or her department. On appointment to office, a new minister will take over responsibility for many departmental policies. The overwhelming majority of these will be just existing ways of doing things. A good many will be enshrined in Acts of Parliament, but these will be accompanied by organizational arrangements, systems of administration and working conventions which will also help to define policy.

It is this existence of policies that determines much everyday practice in a department, and therefore provides the most crucial group of constraints for a new minister. Existing policies keep most people occupied most of the time. Innovations depend on finding opportunities for staff to work on developing new policies. They may also depend on persuading people from within the department to work to change old policies, which have hitherto been regarded as quite satisfactory. Clearly, an innovating minister has to find ways to make a vast operational organization change its ways.

What is perhaps more significant is that a new minister will also find that his or her department is developing new policies. These are not necessarily merely the leftover business from a previous administration. Many of them will derive from weaknesses in existing policies that have been recognized within the department, and that administrators are striving to correct. Some, moreover, will have their roots in changes in the world on which existing policies operate, changes that are making those policies unsuccessful or irrelevant. This group of policies or 'would-be policies' is important. The new minister may find that his or her own, or the party's, policy aspirations mesh with the policy issues on which the department staff are working. In such circumstances, he or she may find it comparatively easy to become, or to be seen as, an innovator. However, he or she may have to face the fact that their own views of the department's policy needs are regarded as irrelevant to the main problems being tackled within it, or even that his or her own commitments lead in quite opposite directions to those being taken by others concerned with policy innovation in the department. Popular discussions of the success or failure of ministers are often carried out in terms of their personalities and their experience. Of course, it is often possible to distinguish 'strong' and 'weak' ministers; but it must not be forgotten that the comparatively temporary incumbent of the top position of a large organization may be just lucky – or unlucky – in arriving when key advisers are likely to agree that exciting innovations are necessary or, conversely, in finding that the consolidation of existing policies, or the confronting of unpleasant realities, is more important than the policy changes he or she cherishes.

An interesting, though painful to the individuals concerned, example of these phenomena was provided after the election of the Labour government in 1997. The Secretary of State responsible for Social Security, Harriet Harman, was given a senior colleague with considerable relevant expertise, Frank Field, to operate as a 'minister' for social security reform. Field found it very difficult to develop an innovatory agenda against a background of expenditure restraints. Harman came under pressure from the Treasury to enact cuts already designed by the civil service. In addition it is alleged that the two found it very difficult to work together (Rawnsley, 2001). Within a year both were out of office.

There are various kinds of policy initiatives. Some policies may be enacted by the passing of a law. Reform of regulatory law, for example, may have slight administrative implications. A second category of policies, with only indirect consequences for the minister's own department, consists of those whose enactment and implementation depend on another agency. Legislation giving powers, and even sometimes duties, to local government comes into this category. An example is legislation to protect the interests of disabled persons and their carers. While it seems to involve the development of a national policy, in practice its dependence on local government makes it a gesture in which central government involvement is comparatively slight. Clearly, it is easier for a minister to accept this kind of legislation than to develop a policy that effectively changes the direction of a great deal of work going on *within* the department. In the above case, the policy making may be more 'symbolic' than real; ministers may hope to derive kudos without really enacting innovations.

On the other hand, once a minister seeks to enact policies that require the expenditure of 'new money', he or she becomes engaged in what is inevitably a more difficult political exercise. Formally, the approval of the Treasury is required, probably together with the support of the Cabinet in one of its priority-setting exercises, where the minister is involved in competition with colleagues who have alternative expenditure aspirations.

What this implies for the minister's relationship with civil servants is altogether more complex. The specific expenditure commitment will, by no means, be the only one the department might undertake. Hence, there will be an intra-organizational battle about the case for that particular innovation. What the outside world sees as a minister promoting a particular project, is probably the end of a long process in which different groups of civil servants within the department have argued about the case for that venture as opposed to other ventures. The political negotiations between a minister and the Treasury ministers will be matched by much more elaborate negotiations between civil servants. A case that is comparatively weak when argued within the department will be faced with further problems in this tough forum, and a minister who successfully overrides objections within his or her own department may well lose in this wider battle. Students of government have, moreover, raised questions about the extent to which civil servants will fight effectively for their minister against the Treasury, in view of the prestige and power of the latter within the civil service as a whole (Heclo and Wildavsky, 1981).

In differentiating different kinds of policies, and in interpreting their implications for ministerial power, it must be recognized that some policies have implications for more than one department. A new approach to assistance with housing costs, for example, may have to be considered both by the Department for Work and Pensions, with its concern for social security policy, and by the Department for Local Government and the Regions with its responsibility for housing policy. The Treasury will also expect to be involved at an early stage, both because of its responsibilities for taxation and because of its concerns about overall expenditure. In addition, local government is likely to be involved. All this adds a form of complexity that greatly enhances the significance of negotiations between civil servants, and the related tendency for the maintenance of the *status quo*.

This discussion has distinguished between policies that ministers can enact with relatively slight implications for their own departments and those that require elaborate departmental involvement. It has implied that, where ideological commitments are involved, a distinction may be made between relatively easy gestures and difficult administrative battles. It may also be the case that some difficult aspects of 'bargaining politics' are involved where policy success depends on the responses of other organizations. The Thatcher government found some of its ideas for tax and social security reform affected by the reservations of small businesses about new tasks for government. The power of the doctors in health policy provides related examples. In this case, the problem comes, if not exactly within the Secretary of State's own department, at least from within public agencies. Also important for the analysis of social policy is the interplay between central government and those other organs of government, particularly local government, who have a crucial role to play in the implementation of policy, but are also themselves in certain respects policy formers. A new minister with an overall responsibility for the health and personal social services within the Department of Health, or for education, or for housing policy, will find an 'established' relationship between the department and local government or the health service with certain key characteristics. There will be a body of enacted legislation, a pattern of grants from central government, a range of procedures relating to the sanctioning of new initiatives including the taking up of loans for new capital expenditure, perhaps a pattern of inspection or policy review, and a variety of policy expectations enshrined in circulars and related messages from the centre. In a few cases, the obligations of the local authorities will be quite clear. In a rather larger number of situations, the authorities will have quite explicit duties but will not have been given detailed guidance on how to carry them out. In yet other important cases, the local authorities will regard themselves as the key policy formers; the central requirements will have been specified in such general terms that the decisions that really dictate the quality of the service given to the public are made locally. Then there will be some situations in which central government has made it very clear that the policy initiative rests with local agencies, by *permitting* activities if they so wish. Finally, there will be a few situations in which local authorities have been almost entirely the innovators, in which they have sought to promote local acts through Parliament or in which they have interpreted general powers given to them in quite novel ways.

The new minister who wants to introduce changes into this pattern has a variety of options open, but each may involve complications wherever there is resistance to new ideas. New policies are expressed as much in ministerial statements, White Papers and circulars to the local authorities as in new statutes. In each case, the minister may be able to bolster a recommendation with indirect weapons: by control over loans and other powers to permit or limit activities, by co-operation or lack of it in situations in which joint central–local action is necessary. The performance indices required of local government under the 'best value' policy (see pp. 63–4) may also be manipulated to this end. In the National Health Service (NHS), the control over funding also facilitates policy change from the centre.

In this section, the discussion has ranged over many of the influences on policy. Using the notion that is particularly associated with representative government, of a new minister with explicit policy commitments, attention has been given to the pressures that frustrate such commitments, or replace them by commitments derived from other sources. It has been stressed that there are strong forces in favour of the maintenance of existing policy, and that many new initiatives are, in fact, derived from concerns not so much to innovate as to correct the imperfections of existing policies.

Braybrooke and Lindblom (1963) drew attention to the extent to which the policy process is 'incremental'. That is, they were particularly concerned to attack that portrayal of the policy process which perceived it as, or able to become, a rational appraisal of all the alternative consequences of alternative policies followed by the choice of the best available. If incrementalism is perceived in these terms, there is little difficulty in understanding its applicability to social policy. As the historical chapter showed, the development of social policy has been very much a process of piling new initiatives on top of older policies, without ever clearing the ground to facilitate a fresh start. Then, as this piling-up process has proceeded, it has created new interests which future developments have to take into account. Since political values have often been at stake in conflicts over social policy, the very character of the ideological issues has precluded a cool appraisal of all the policy options.

Policy making is not a pure exercise in rational decision making. Nor is it simply the putting into practice of ideologies, or a quite incoherent process of bargaining and muddling through. Rather it is a mixture of all three, with perhaps the first being least apparent and the third most in evidence.

SUGGESTIONS FOR FURTHER READING

For those who need a basic account of political institutions, Jones et al. (2001) is recommended. Budge et al. (2000) and Dunleavy et al. (2002) offer a review of contemporary political issues. M. J. Smith (1993) and Marsh and Rhodes (1992b) explore the issues about 'policy networks' and 'policy communities'.

An account of devolution and other recent constitutional changes is provided in Jowell and Oliver (2000). Tony Byrne's regularly updated textbook on local government is a good source on that subject (2000), while those who want to follow up the issues concerning the financing relationship between central and local government should look at Glennerster et al. (2000). While it is not appropriate to recommend wide reading on the EU here, Kleinman (2002) is a good source on the issues about its role in social policy.

My book *The Policy Process in the Modern State* (Hill, 1997a) explores many of the theoretical issues to do with the study of policy making.

Chapter 4

Implementation

- Introduction
- Structures for policy implementation
- Analysing policy implementation
- Issues about the implications of the way policy is formed
- Issues about 'layers' in the policy transfer process
- Factors affecting the responses of implementation agencies
- Horizontal interorganizational relationships
- The social, political and economic environment
- Conclusions
- Suggestions for further reading

Introduction

Why devote a chapter in a book on social policy to the study of policy implementation? What is the significance of this issue for our subject? There are several reasons why it is important. As was made clear in the last chapter, the making of policy can be seen as involving a combination of 'formation' and 'implementation' in which there is a continuing interaction between the two and it may be the latter as much as the former that crucially determines its shape. Hence concern with the ineffectiveness of policies is now recognized as requiring the asking of questions both about the character of policy and about the implementation process and the organizations responsible for implementation.

There is a widespread 'top–down' perspective from which questions emerge like: Why don't those who are expected to carry out policies do what is required of them? But that question may be turned on its head since many people concerned with policy delivery may equally ask, from their 'bottom–up' perspective: Why are we being expected to carry out policies that are inappropriate for the issues and problems we confront? Both kinds of questions are equally valid and any sound discussion of implementation needs to take into account the legitimacy of both perspectives and the realities of implementation processes in which influences from the top, bottom and indeed the middle of the system are likely to be present. To these must be added some important issues about the impact of policy process upon people who are the recipients of its outputs.

Structures for Policy Implementation

This section provides a brief account of the main groups of people responsible for social policy implementation in the UK. Since the organizational arrangements vary within the constituent countries of the UK, the comments in this section should be taken to apply only to England unless there is an observation to the contrary. However, in the cases of social security and employment there is a single system for Britain, and the system in Northern Ireland is in most respects a copy of that.

Social security benefits are calculated and paid to the public by a large number of civil servants based in regional and local offices. These people now come under public 'agencies', carrying out functions delegated to them by the Department of Work and Pensions, to whom they are ultimately answerable. Until the formation of that new department the key social security agency was called the Benefits Agency. Since 2001, however, a restructuring process has been started bringing pensions administration under a new agency called the Pensions Service while the administration of those benefits that have not moved to the Inland Revenue are being brought under Jobcentre Plus, integrating them with the administration of policies for job seekers.

Tax credits and child benefit are the responsibility of the tax system run by the Board of Inland Revenue, an organization that has a long history of relative autonomy but which essentially takes its policy mandate from the Treasury. The Inland Revenue is also responsible for the collection of National Insurance (NI) contributions.

Another social security agency which has been the subject of considerable controversy is the Child Support Agency, set up to administer legislation enacted in 1991 to strengthen the system for securing contributions to child support from absent parents (mainly fathers).

To relate to local implementation systems, a number of central government departments have regional offices. Examples relevant to social policy implementation are the system of regional offices of the Department for Local Government and the Regions which handles many aspects of relationships with the local authorities, and the Department of Health's regional social services inspectors who advise and supervise local authority social services.

The implementation of health policy in England and Wales is devolved in a complex way. At national level, there is a National Health Service Executive. This is staffed by civil servants from the Department of Health and may, in many respects, be regarded as an extension of that department with direct accountability to the Secretary of State. Some of the Executive's activities are organized on a regional level.

Responsibility for the provision of all services at the local level including family practitioner services has been, or in some areas (at the time of writing) will be, brought under Primary Care Trusts. These both provide primary care services and commission secondary care. The latter is provided by other Trusts, which administer hospitals and some community services. Community health services appear, with arrangements varying from place to place, in Trusts on either side of the primary/secondary divide.

These arrangements operate within a structure over which Strategic Health Authorities have an overarching responsibility. This particular arrangement came into operation in April 2002. At the time this book is being drafted there is considerable uncertainty about how this new system will operate in practice. It has replaced a structure in which Health Authorities, with smaller territorial areas, operated as the key commissioning organizations with Trusts of various kinds as the service providers.

Both Health Authorities and Trusts, of all kinds, are quasi-autonomous organizations with directors (executive and non-executive) appointed by the Secretary of State, but with their own employees.

A controversial issue within health services concerns the extent to which commissioning bodies may go outside the normal NHS provider bodies to seek services from the private sector.

Health policy is an area of social policy in which professionals – particularly doctors – have extensive degrees of autonomy. It is often difficult to make the distinction between policy making and implementation with reference to a service operated by professionals. Day-to-day service-provision decisions may actually determine, or pre-empt, priorities. In this sense, they can be described as policy-formation decisions. While developments in the 1990s seemed to involve attempts to strengthen managerial authority over the professions, at the time of writing there seems to be a shift towards an alternative approach to health management which expects health personnel (particularly doctors), in bodies like the Primary Care Trusts, to increase their participation in decision making on local policy issues.

Responsibility for environmental health issues and for other non-medical influences on health such as food policy lies with the Department for Environment, Food and Rural Affairs. Much of the work of this department is done through agencies, such as the Environment Agency, or through local government. Local authorities have specific responsibilities for environmental health issues.

The personal social services are, relative to the NHS, very much a small proportion of the policy concerns of the Department of Health. One implementation complication here is that the central department responsible for local government is the Department for Local Government and the Regions. This department, together with the Treasury, deals with the main financial and legal links with local government, but has no responsibility for education, social services or environmental health policy. This exacerbates a tension, at the local level, between the demands of an integrated and corporate approach to local government and the separable service interests of heavy-spending activities. Arrangements in Scotland and Wales may be better co-ordinated.

The personal social services in Britain are usually the responsibility, inasmuch as they are under public rather than voluntary control, of social services departments (social work departments in Scotland) within local authorities. However, some local authorities have developed alternative ways of organizing these services, linking their management to that for other community services or housing. The increasing recognition of a need to co-ordinate social services with health services at the local level is also leading to innovations which link health service staff into care-management arrangements. It may be the case that there will eventually be radical organizational changes that will move some or all personal social services into the health service. We will return to this theme in chapter 7.

Since 1993, local authorities are required to operate, in respect of their community care services but not their child care services, a purchaser/provider system in which they seek the 'best value' (see pp. 63–4) service. Providers may be sections within the local authority department, required to operate with some degree of managerial and, particularly, accounting autonomy. They may also be voluntary or profit-making organizations; or they may be health service Trusts. The government has been concerned that providers from outside the local authority shall have a good chance of competing for personal social services contracts. In the area of the provision of residential care, which was already heavily privatized, local authority direct provision is rapidly disappearing. Some authorities also contract out some parts of their child care services. There is a quasi-autonomous Care Standards Commission that supervises most care services, both public and private.

Many directors and senior staff in social services departments are professionally qualified social workers, but a relatively small proportion of the staff is engaged in social work. Other key workers include home helps, residential care staff and occupational therapists. Policy implementation is often influenced by the character of co-operation between these different occupational groups.

Responsibility for the implementation of education and skill-training policy is divided between local authorities and a series of arrangements for links between the central ministries (Education and Skills) and the schools and colleges.

Many of the implementation issues in the local authority education service concern the relationship between the authorities and the schools. While the chain image is not entirely appropriate, since varying responsibilities and degrees of autonomy are involved, and individuals in the chain may be bypassed, it is important to acknowledge that implementation may depend on a series of links: the elected members of a local authority, the chief education officer and his or her administrative staff, local authority inspectors and advisers, school governing bodies, head teachers, departmental heads within the schools, and class teachers. The examination of policy implementation in the education service raises a number of interesting questions about local authority autonomy, the role of school management and the place of professional discretion.

The 1986 Education Act strengthened the powers of the governing bodies of local authority schools, laying down rules to determine their budgets and giving them autonomous responsibilities. It also enabled schools to apply to the Secretary of State to become 'grant maintained schools', directly accountable to him or her rather than under local authority control. After 1997 the new government abolished this form of school autonomy, but it put in its place a complex variety of alternative models for school management involving various degrees of autonomy from local government control (see further discussion in chapter 8). While the government has seen this as a form of decentralization, increasing the feasibility of parent power, the weakening of local political control can equally be seen as increasing centralization (Glennerster et al., 1991). The latter impression is further reinforced by the development of the national curriculum and by the power given to an independent inspectorate (Ofsted) accountable to central government.

In the case of post-school education the central/local links are complicated by a plethora of intervening and advisory bodies, in what Ainley shows to be a very complex and 'inherently unstable system' (Ainley, 2001, p. 474). Of key importance are a newly established Learning and Skills Council in England and a National Council for Education and Training in Wales with responsibility both for post-16 education in schools and also for further education. They direct the work of a network of local Learning and Skills Councils.

Higher education in Britain has required special forms of organization designed to take into account the fact that many colleges serve more than the local authority area in which they are based. For the university sector, a special intermediary body has long existed. However, the 1986 Education Act replaced the comparatively independent University Grants Committee by a more directly government-controlled Funding Council.

Local authority housing in Britain is the responsibility of the unitary or lower-tier local authorities. In Northern Ireland, protests about discrimination by local authorities led to the creation of a province-wide Housing Executive; and in Scotland there is an important nation-wide 'public' housing association to supplement the work of the local authorities. There is also, in England and Wales, a Housing Corporation, responsible for the provision of funds for housing associations. A feature of recent government policy has been a quest for new ways of managing and financing housing. This is increasing the importance of bodies like the housing associations, financed by public money or by a combination of public and private money.

The implementation of housing policy is fragmented not only because of the mixture of kinds of housing authorities but also because this is an area of social policy in which many significant decisions are made by private agencies. Since there are three main types of housing tenure – renting from a local authority or housing association ('social housing'), owner-occupation, and renting from a private landlord – and the government intervenes, or has intervened, to try to influence the quality and cost of each type, policy implementation is often a very complex matter. In studying it, attention has to be given not only to the relationship between government and the local authorities, but also to government attempts to influence the behaviour of building societies, landlords and private house builders. There are also some other public–private interactions of some significance for housing policy. For example, there have been government efforts to influence the price of land and to curb land speculation, government interventions in the money market, and government manipulation of the costs and benefits of various statuses in the housing market by means of taxation and social security policy.

Support for the housing costs of low-income tenants comes from housing benefit. In Britain, policy responsibility for this lies with the Department of Work and Pensions but local authorities administer the scheme. They receive direct reimbursement of most of their costs, except in respect of a few rather difficult issues (such as the treatment of some high rents) where they are given discretion at their own expense.

Finally, it should not be thought that the relationships between government and the various private sectors are of no concern to the local housing authorities. The latter increasingly seek to influence housing opportunities of all kinds in their areas, and to give advice to those they do not house themselves. Moreover the housing authorities, of course, have a significant interest in land prices, and have planning responsibilities to relate housing activities to other kinds of developments and land use in their areas. Housing policy implementation thus has many dimensions.

This whole section has shown that the machinery for policy implementation in the UK is complicated. Indeed it is steadily becoming more complicated. There has been a movement away from dependence on simple bureaucratic models – a single social security ministry, a National Health Service hierarchically organized, local authorities expected to be organized departmentally – to a range of models involving contracting, cross-system partnerships and output surveillance. There has been a succession of experiments:

- new bureaucratic organizations in the 1960s and 1970s;
- efforts to create market or quasi-market arrangements in the 1980s and 1990s;
- a confusing pragmatism in the 1990s and 2000s with emphases upon the idea that only 'what works' matters and on a need for 'joined up' government together with a continued quest for new ways to control (see Newman, 2001).

Each fashion in 'governance' has left legacies behind to confuse the overall picture.

Analysing Policy Implementation

While any subdivision may be arbitrary it is useful to categorize the issues about implementation into the following:

1 issues about the implications of the way policy is formed;
2 issues about 'layers' in the policy transfer process;
3 factors affecting the responses of implementation agencies (their organization, the extent of autonomy amongst their staff, etc.);
4 horizontal interorganizational relationships (relationships between parallel organizations required to collaborate in implementation);
5 the impact of the social, political and economic environment.

Issues about the Implications of the Way Policy is Formed

The policy-formation process is like the design of a building for a specific occupant by an architect; the implementation process affects policy design quite early on and will continue to influence some details of it even after implementation has begun, just as modifications are made to buildings after occupancy. The content of that policy, and its impact on those affected, may be substantially modified, elaborated, or even negated during the implementation stage. Nevertheless policy is originated by specific groups of people, very often the actors at national government level discussed in the previous chapter, and those people are likely to have specific concerns about the way it may subsequently be elaborated.

Many policies will be formulated in a complex way; setting out to achieve objectives x, x_1, x_2 ... under conditions y, y_1, y_2, ... These complexities may well influence the implementation process. Some policies will involve vague and ambiguous specifications of objectives and conditions. These will tend to become more specific during the implementation process.

While it is possible, in the abstract, to treat policies in isolation from other policies, in practice, any new policy will be adopted in a context in which there are already many other policies. Some of these other policies will supply precedents for the new policy, others will supply conditions, and some may be in conflict with it. These will therefore contribute to the modification of policy as it is implemented.

Policy goals are often specified, as has been pointed out, in general, or unclear, terms. We may identify a number of different reasons for this lack of clarity. First, it may be simply that those who initially formulate policy are far from clear about what they really want. The lack of clarity may be so total that it is comparatively meaningless to seek to identify a policy or to study its implementation. Some of the 'policies' of this kind derive from political aspirations to demonstrate a popularly desirable commitment.

Secondly, it is important to take account of the extent to which a lack of clarity about policy stems from a lack of potential consensus. Policies emerge that are not merely compromises, but also remain obscure on key points of implementation. Where this occurs, it is likely that there will be a lack of consensus among the implementers, too. Hence, wide variations in practice may emerge, together with a range of conflicts surrounding the implementation process. A study of the provision of care and education for children under compulsory school age by Liu (2001) illustrates very clearly how conflicts between those concerned about 'care' and those concerned about 'education', and conflicts about the respective roles of the public and private sectors, have inhibited effective policy development in this way.

Ambiguity arising from lack of consensus about policy goals provides opportunities for those who are opposed to their general thrust, or who wish to divert them to serve their own ends. Bardach (1977) has developed an extensive analysis of the various 'implementation games' that may be played by those who perceive ways in which policies may be delayed, altered or deflected. While some policies contain few features that their opponents can interfere with – laying down, for example, a clear duty to provide a particular service or benefit – others, such as the Department of Health's commitment to the development of community care for mentally ill people, depend heavily on the commitments of implementers, and are relatively easily diverted in other directions or even rendered ineffective.

While acknowledging that many policies are made complex and ambiguous by the conflicts within the policy-making process, it is important to recognize that it is intrinsically difficult to specify some policy goals in terms that will render the implementation process quite clear and unambiguous. This is one important source of discretion for implementers. Jowell (1973) has drawn attention to examples where the concern of policy is with 'standards' that are not susceptible to precise factual definition. He argues that standards may be rendered more precise by 'criteria', facts that are to be taken into account, but that 'the feature of standards that distinguishes them from rules is their flexibility and susceptibility to change over time'. Questions about adequate levels of safety on the roads or in factories, or about purity in food, are of this kind. So are many of the issues about need in social policy; see the discussion on pp. 195–7. Discretionary judgement is likely to be required by policy implementers, alongside the more precise rules that it is possible to promulgate. We will return to the topic of discretion below.

Issues about 'Layers' in the Policy Transfer Process

Many policies are formulated by one layer in an administrative system but implemented by another. Some writers speak of one layer 'mandating' another. There is thus a 'transfer' process involved. In the UK, central government will generally have been involved in the policy-formulation process, but implementation is often delegated to other organizations, with the centre generally maintaining an interest in the implementation process. It is thus important to consider questions about the ways in which policies are expressed, and the evidence required to establish the extent of implementation. Policies may be conveyed to local implementers in a range of ways from, at one extreme, the explicit imposition of duties and responsibilities to, at the other end of the continuum, the loose granting of powers that may or may not be used. We can contrast, for example, the comparatively strict ways in which regulations under social security legislation instruct local authorities in the administration of housing benefit, with powers given (originally in the 1963 Children and Young Persons Act, now in the 1989 Children Act) to local authorities to make money payments, in exceptional circumstances, to prevent children being taken into care, where no attempt has been made to prescribe how this should be done.

This mandating process will often be accompanied by financial transactions between layers. In the UK the split between central government as a policy initiator and local government in the role of implementer produces a situation in which central intentions appear to be thwarted by local scarcities. Yet it is generally, as was shown on pp. 65–6, central government that determines the level of local resources. In the area of community care, local authorities in the mid-1990s received some additional funds to enable them to meets costs which were previously met by central government from the social security budget. At the same time, they were subjected to centrally imposed limits on their capacity to raise local revenues. Many considered that their resources fell far short of their responsibilities under the new legislation. There is a certain political duplicity in legislation that expects local agencies to provide benefits that the centre makes them unlikely to be able to afford.

The 'agencies' set up to administer central services – like the Benefits Agency – seem, *prima facie*, to have clearer mandates. They are governed by framework agreements that seem to make their implementation responsibilities explicit. Yet the intrinsic difficulties in drawing a clear distinction between policy formation and implementation mean that anything they may do to alter the service they provide to the public may raise political concerns. Furthermore, as the case of the Child Support Agency (see chapter 5, pp. 121–2) shows, when something goes wrong, there will be argument about whether an agency has failed to fulfil its mandate or whether that mandate was flawed. In fact, as was the case in this example, their apparent separation enabled their chief executives to be offered as sacrifices for ministerial mistakes.

One issue deserving of attention is the 'special' agency set up to concern itself with policy making and implementation in a specifically limited policy field. Three motives can perhaps be identified for the creation of special agencies in the UK, although there are, of course, dangers in taking ostensible motives as real ones: to create an effective separate and accountable 'management system', to reduce political 'interference', and to provide for the direct representation of special interests. In the UK there have been a variety of efforts to design arrangements for local control over further education and training policy designed to involve local employers and other relevant interest groups (see Ainley, 2001).

The removal of some aspects of the elaboration of policy from direct political influence, particularly when there are powerful special interests within the quasi-autonomous body, introduces complications that make it particularly difficult to distinguish policy formation from implementation. These agencies may be seen alternatively as implementers that affect the character of policy or as independent creators of policy forever in a relationship of tension with the 'centre'. It is this tension that can then sometimes be seen as leading to central efforts to curb the independence of agencies whose initial freedom was provided by government.

This whole subject is made more complicated by issues about accountability and the right to control. These have always been areas of controversy for social policy in the United Kingdom, but that controversy has been given a new twist by the development of approaches to government that involve a rejection of simple hierarchical modes of control. What has happened is that discontent with older hierarchical or 'bureaucratic' models for policy implementation has led to a range of experimentation with alternative models (Hood, 1991). During the 1980s and 1990s that experimentation was very influenced by a view that 'market' rather than 'hierarchy' models (Williamson, 1975) should be adopted, with services contracted out to private agencies or run by autonomous public agencies in a quasi-market relationship to a public sector 'purchaser'. That perspective has gradually been replaced by a more pragmatic stance that involves a continued distrust of hierarchy, a conditional acceptance of market arrangements (if they work) and an interest in exploring other ways of delegating responsibility to the lowest possible level. The last named development involves, for some, a commitment to new participatory forms of democracy, involving services' users in service management.

Janet Newman, in her study of governance in Britain under 'new Labour', has argued that governance is 'always likely to be characterised by multiple and conflicting models' (2001, p. 39). She describes that conflict as involving tension between continuity and innovation, on one dimension, centralization and differentiation on the other. From those dimensions Newman distils four models of governance (ibid., p. 38):

- the self-governance model, towards devolution based on citizen or community power;
- the open-system model, towards flexibility, based on the flow of power within networks;
- the hierarchy model, towards control, based on formal authority;
- the rational goal model, towards output maximisation, based on managerial power.

Newman says of the Blair government:

> Labour sought to create both a new social settlement based on consensus and inclusion, and a more coercive and conditional welfare regime. It attempted to ensure the consistency and efficacy of policy delivery by setting and enforcing performance standards, while at the same time seeking to institutionalize new forms of co-steering and co-governance through partnerships and community capacity building. It sought to send out a strong and consistent set of messages from the centre, while also fostering public

participation and drawing a wider range of actors into the policy process. (Ibid., pp. 163–4)

Newman's analysis thus suggests that there is a search going on for new approaches to control over implementation, characterized by conflict over the desirability of decentralization. An alternative way of looking at this is to see that there are choices to be made between alternative models. Drawing upon a variety of attempts to supplement the hierarchy/market dichotomy outlined above with a third alternative involving higher levels of participation (called 'persuasion' by Lindblom, 1977, and 'community' by Colebatch and Larmour, 1993), the author and Peter Hupe (Hill and Hupe, 2002) have arrived at a typology of modes of governance involving different implementation expectations, as follows:

- 'authority': where rules are laid down in advance;
- 'transaction': where certain outputs are expected, often as specified in contracts;
- 'persuasion': where the essential mode of operation involves collaboration and networks or what may be called 'co-production'.

Choices between the alternatives will depend both upon the ideologies of those (at both levels) who are able to make those choices and upon considerations about the 'best' ways to organize any specific policy-delivery process. The latter considerations rest upon what is being attempted, with it being recognized that very different considerations will apply, for example, between situations in which implementation involves delivering specific cash benefits, or offering complex services, or regulating behaviour.

Factors Affecting the Responses of Implementation Agencies

While traditional approaches to public administration involve notions of prescription of activities from legitimate policy makers to public 'servants' expected to defer to authority – within organizations as well as between – many studies of organizational behaviour suggest that there are finite limits to the prescription of subordinate behaviour. Detailed rule-making is a difficult and time-consuming activity. If it requires close supervision and control, a point may be reached where such activities are self-defeating. It is interesting to note how much manufacturing industry has moved away from what has been described as the 'Fordist' model of routine mass-production work. Managerial gurus like Peters and Waterman (1982) extol the virtues of flexible forms of organization, engaging the commitments of employees and enabling them to innovate and cope with organizational change. This approach has been seen as relevant to government too (Pollitt, 1990; Butcher, 2002).

In many areas of social policy, there will be a strong element of discretion in tasks. Earlier in this chapter references have been made to what may be described as sources of discretion:

1 deliberate recognition of local autonomy;
2 'political' difficulties in resolving key policy dilemmas;
3 'logical' problems in prescribing 'standards'.

To these must be added:

4 the inherent limits to the regulation of tasks;
5 the human motivation problems which follow from trying to regulate them.

In practice, prescriptions for policy implementation convey discretionary powers to field-level staff for reasons that are combinations of these 'sources' of discretion.

An alternative way of looking at the phenomenon of discretion is to see the field official (including the teacher or social worker) as a 'street-level bureaucrat' (Lipsky, 1980). His or her job is characterized by inadequate resources for the task, by variable and often low public support for the role, and by ambiguous and often unrealizable expectations of performance. The officials' concerns are with the actual impact of specific policies on their relationships with specific individuals; these may lead to a disregard of, or failure to understand, the wider policy issues that concern those 'higher up' in the agency. The 'street-level' role is necessarily uncertain. A modicum of professional (or semi-professional, see below) training defines the role as putting into practice a set of ideals inculcated in that training. Yet the 'street-level' bureaucrat is also the representative of a government agency that is itself subject to conflicting pressures. In day-to-day contact with clients and with the community at large, he or she becomes, to some degree, locked into the support of individuals and groups who may be antipathetic to the employing agency. In such a situation of role confusion and role strain, a person at the end of the line is not disposed to react to new policy initiatives from above as if he or she were a mere functionary. New policies are but factors in a whole web of demands that have to be managed; see Hudson (1997) for some British social-policy examples of this.

There are 'two faces' to street-level bureaucracy. It may be seen as the effective adaptation of policy to the needs of the public, or it may be seen as the manipulation of positions of power to distort policy towards stigmatization, discrimination and petty tyranny. Which it is will vary according to the policy at stake, and the values and commitments of the field workers, but this will also depend on the scope accorded by the organizational control system, for this phenomenon is not necessarily independent of 'biases' built into the policy-delivery system. Workers may more easily manipulate their 'system' in favour of, or against, some clients in situations where their agency grants them licence to deploy such commitments.

Consideration of discretion and of the roles of 'street-level bureaucrats' must also involve looking at the implications of professionalism for implementation. Three interrelated points may be made about professionalism:

1 it may entail a level of expertise that makes lay scrutiny difficult;
2 professionals may be, for whatever reason, accorded a legitimate autonomy;
3 professionals may acquire amounts of power and influence that enable them to determine their own activities.

These sources of professional freedom clearly have a differential impact depending on (a) the profession involved, (b) the organizational setting in which professionals work, and (c) the policies that they are required to implement. The importance of the level of expertise for professional power has led some writers to make a distinction between professions and semi-professions (Etzioni, 1969), with doctors and lawyers in the former category but social workers and teachers in the latter.

The issues about expertise are, however, complex. They interact significantly with the phenomenon of 'determinacy' – the extent to which the professional response can be pre-programmed. The more complex professional tasks are a mixture of activities which can be routinized together with situations in which the professional must have the capacity to respond to the unexpected. For example, much doctoring is routine – many patients present clear symptoms for which there is a predictable response or there are logical testing procedures to go through to reach a diagnosis – but a good doctor has to be able to spot the exceptional condition and react to the unexpected response to treatment. Should health care systems therefore lay down 'protocols' and monitor to ensure that standard procedures are followed? Or should they allow doctors to exercise their discretion, so that they feel they are able to respond flexibly to the unexpected rather than operate as 'Fordist' workers practising 'cookbook' medicine? This is, of course, not an either/or matter; the problem is how to find the ideal path between the extreme positions. It is a very live one for the management of the NHS; at the time of writing, it is manifest in efforts to develop a system of 'clinical governance' to fuse professional freedom with public accountability.

The second point above, on autonomy, has been the subject of controversy about the impact on professional activities of organizational, and particularly public, employment. The conclusion would seem to be dictated by some of the considerations in the previous paragraph. That is, in short, that 'it depends on the profession and on the organization'. On the third point, once again, a good deal depends on the nature of the policy involved.

In a large number of situations, it is expected that professional judgement will have a considerable influence on the implementation process. Clearly explicit in many policies is an expectation of this. It applies to many decisions made in face-to-face relationships between professionals and their clients. Many of the issues involved are increasingly the subject of controversy, involving arguments about 'rights' versus 'discretion'. Within these arguments, disputes occur about the significance of expertise and about the scope for effective limitation of discretionary power. Their effective resolution would also impose many difficult policy questions – about moral rights to choose (for example, with reference to abortion) and the best way to allocate scarce resources (for example, with regard to kidney machines) – which are, at present, partly masked by professional discretion.

There are also some important questions here, which are difficult to resolve, about the way to link together professional autonomy in dealing with an individual relationship with a client, and a policy-based concern (or 'public concern') about the way in which professionals allocate their services as a whole. Professionals have been found to be reluctant to confront priority questions; they often prefer to deal with each patient or client as an individual in need without any reference to a collective ethic that requires some degree of priority ranking. A consequence of this may be lengthening waiting lists. The political response to these has been to treat waiting lists as crucial indices of services to the public (with targets enshrined in charters, and published). Yet doing this does not solve the problems of competing priorities. It either forces a watering down of the service offered to all or, more likely, forces attention to be given to certain issues (like the rapidity with which patients secure a certain routine operation) at the expense of others where the quantitative indices are not available or cannot be so easily interpreted. There are also problems about the extent to which indices of this kind can be manipulated by altering procedures and recording practices rather than by improving the overall service.

This section has explored the many sources of autonomy on the part of implementing agencies. This autonomy is controversial because it occurs against a background of conflict over accountability, about the rights of various actors to exercise control – politicians at the top, organizations and professions in the middle, workers at the 'street level' and, last but not least, the public themselves as the recipients of policy outputs.

Horizontal Interorganizational Relationships

A further important complication for the operation of individual agencies is that many activities depend on the co-operation of two or more organizations. We describe these as 'horizontal' relationships since the organizations are in no sense 'accountable' to each other. The relationships between layers analysed above are complicated by deviations from the simple model in which there are single organizations at each level – a single central government department relating to a single implementing agency, or to a number of local authorities in each of a series of distinct geographical areas. Policy implementation often depends on co-operation between separate organizations where responsibility at the local level is (a) delegated to several organizations with separate territories, and (b) dependent on co-ordinated action between two or more local organizations.

Many organizations are involved in a web of relationships, which vary in character and intensity according to the issue. Some activities require considerable co-operation between levels while others require very little. However, it may be misleading to lose sight of the overall pattern since the outcome of one relationship will affect responses to another. Relationships are ongoing; each will have a history that conditions reactions to any new issues. Equally, each organization will have developed its own sense of its task, mission, and role in relation to others. These will affect its response to anything new.

It is widely recognized that different services to individuals need to be integrated. This issue is particularly salient in the area of health and personal social services policy. Many individuals need varying combinations of health and social care. The search for the best way to organize to make these combinations effective is explored further on pp. 191–4. There are no easy answers. While various attempts have been made to create structures that do this, it is perhaps the case that what is crucial is that ways are found to encourage different professionals to work together at the 'street level' regardless of their organizational locations (see Hudson and Henwood, 2002).

The Social, Political and Economic Environment

Policies may be interpreted as responses to perceived social needs. They are evolved in an environment in which problems emerge that are deemed to require political solutions, and where pressures occur for new political responses. Government is concerned with 'doing things to', 'taking things from' or 'providing things for' groups of people. Putting policies into practice involves interactions between the agencies of government and their environment.

Many policies may be seen as providing for 'outputs' that may or may not deliver what are regarded as desirable final 'outcomes'. The latter may be determined by factors other than the policy under scrutiny. Policies may seem to aim at outcomes – improving health, reducing poverty, increasing literacy etc. – but in fact fail to do so. This may be because of environmental factors that are hard to control.

However, in looking at social policy, we must also question whether the distinction between the policy system and its environment can be easily made. In chapter 1, it was established that it is misleading to see any simple equation between the activities of the social policy system and the enhancement of social welfare. Yet, just as the policy determinants of welfare are multiple, and sometimes unexpected, so individuals' welfare is influenced by phenomena that have nothing to do with the activity of the state. As pointed out, the determinants of an individual's welfare can be broadly classified as depending on their own capacity to care for themselves, combined with (a) market activities and relationships, (b) the behaviour of 'significant others' as providers of 'informal care', among whom family members are likely to be the most important, and (c) the role played by the state. To study welfare requires attention to all 'determinants'. Changes in the way in which welfare is provided are particularly likely to involve shifts in the roles played by these 'determinants' and shifts in the relationships between them. In other words, the process of interaction between policy system and environment is a very active one, and those interactions occur across an ambiguous, shifting boundary. To give a concrete example, personal social services care is only one element in individual care systems in which family, neighbour and purchased care are likely also to play a part. A shift in the availability, or character, of any one of these care ingredients is likely to have an impact on the others. Day-to-day policy implementation in the state-provided sector involves the management, or indeed sometimes mismanagement, of its relationships to the other elements. Accordingly analysts of social policy have conceived of the system as a 'mixed economy of welfare' (Webb, 1985). The implementation of many contemporary policy initiatives – privatization, the limitation of social expenditure, the extension of social care – involves changing the balance between the various ingredients in the 'mixed economy of welfare'. Where government withdraws or reduces its direct contribution to welfare, it may still make an indirect contribution, for example, if the social security system subsidizes private provision; or it may have to acquire a new range of regulatory concerns about the quality of private services; or it may face increased problems in the other areas of concern, because of the new pressures placed on individuals and families.

Conclusions

This chapter has portrayed the implementation process as a complex one, in many respects inextricably entwined with the policy-making process. It has suggested that, in the study of social policy, it is important to give attention to implementation problems that arise directly from the way policy was formulated, but to recognize also that there is a complicated interrelationship between these and a range of inter- and intra-organizational factors. Finally, all these complications interact with a complex environment.

Relationships between the public and the organizations delivering public policies may be studied with a view to ascertaining and explaining what people actually get from the social policy system. Clearly, questions about bias in the behaviour of public officials, the mechanisms by which scarce benefits or services are rationed, the roles played by 'gatekeepers' and the problems of securing effective 'take-up' of some benefits are issues of concern for the implementation of policies. In the study of these matters, many of the issues about the motivation of implementers concern the interaction between the nature of policy, the implementation system and the characteristics of the public. Policy delivery is not easily made an 'even-handed' process; class, gender and race differences influence access to professional services; some social security applicants are less well-informed and more easily deterred than others; and 'street-level bureaucrats' who may be regarded as highly responsive to local needs in a white neighbourhood may be seen very differently in a black one. Are these biases in the system attributable to faults in policy or faults in its implementation? The answer is very often that both may be responsible. Their interaction needs to be examined very carefully.

While we all experience the effects of the implementation process, and many of us participate in various ways in it, very few of us are involved in policy formation. Yet, it is this policy formation, often particularly that which occurs at the highest level, that receives much more attention. It is hoped that, in considering the detailed discussions of particular areas of policy contained in the next section of this book, readers will bear in mind the importance of the interaction between the policy-formation process and the implementation process for the actual impact of social policies on the public.

SUGGESTIONS FOR FURTHER READING

Tony Butcher's *Delivering Welfare* (2002) offers an excellent overview of the organizational arrangements for social policy delivery in Britain, with a strong emphasis on contemporary developments. I have contributed to further discussions of the theoretical issues raised in this chapter, in chapters 6–9 of my book *The Policy Process in the Modern State* (Hill, 1997a) and in a book with Peter Hupe, *Implementing Public Policy* (2002). Contributions to parts IV and V of my edited collection *The Policy Process: A Reader* (1997b) are also relevant.

A large literature is emerging on the new approaches to the management of policy delivery, and its implications for professionalism. The following are recommended in addition to Butcher's book mentioned above: Clarke, Cochrane and McLaughlin's edited collection *Managing Social Policy* (1994), Rao's *Towards Welfare Pluralism* (1996) and Newman's *Modernising Governance* (2001).

Much information about the organization of the implementation system can be found in the websites for government departments and other public organizations accessible via www.ukonline.gov.uk.

Chapter 5
Social Security

Introduction

The term 'social security' is used here to cover all the state systems of maintenance in the UK. These fall into five categories:

1 contributory benefits;
2 benefits that the state requires employers to provide;
3 non-contributory benefits which are not means-tested but are contingent on the individual being in some specific category;

4   means-tested benefits;
5   tax credits.

The responsibility for social security benefits is divided between the Department for Work and Pensions and the Inland Revenue. The Department for Work and Pensions delivers benefits through agencies. As a result of the government restructuring after the 2001 election the agency system for the delivery of benefits is being reshaped at the time of writing. Pensions are coming under an agency called the Pensions Service. Benefits for adults under pension age, which have been the responsibility of the Benefits Agency, are being brought under an organization called Jobcentre Plus. The latter change implies a direct linking of benefit administration for all under pension age with employment services in a reconstructed network of local offices. There is also the Child Support Agency, which collects contributions from absent parents towards the maintenance of children in families dependent on 'income support'. The Inland Revenue collects national insurance (NI), pays tax credits and administers the child benefit system. Housing benefit and council tax benefit are administered by the unitary, or lower-tier, local authorities, using a rule structure laid down by the Department for Work and Pensions.

Contributory Benefits

The Beveridge plan for contributory benefits (Beveridge, 1942) envisaged that these should provide the main source of provision for income mainten-ance in the event of old age, sickness, unemployment and widowhood. The legislation of the 1940s, picking up the main pieces from earlier contributory social security schemes, attempted to provide this coverage. The few surviv-ing contributory benefits date from that time, but the system of contribu-tions, the nature of the benefits and the character of the alternative benefits available to back up the contributory system have all changed a great deal.

All employees, together with the self-employed, are required to pay NI contributions. These are calculated as a percentage of earnings, but there is a low-income threshold below which they are not required, and an income level above which additional income is not taken into account. Normally employees' contributions are deducted from their pay by employers, who also have to pay employers' NI contributions on a similar basis for those they employ.

The original NI scheme set up in the 1940s specified a clear relationship between contributions and a wide range of benefit entitlements. This is no longer the case. The link between contributions and benefit entitlements has been steadily eroded since 1979, so that it is now more appropriate to see contributions as simply a tax. The limited remaining contributory benefit entitlements are discussed in this section.

There is a flat-rate pension to which insurance contributors are entitled on reaching the age of 60 if they are women, 65 if they are men (the female qualifying age will be increased to 65 by a phasing-in process in the period 2010–20). The actual pension rate depends on the length of working life.

After 1977, there was put into operation a state earnings-related pension scheme (SERPS) that provides earnings-related pensions. Individual employees had to contribute either to this scheme or to officially approved private schemes. Those who 'contracted out' secure only the flat-rate retirement pension from the state (though benefits from a limited interim scheme that operated between 1961 and 1975 provide small additions for some people). In 2002 the government replaced SERPS with the 'state second pension' (see p. 114). There are arrangements for carrying forward SERPS contributions.

The employee who is unable to work on account of sickness is initially dependent on his or her employer for support. The latter is, with some exceptions, required to provide sick pay at least at the minimum levels prescribed by Parliament, for 28 weeks. This is, of course, not a contributory benefit *per se*, but this scheme replaced the former NI one, and small (formerly all) employers obtain some rebate of their NI contributions in respect of sick employees.

Those who become sick when not in employment may receive a contributory benefit if they were insurance contributors for a period until shortly before, a benefit that is now called 'short-term incapacity benefit'. During this period, claimants must establish that they are unfit to return to their normal occupation.

After the first six months of sickness, anyone still unfit for work moves on to a higher rate of short-term incapacity benefit, which continues until they have been sick for a year. After a year of sickness, people may move on to long-term incapacity benefit. The rate of payment is a little higher than that of the short-term benefit.

The qualification rules for incapacity benefit are very strict. There is an elaborate 'personal capacity assessment' procedure under which ability to do work of any kind is assessed. The government's objective here is to prevent people settling down on this long-term benefit unless it is quite clear that they cannot re-enter the labour market, even with training and other forms of support.

In addition to the incapacity benefits described above, there are special, in general more generous, provisions applying to those whose incapacity for work arises from an industrial accident or a prescribed industrial disease. These will not be considered in detail here.

There is a system of statutory maternity pay, like statutory sick pay, payable for 18 weeks. This must be paid by employers if their employees have been continuously with them over half a year. This is backed up by a reduced state maternity allowance for women with recent work records who do not qualify for pay from their employers.

The benefit for unemployed people is called 'jobseeker's allowance'. As the name suggests, to qualify a person has to make a clear undertaking, signing a 'jobseeker's agreement', on the steps he or she will take to try to find work. However, contributory benefits for unemployed people have always been limited by strict previous contribution conditions, by rules which disqualify a person if there is evidence that the unemployment may be to some extent their own fault, and by a time limit to entitlement. With the introduction of the jobseeker's allowance, the latter has been reduced to six months. After six months, or if the previous contributions and other tests are not satisfied, jobseeker's allowance is means-tested (its rules being broadly those applying to 'income support'; see p. 107).

A contributory scheme for those out of work, which has initial qualifying rules and the exhaustion of entitlement after six months, leaves many in need of means-tested benefits. In particular, young new entrants to the labour force are unprotected by the contributory benefit scheme.

There is a lump-sum bereavement payment of up to £2,000 where a spouse who has fulfilled specified NI contribution conditions, dies. There is also a bereavement allowance payable for a year to bereaved people between 45 and pension age. There are also provisions under which widows and widowers may inherit a pension entitlement. Widows and widowers have a contributory benefit entitlement, based on their deceased spouse's contributions, to an allowance if they have children to support. This benefit is lost on remarriage or 'cohabitation'.

There are no provisions for benefits to cover the ending of marriage other than through death, or to provide for the consequences of the ending of unmarried 'partnerships' due to any cause (including death). Benefits in these cases depend on means-tests.

Benefits that the State Requires the Employer to Provide

The main benefits in this category were mentioned in the discussion above, since they evolved out of the earlier insurance benefits for sickness and maternity and need to be seen as still linked to related residual benefits: these are statutory sick pay and statutory maternity pay.

In addition employers have a liability to make redundancy payments. The minimum amounts of these are determined by a formula taking into account the rate of pay and length of service.

It is also appropriate to mention private pensions here inasmuch as the alternative to the state second pension is contributions to private schemes. There are regulations, backed up by special agencies, to supervise all private pensions. In 2001 legislation provided for new kinds of private pension schemes, to be under much stricter state supervision, known as 'stakeholder' pensions. The government expects stakeholder pensions to be available to all but the very low paid; it requires employers to make them available to employees but does not compel people to contribute to them.

Non-contributory, Non-means-tested, Contingent Benefits

Child benefit is paid to the parents or guardians of all children under sixteen years of age and of children between sixteen and eighteen who are still at school. The only qualifying condition is a residence one.

There are some non-contributory benefits available to long-term disabled people, which must not be confused with the industrial injury disablement provision or with incapacity benefit. These are the disability living allowance and attendance allowance. These are set at various rates depending on the extent of need for care by another person. There is a range of detailed rules concerning these benefits which cannot be discussed in the space available here. People who claim before they are twenty years old, in other words those never able to enter the labour force and become NI contributors, are also entitled to incapacity benefit.

There is also a benefit available for carers who are not gainfully employed and have to devote a substantial amount of time to the care of someone disabled. This is invalid care allowance, and its rate of pay is low.

Means-tested Benefits

A comparative study of social assistance schemes described the UK as having an 'integrated safety net' built around 'income support' which is seen as 'a large, national, general programme providing an extensive safety net at or below social insurance levels' (Eardley et al., 1996, p. 169). This extensive means-testing is necessitated by the various restrictions on the availability of contributory benefits described above. It also arises because the levels of some of the contributory benefits (flat-rate pensions, short-term incapacity benefit and jobseeker's allowance) are such that claimants will often qualify for further means-tested support as well, at least in respect of housing costs. At the time of writing there are grounds for doubt about the extent to which that word 'integrated' in the quotation above is still appropriate. Clearly the government still expects the whole means-testing system to function in an integrated way but the development of the system of tax credits (see the next section) administered by the Inland Revenue is making some aspects of that integration more difficult.

The main means-tested benefit is called 'income support'. Its means test is based on a simple personal allowance structure, enhanced in some cases by 'premiums'. The specific personal allowance rates are for a couple, a single person over 25, a person between 18 and 24, and there are three age-related rates for children (but bear in mind the implications of the introduction of the Child Tax Credit for this aspect of the scheme after April 2003 – see below p. 109). Then, there are different premiums for families, lone parents and disabled people. The idea throughout is that the determination of the appropriate overall entitlement for a household should be a simple, predictable process. Additions for special needs have been abolished. Rules determine how any income should be taken into account. People in full-time work (defined as doing sixteen or more hours in employment per week) are disqualified from receiving income support, but part-time workers may obtain it. To deal with this, an earnings rule is used, based on net income, which involves disregarding a small amount and then deducting the rest from any entitlement. Similar 'disregards' are used for some other kinds of income, but state benefits are taken into account in full. There are special rules dealing with savings, disregarding small amounts, then applying a sliding scale, reducing benefits up to an upper limit at which they disqualify a person from benefit entirely.

The means-tested support for pensioners provides higher rates of benefit. It has, since 1997, been described as a 'minimum income guarantee'. After 2003 it will be called a 'pensioner credit', and will be further complicated by provisions to reduce the deductions hitherto applied when people have small savings and private pensions.

The housing benefit scheme has been designed to be compatible with income support. The income support rules are used in the calculation of benefit so that anyone with a rent to pay who is at, or below, the income level that would qualify them for income support may receive the full housing benefit entitlement. Housing benefit provides support for rent; it does not provide support for house buying. However, owner-occupiers on income support may receive some help towards mortgage interest payments.

The housing benefit scheme is, in effect, extended to local taxation. Low-income council tax payers may apply for a reduction in their payments known as 'council tax benefit' (calculated in a similar way to housing benefit).

The housing benefit maximum is generally the full rent (though there are various rent restriction rules – applied to single persons under 25 and to accommodation deemed to be either too large or too expensive) minus contributions from other adults (apart from the claimant's 'spouse'). There are some complicated rules dealing with all these qualifications. The maximum is payable to those whose incomes are at, or below, the 'income support' or 'minimum income guarantee' qualifying level. Similarly, for those with incomes at, or below, that level and with no adult non-dependent family or householder members, the council tax benefit will provide for the remission of the whole tax liability. Where incomes are above income support level, benefit tapers off proportionately, at the rate of 65 per cent for housing benefit and 20 per cent for council tax benefit.

Chapter 10 shows how housing benefit has become the main approach to the provision of housing subsidies to low-income tenants. As a system run by local authorities on behalf of the Department for Work and Pensions, it is not always well co-ordinated with the rest of the benefits system. It is administratively costly. It is also rather vulnerable to fraud, particularly in the private rented sector where there can be collusion between landlord and tenant to try to maximize benefit. The government is seeking ways to simplify the system. These may involve the introduction of formulae that extend the tendency to offer less than full support to rent payments.

Under the supplementary benefit scheme operative until 1988, there were provisions enabling single payments to be made to help people with exceptional expenditures – removal costs, furnishing, house repairs and so forth. An elaborate body of rules dealt with these entitlements. The 1986 Social Security Act swept away these single-payment entitlements but, in their place, set up the social fund, administered by a specially trained group of staff. There are two kinds of grants available from the fund as of right to people on income support: a lump sum maternity-needs payment and a funeral-needs payment (the amount of which depends on funeral costs). There is also provision for grants to be made from the social fund to assist with the promotion of community care. These may be available when people need help in establishing themselves in the community after a period of institutional care, to assist with some travelling expenses to visit relatives in hospitals and other institutions, and to improve the living conditions of defined 'vulnerable groups' in the community. Elaborate guidance is provided to social fund officers to help them to determine needs of this kind. They are expected to liaise closely about such matters with social services and health services staff, and to take into account powers these other departments may have to provide assistance in cash or kind. All other help from the social fund is by way of loans, normally repayable by weekly deductions from benefits. Again, officers have been given elaborate instructions on the circumstances in which they may provide loans. The social fund, excluding the two items of benefit as of right, is 'cash limited'. Within this budget, 30 per cent is available for community care grants and 70 per cent for loans. This means that local offices have annual budgets, and are expected to apply a set of rules about priorities, linked to the total sum available.

One quite important means-tested benefit administered by local authorities, entitlement to free school meals, is available to children whose parents are on income support.

Other means-tested benefits include education grants, relief from payment of National Health Service charges, and legal aid. Local authority social services departments also use means tests to determine charges for residential care and domiciliary services (see chapter 8).

Tax Credits

Tax credits represent a new element in the government's battery of social security measures for lower-income earners below pension age. At the time of writing they consist of:

- Working families tax credit introduced in 1999 to replace a means-tested benefit called 'family credit'.
- A child-care tax credit that accompanies working families tax credit to enable low-income working parents to get some help with child care costs.
- Disabled person's tax credit, also introduced in 1999, to enhance the income of low-income workers who are disabled.
- Child tax credit, introduced in April 2001 for all but higher-rate taxpayers.

After April 2003 they will be replaced by:

- An integrated child tax credit bringing the working families tax credit, the child care tax credit, the child tax credit, the child support element in the disabled person's tax credit and the additions to means-tested benefits for children together into a single scheme.
- A working tax credit for low-income earners without children, which will embrace the disabled person's tax credit.

The emphasis upon tax credits is particularly linked to the Blair government's concern about labour-market participation. Credits are intended to increase the likelihood that returns from low-income work will be higher than those from the benefits for those out of work.

Tax credits are different from tax allowances, which reduce tax liability and thus only benefit those with high enough incomes to pay tax. There is, of course, a sense in which these tax allowances are social security benefits too, even though they do nothing for the incomes of the poorest. Classical essays by Titmuss (1958) and Sinfield (1978) drew attention to the 'social divisions of welfare' in which tax allowances feature among the 'welfare benefits' available to the better off. However, they do not feature in official definitions of social security.

Statistics on the Benefit System

Table 5.1 sets out data from the financial year 2000–1 on numbers of recipients of the main benefits and the amount of government expenditure on each of them.

Social security expenditure is a very large item in government expenditure (approaching 40 per cent). It has tended to grow rapidly. In 1977–8 it was £50 billion (in 2000–1 prices), in 2000–2 it was £104 billion (National Statistics, 2002b, p. 137). Those figures are based on 2000–1 prices to eliminate the distorting impact of inflation. Two crucial factors driving social security expenditure upwards were the ageing of the population and unemployment. At the very end of the twentieth century the growth in the number of pensioners had temporarily slowed down and unemployment fell. Since 1997, therefore, social security expenditure has been relatively stable.

Table 5.1 Social security benefit and tax credits: recipients and costs, 2000–1

Benefit or credit	Recipients (thousands)	Cost (£ millions)
Child benefit	7,108	18,635
Income support	3,811	15,402
Jobseeker's allowance	973	441
Working families tax credit	1,195	4,648
Housing benefit	3,952	11,172
Council tax benefit	4,371	2,589
Incapacity benefit	1,504	6,619
Disability living allowance	2,131	6,050
Attendance allowance	1,250	2,659
Invalid care allowance	385	863
Retirement pension	10,991	8,824
Overall total cost		**101,015**
(includes benefits not listed above)		

Source: Calculated from data from www.statistics.gov.uk/ukinfigs/social.asp (2002a).

The Distinctive Characteristics of the UK System
of Social Security

The UK National Insurance scheme today bears little resemblance to commercial insurance. There is no 'funding' and investing of contributions. Entitlements bear little relationship to contributions, and have been severely eroded. Annual government income from NI contributions exceeds expenditure on contributory benefits, and the separate government contribution to the fund promised in the original legislation is no longer made. According to the 2001 budget statement, the government expected to raise around £63 billion from NI contributions, around two-thirds of the social security budget and therefore substantially more than the cost of the remaining social insurance benefits (largely embedded in the figures given in table 5.1 as spending on the retirement pension, incapacity benefit and part of the jobseeker's allowance).

The presence, in the UK system, of a safety net group of means-tested benefits to back up the contributory scheme is by no means peculiar to this country. Such assistance schemes are widespread; in many countries they remain under local control and more closely resemble the UK scheme's predecessor, the Poor Law. What is perhaps peculiar to the UK scene is the complex overlap between the two systems. In the UK, the contributory scheme has to be supplemented in a large number of ways.

The UK system of social security has been built up by the development of a contributory system together with a limited system of family benefits, which were conceived to minimize dependence on means-tested benefits. However, the means-tested benefits have not been reduced to the safety net role envisaged for them by Beveridge and others. Indeed, in recent years an alternative strategy has been to confine expenditure on social security, by putting the emphasis on means-tested benefits and tax credits. While the main issue for debate about the system seems to be the conflict between the case for a comprehensive system of non-means-tested benefits, probably founded on contributory principles, and the alternative means-testing approach, this conveys an oversimplified notion of its character. In fact, the two approaches are mixed together in the system, and the overall picture is further confused by a range of *ad hoc* responses to special issues and problems: the needs of disabled people, the compensation of industrial injury victims, the requirements of support for students and schoolchildren, and so on.

The 1986 Social Security Act simplified the means-tested part of the system. This eased administration. It limited the opportunities for errors, differential rule interpretation and outright discretion within the main means tests. However, the staff reductions that have occurred, the increases in the numbers of claimants and the high performance targets imposed on staff have meant that error rates in the calculation of benefits have remained high. Moreover, such simplification inevitably implied rough justice, gainers being counterbalanced by losers.

When the Labour Party indicated in its election manifesto for 1997 that it would be 'the party of welfare reform', it inevitably set up a debate about what that should mean. The approach to this which would probably have found most favour with Labour Party rank-and-file members is what may be described as a 'back to Castle' option. The crucial reference point here is the period when Barbara Castle was Secretary of State in the Wilson government of 1974–6. In this period, family allowance was replaced by child benefit, SERPS was introduced, and the main principle used for uprating benefit became indexing to prices or earnings according to which of these rose faster. Later, the Thatcher Governments seriously undermined SERPS and changed the uprating principle to a link only with prices. The 'back to Castle' option in respect of pensions policy was advocated powerfully by Barbara Castle herself in a speech to the Labour Party conference in 1996 and in a pamphlet with the emotive title *We CAN Afford the Welfare State* (Castle and Townsend, n.d.).

The 'back to Castle' option itself can be seen as a development of what has been called 'the back to Beveridge' or 'new Beveridge' approach to social security policy, which sees the ideal way forward to be a combination of the restoration of those parts of the original Beveridge social insurance edifice undermined by the Conservatives, the restoration of the earnings-related additions Labour put in during the 1960s (together with the restoration of SERPS to its original form), with the development of new ways to put into the social insurance framework protection for those who have difficulties in building insurance entitlements (carers, part-time workers, etc.). The comparative ideal here is the strong, and largely inclusive, Swedish social insurance system with its good minimum provisions for those unable to contribute.

A variant on this approach to the reform of social security is an even more radical option, the advocacy of a 'citizen's income' or 'basic income' for all. Such a system would involve a state-guaranteed minimum income paid to all citizens. Then those who were able to secure earned incomes to supplement this state minimum would have these taxed, inevitably more heavily than is currently the case (Walter, 1988; Parker, 1989; Fitzpatrick, 1999). This would be a radical departure from our current system. What is important about this approach is that it sees both means tests, with their deterrent effects, and social insurance, with its contribution tests as irrelevant and difficult to administer in a world in which much work is temporary, part-time and insecure. It finds little support close to the corridors of power; in government policy the strong contemporary emphasis upon employment embodies little acceptance of fears that work is insecure. There is, however, also a version of the basic income perspective which involves arguing for a 'participation income' for specific contingent groups such as the elderly or the sick (Atkinson, 1994).

Both a return to effective and redistributive social insurance and the establishment of some variant of the basic-income approach would constitute a satisfactory basis for a 'radical' reform of social security. They have been rejected because of their costs. A good idea of the cost implications of these options can be gained from looking at one of the most modest proposals from the 'back to Castle' perspective. If the link between wages and basic insurance pensions had been restored to parity with the ratio between pensions and earnings established by 1979, it would have meant, in 1997, an increase for every pensioner of at least £20 per week (Lynes, 1997a). That would mean an addition to the social security budget of over £10 billion a year. That was an unacceptable prospect to a government committed to public expenditure restraint.

Instead of the ideas set out in the last few paragraphs two others dominate the current social-security-reform agenda: the development of tax credits, and more privatization. These will be discussed further below.

Pension reform

As far as pensions are concerned the UK is already a long way down the privatization road. Private pension schemes have always been salient elements in the system. By 1963, about 48 per cent of employees were enrolled in occupational pension schemes. The percentage has remained much the same ever since (Lynes, 1997b, p. 323).

The Green Paper *Partnership in Pensions* (Department of Social Security, 1998b) sought to offer a mixed deal on pensions. The characteristics of this deal were:

- more now for the poorest pensioners;
- more (though not compulsory) privatization but under stronger state protection;
- and a deal for low-income workers (including part-time workers and those with periods out of the labour market as carers) which will be better than the State Earnings Related Pension scheme (SERPS) set up in 1976 but seriously damaged by modifications imposed in 1986.

More precisely what was involved was:

- maintenance of the basic flat-rate contributory pension;
- voluntary 'stakeholder pension schemes designed to offer an alternative to entirely private pensions for those on middle incomes (between roughly £9000

and £18,500 a year)' (ibid., para. 27) which are low-cost, flexible and secure, involving private investment under statutory surveillance and with generous tax concessions from the government;

- a state second pension for those unable to get into private or stakeholder schemes, essentially earners of below £9000 a year and those in caring roles, which the government claims will offer a better deal than SERPS;
- a 'minimum-income guarantee' (after 2003 called the 'guarantee credit') for current pensioners;
- a 'savings credit' scheme to supplement the incomes of those with relatively low private pensions (including stakeholder pensions) but who are nevertheless above the level to qualify for the full 'guarantee credit'.

All of these measures are being put in place by the time of writing, with the last expected in 2003.

The issues about these measures can be divided into:

- their effect upon the welfare of contemporary pensioners;
- the prospects for future pensions, once the new contributory schemes mature.

The 'pension credit' or 'minimum income guarantee' is, in practice, social assistance for pensioners. It is subject to both means-testing and asset-testing, even though the approach to the latter will (after 2003) treat these more generously than before. The government has deliberately chosen to enhance this benefit rather than the NI pension. It initially maintained the previous administration's practice of only raising the NI pension rate in line with the rise of prices. The result was that the gap between the social assistance rate and the NI pension rate widened significantly (see table 5.2). The very low increases in the NI pension rates attracted substantial criticism. The Labour Party's relatively poor results in local elections in May 2000 were widely blamed upon discontent about 'a mere £0.75 on the basic pension'. The government was doing very little for pensioners with incomes just above the levels at which social assistance entitlements arise. This was seen as an injustice to insurance contributors and a disincentive to saving.

The government bowed to political pressure and announced an NI pension rate increase above the rate of price increases, of £5 for a single person and £8 for a couple, in April 2001. However, the increase in the minimum-income guarantee rate was much greater, £13.70 for a single person and £18.60 for a couple. Hence, as table 5.2 shows, the gap between the support offered by NI and that offered by the means test increased much further. However, in November 2001 the Chancellor, Gordon Brown, announced that future NI pension increases would 'always' be 2.5%, or more if inflation is higher, amounting to at least £100 a year for a single pensioner and £160 for couples. 'Always' is in inverted commas

Table 5.2 Relative weekly rates for National Insurance retirement pensions (RP) and minimum-income guarantee (MIG) for couples (amounts in £s)

Rate set in April	Retirement pension rate for a couple	Basic minimum-income guarantee for a couple*	Excess MIG over RP
1997	99.80	106.80	7.00
2000	107.90	121.95	14.05
2001	115.90	140.45	24.55
2002	120.70	149.80	29.10

* There are higher rates for older pensioners

here as even if this Chancellor will not break his word he cannot commit his successors.

The pension credit scheme may help to deal with the fact that people with incomes only just above the 'minimum-income guarantee' are losing ground in relative terms. However, it will encounter the problem facing such variable-income enhancement schemes: that the rules to govern the way the supplement 'tapers off' as income rises, are likely to engender new inequities and disincentive effects.

Any evaluation of the new contributory pension schemes (the stakeholder pension and the second state pension) requires a prediction of long-term effects. The arrival of the stakeholder scheme in April 2001 was greeted by a number of newspaper articles, many of them offering advice to people who might be deciding to start to purchase these pensions. There was widespread doubt about whether they offer a good deal to low-income workers. The problem is that investment in one of these pensions can involve forgoing a substantial amount of current income for a comparatively low return that may compare unfavourably with the levels of benefit offered by the minimum-income guarantee. Certainly there is agreement that stakeholder pensions are likely to be a bad buy for people who are already half way through their working lives.

Estimates of what the stakeholder pensions will offer depend upon taking current returns on private pension schemes and current annuity rates and projecting them into the future. Both of these rates have fallen in recent years and could fall still further in an era of low inflation and limited economic growth. But predictions of this kind – if used to offer advice to potential purchasers – need also to deal with the future work prospects for people (especially women) in the more vulnerable parts of the labour market. On top of all this, trying to predict whether these quasi-private schemes will offer a better deal than anything the government may provide requires guesses about how governments will behave across a period of 30–40 years. The past behaviour of UK governments offers no basis for any expectation of a stable future for pension schemes.

By early 2002 not only was there increasing evidence that stakeholder pensions were not proving as attractive as the government expected, but there was developing alarm at changes being made to existing private pension arrangements. A particularly attractive feature of private pension arrangements for many employees of larger enterprises, and for public employees, has been that pensions are based upon formulae providing a benefit offering a proportion of the final salary, calculated in terms of the number of years in the scheme. For many workers this implies a combined pension and lump sum representing about two-thirds of the final salary. An increasing number of companies have decided that they cannot guarantee these sums. They have therefore closed their final-salary schemes to new entrants, or even demoted the expected benefits for existing pension-scheme members. The alternative being offered is that already provided by many of the less advantageous schemes, money-purchase pensions whose ultimate value will simply depend upon the growth of the actual sums invested.

These developments have followed from the state of the stock market and the declining returns from investments. Actuarial calculations suggest that contributions to money-purchase pensions, including stakeholder pensions, will have to be a proportion of current income of around 20 per cent to provide pensions comparable to existing final-salary schemes. Of course, these estimates depend upon projecting forward the current returns on investments. These may change. In the past the high return on investments had led some employers to reduce their contributions to final-salary schemes on the grounds that these would not be necessary.

The purpose of this rather technical discussion of private pensions is to suggest that the government's strategy of seeing privately funded pensions as a key tier of pension arrangements for the future may be beginning to collapse. This is leading to arguments that the government must make more explicit underpinning arrangements for stakeholder pensions, or that public-expenditure implications comparable to those embodied in the 'back to Castle' strategy outlined above will have to be accepted in the end.

Meanwhile all the remarks about the bad deal the stakeholder scheme offers to low-income and insecure workers, relative to the minimum-income guarantee, may also be pertinent to the state second pension scheme (see Agulnik et al., 1999).

Problems with Means Testing

There is an extensive literature on the problems of means-testing. Much that has been written on this subject comes from those who advocate, as an alternative, strengthening the contributory benefits system so that it becomes more universal in its coverage and provides better benefits. We have seen already some of the political objections to this approach, and noted the development of tax credits as the officially preferred approach to social security reform.

The development of tax credits may be seen as incremental moves towards 'negative income tax' (Minford, 1984). The UK's 'pay-as-you-earn' (PAYE) system for the deduction of tax would seem to be the ideal vehicle for the development of a system whereby additions, rather than deductions, could be provided in some cases. However, the basis for the assessment of tax is an annual one. Where the objective is to deal with the needs of people on a low income whose circumstances change frequently, annual assessment is very inflexible. Hence for a long while the income tax system itself remained 'untainted' by social security considerations. Although the establishment of a number of tax credits has changed the situation, it is still a little too early to judge how easily tax credits sit alongside income tax.

However, in many respects, a tax credit is no more than a means-tested benefit administered through the tax system. What is involved is a maximum rate, payable to those with very low incomes, which tapers off as income rises until they reach the point at which they are taxed instead.

The general case against means tests is that they confuse, deter and stigmatize those who need help. People prefer benefits to which they have clear-cut rights, and about which they can obtain unambiguous information. Those who have to claim help are often already in trouble, about which they are ashamed or for which their neighbours criticize them; to have to reveal intimate details to an official so as to obtain benefits deepens the sense of 'stigma'. The low take-up of some benefits is attributed both to this stigma and to the complexities surrounding the administration of means tests.

It is undoubtedly the case that take-up levels for means-tested benefits are lower than for many other benefits, but there are also marked variations between the various means-tested ones. The Department for Work and Pensions publishes estimates on the take-up rates for some benefits. It distinguishes take-up in terms of the caseload (additional claims that could be made) (col. 2 in table 5.3) and in terms of expenditure (the amount of benefit left unclaimed) (col. 3). This distinction is based on the fact that many non-claimers will have relatively low entitlements. Table 5.3 sets out

Table 5.3   Estimates of non-take-up of benefits

	By caseload	By expenditure
Income support	13–23%	6–13%
Jobseeker's allowance (income based)	22–33%	16–26%
Housing benefit	5–11%	3–8%
Council tax benefit	20–7%	17–24%

Source: Date reported in *Income Related Benefits: Estimates of Take-Up in 1999/2000* (Department for Work and Pensions, 2001).

official estimates of the proportions of unclaimed benefits in the year 1999–2000.

There are some crucial issues about take-up on which there are not yet any official estimates. In the past there were take-up problems in respect of family credit, the benefit then available for low-earners with dependent children. This has now been replaced by tax credits. The linking of benefit entitlement with tax assessment ought in principle to reduce the take-up problem. On the other hand the new system puts a considerable onus upon employers to identify situations in which there may be a tax credit entitlement. It will be important, once the new arrangements have settled down, to assess the take-up issues in respect of all the tax credits. At the time of writing there is no good evidence available on this.

A factor that facilitates take-up of benefits is that income support is regarded as an automatic 'passport' to other benefits. This is most evidently the case with relief from NHS charges. However, this implies a cause for concern about the needs of those just above income support levels, together with those who, in not claiming small amounts of income support, may also be shutting themselves out from ready access to other benefits.

One particular problem with the multiplicity of means tests is that, operating together, they may create a poverty trap (or poverty plateau). This is a kind of 'tax effect' whereby an individual whose earned income rises may find that tax and NI contributions increase while benefit income decreases, together diminishing any actual gain to a very low level. One of the main advantages of the 1986 Act was to be, according to the government, that, by taking into account earned income after tax and NI deductions and having the main means tests operate with a common framework, they would eliminate the poverty trap problem for most people. However, the increases in tax and NI contributions when combined with the tapers in housing benefit and council tax, and the family credit scheme then in operation, often limited the gain from an extra £1 of gross earnings to 3 pence. That could be expressed as the equivalent of a 97 per cent tax rate (a loss that is more than twice the marginal rate of income tax on people with the highest incomes!). The taper rates for the new tax credits are set lower, but in the absence of a change in the housing benefit taper rate, the gain on the shift to 'working families tax credit' was only 2 pence in the pound. Additionally, the whole situation is complicated in practice by the desire of the Inland Revenue to operate an approach to determining entitlement that is premised upon the assumption that individual household arrangements, and incomes other than via employment, are stable so that reassessment can be an annual matter.

It is important to bear in mind that the poverty trap applies with part-time work, or when either of a couple on benefits together finds work, and to temporary work. In other words, there are some complex issues about disincentives to labour-market participation, which flow directly from the poverty-trap effect.

The poverty-trap problem must afflict any unified means-testing system. If the tapering-off effect is to be reduced, benefit receipt will logically spread further up the income distribution, adding to the cost of the scheme. In the last resort, this can only be compensated by increasing tax rates, either across the board or through alterations to the higher-rate bands.

A study by Alcock and Pearson (1999) shows that the problem of the poverty trap may be intensified by public services for which charges are related to income. They show that this is true of a range of local authority services – social care services, charges for extra education benefits (music lessons, for example), travel passes, entry to swimming pools, etc. The problem can only be avoided if less-targeted status considerations rather than income tests are used in determining concessions (age, for example). Alcock and Pearson also indicate the way in which rules about capital holdings may impose a similar 'savings trap'.

The complexities associated with means-testing have necessitated the development of aid and advice services to help people secure their entitlements. Pioneers of this work, often described as 'welfare rights work', have been voluntary organizations, particularly the Child Poverty Action Group, and some local authority social services departments (Fimister, 1986). There has been an extensive controversy within social work about the extent to which that activity should include such work, with some people seeing it as essential for an effective service for clients who are very often poor, while others feel that it distorts their activities and pulls them away from 'real' social work (Becker and Silburn, 1990). Increasingly, now, such work is concentrated in voluntary agencies and advice bureaux.

Social Security Assumptions about Family Life and Women's Roles

The assumptions about family life incorporated in the Poor Law involved a household means test whereby all a household's needs were taken into account and also its resources, so that adult children of a needy couple were expected to contribute to their maintenance. The contributory benefits developed in 1911 treated the insured claimant as the sole beneficiary, providing flat-rate payments at the same level, regardless of his or her family commitments. However, in the 1920s, the principle of additions to benefits, taking into account the needs of wives and children, was introduced. The improved contributory scheme developed in the 1940s carried forward this principle, while means-tested assistance shifted from a household means test to a family one. Broadly, then, UK social security policies have been developed on the assumption that the typical claimant is a married man with a non-working wife and dependent children. That is not, of course, to say that the system cannot cope with claims from single people, but that it has had difficulty in coming to terms both with female employment and with family arrangements constituted other than on the basis of legal marriage.

Until the 1970s, married women were required to pay lower contributions and to receive lower benefits than men. While this anomaly was then eliminated, others remain. Married women cannot claim contributory benefit increases in respect of dependent husbands. The continuation of provisions for non-employed wives to be treated as 'dependants' for whom husbands can claim additions to benefits implies that the return which an employed woman receives on her contributions may, in some cases, be worth only the difference between the full pension or benefit and the addition for a non-working wife. In other words, there are difficulties in securing a fair balance in a scheme that tries, on the one hand, to make provision for dependent wives and, on the other, to enable the married woman to be a contributor and claimant in her own right.

The position with regard to means-tested benefits is even more complicated when men and women live together, and perhaps have children, but are not married. A family means test requires judgements to be made about whether a family situation exists. Generally, this is straightforward; claimants agree with official interpretations of their situations. Indeed, it is to the advantage of a male claimant living with a non-employed 'wife' and children (even if they are not his) to claim them as his family. However, difficulties arise when claimants, usually female, wish to be treated as independent, but find that the social security and housing benefit authorities regard them as the 'wives' of male friends. The government has tried to develop a definition of 'living together as man and wife' which distinguishes stable relationships from more casual ones, but difficulties and disagreements still occur. It is only heterosexual relationships that are treated in this way; in all other cases, claimants' needs are assessed separately. The issue here, as was pointed out on p. 105, also applies to widow's or widower's benefits, and arises from the family-based approach to benefits. While it would be possible to treat unmarried 'couples' differently from married ones, the only fair way to avoid problems of this kind is to cease to make assumptions about family patterns of support, and instead have a structure of *individual* entitlements.

A related issue concerns the treatment of single-parent families, most of which are, of course, headed by women. The UK treatment of this group has been relatively generous, by comparison with other countries. Income support has been available. Mothers have not been required to become labour-market participants until their children reach sixteen years of age. Absent fathers have been expected to make contributions, though the system has found it difficult to secure these because many of the fathers have low incomes and commitments to new families.

Charles Murray's (1984) tirade against the single-headed household in the USA was taken up in the UK. Politicians began to attribute the growth in single parenthood to the availability of benefits and housing. This has stimulated a debate, reaching beyond the ranks of the extreme Right, about (a) work opportunities for single parents and (b) contributions from absent parents. Attention to the first issue involves encouraging single parents without children under five to seek employment, and it may be that this will become compulsory. Efforts to improve the in-work benefits available to low-waged parents offers a more positive contribution to this strategy.

In the 1990s the Major government decided to tackle the issue of contributions from absent parents by means of a comprehensive, formula-driven scheme to replace both the assessments made as part of the administration of the existing means-tested benefits and the assessments made by the courts in determining maintenance on the breakdown of a relationship. It enacted the Child Support Act in 1991, setting up an agency to administer it. That legislation ran into severe implementation problems. There were four main objections to the new legislation:

1 That it was retrospective in effect – agreements, including court settlements, made in the past were overturned (a particular problem here was the overturning of agreements in which the absent parent relinquished an interest in a house in return for a lower maintenance expectation).
2 That where the absent parent had obligations to a second family, these were given relatively low weight in the calculations.
3 That the parent with care of the child had nothing to gain from collaborating with the agency if she (it is nearly always she in this situation) was on income

support, since everything collected went to reimburse the state; a special problem here was the expectation of co-operation in the supply of information unless there were strong reasons to protect a woman from further indirect dealings with the father of her child.

4   That the operation of a rigid formula was unfair when there are regular contacts with the absent parent and a variety of connected expenses.

The enforcement of the Act was not helped by the income targets imposed on the agency and a programme of work which meant that it started with families on 'income support' and had incentives to tackle the easier cases (that was, the more compliant absent parents).

In 1995, the government brought in amending legislation. It bowed to a vociferous male lobby. It did not change the basic principles of the Act, but it did give the agency some limited leeway to modify its application in relation to the points made in (1), (2) and (4) above. However, there are still difficulties. Further amending legislation in 2000 simplifies the formula for the determination of liabilities. It also gives attention to point (3) above by allowing parents with care to retain some proportion of the contribution from the other parent, even when they are on state benefits.

Social Security Benefit Levels and Poverty

Clearly, it is important in assessing a system of social security to look not merely at the structure of the system but also at the level of benefits provided by it. In the UK, debate about the social security system has been dominated by concerns over the levels of benefits relative to income levels that are deemed needed to prevent poverty. In this sense there has been, ever since the Beveridge report, a concern to assess benefits in terms of their minimal adequacy, not in terms of the replacement incomes they offer. Hence, a great deal of debate about poverty is concerned not with the contributory benefits as such, but with the means-tested benefit levels and about the people and families whose incomes fall below those levels.

It is obviously important to look at benefit levels in terms of their impact upon poverty. However, there are two important considerations to bear in mind about the relationship between social security and poverty:

1   Social security should not only be seen as a policy designed to prevent poverty. There are various arguments for social security policies as mechanisms to share or spread incomes. Benefits may be evaluated in terms of the extent to which they offer individuals income replacements, as percentages of their original incomes. They may also be evaluated as mechanisms to spread resources between people, since there are a variety of justifications for ensuring that incomes are not simply derived from earnings. The question here is whether we

should see redistribution by other than market methods as only justifiable in order to prevent poverty, or whether we consider that there are other justifications for state interventions to influence income distribution.

2   It is important to see social security as only one of a range of phenomena that influence income distribution and have an impact upon the incidence of poverty. Analytically it is often appropriate to see it – alongside taxation – as operating *after* other influences upon income distribution. Furthermore, whilst market forces are likely to be a key influence upon incomes *before* tax and social security they will not be the only ones. Public policies influencing and regulating market behaviour may also be very important. As far as the prevention of poverty is concerned, measures to influence what people are paid (minimum wage laws, equal opportunities legislation etc.) may be important. So may job-creation measures. We will return to these issues in chapter 6.

There are various ways to approach the analysis of poverty. In the first half of the twentieth century there were studies which attempted to relate poverty to an absolute standard, based on the cost of providing a basic minimum of necessities. Towards the end of that century this approach was shown to be unsatisfactory. One particular researcher, Peter Townsend, led the way in showing that poverty is a meaningful concept only when individual standards of living are related to those widely taken for granted in a society (Townsend, 1979, 1993). The bare minimum in the UK could certainly equate with a good absolute standard of living for poor people in the less developed countries of the world. At the same time, views about what is necessary for an adequate way of life change over time. These changes are related to developments in living standards within the nation as a whole. When the national assistance scales – which today, much updated for inflation, form the basis for the income support scales – were first set, in 1948, television was not generally available, and few households had refrigerators, washing machines or central heating systems. If a definition of the poverty level is to take into account these considerations, the key questions are, for example: to what extent should those on the official poverty line have incomes that make it difficult for them to share the way of life of the majority of the people? Or, alternatively, how large should the gap be between the incomes of those on the poverty line and average incomes?

Townsend pioneered an approach to the study of poverty which looked at deprivation in terms of the inability to afford a lifestyle taken for granted by others. He persuasively made a case for regarding large numbers of people in the UK, including both people dependent on social security and many on low wages, as living in poverty (Townsend, 1979). More recent studies (Mack and Lansley, 1985; Gordon and Pantazis, 1997) lend support to Townsend's argument. They demonstrate the extent to which people on a low income lack things which, according to public opinion surveys, are regarded as necessities.

An approach to the understanding of poverty that recognizes that some people may not be able to participate in activities and a way of life taken for granted by others also highlights crucial additional problems. People with low incomes may have other difficulties that will not be self-evident from a simple examination of their resources. If you can only afford cheap housing this is likely to be of poor quality and costly to heat and keep in a good state of repair. If you live in an area where many people have low incomes, the best – and ironically the cheapest – shops may be inaccessible. The cost of transport to places where shops, entertainment facilities, even work and education, are more available may make further inroads into your slender income. Moreover, if you cannot afford a car you will be dependent upon limited and unreliable public transport. All these considerations will apply to poor people living in urban areas where deprived people are concentrated. But they may also apply to the isolated poor, in rural areas. Hence it is likely that poor people will get less value than others for each pound they spend and will find that their low income has 'knock on' effects upon their lifestyles.

While a common-sense response to some of those problems would seem to be to make free or cheap facilities available to the poor, this has the consequence of intensifying the problems about means-testing discussed above, particularly the poverty trap. An alternative approach involves forms of territorial targeting of specific services – giving deliberate attention to the improvement of services in areas where deprived people live. This has been seen as a good non-discriminatory approach to deprivation. The drawback is that these measures are indirect and may not readily benefit those most in need. The phenomenon of rural poverty, where people are isolated and may often be located in areas where many of the rest of the population are prosperous, is particularly intractable in this respect (see Cahill, 2002, ch. 6).

While a sensitive official approach to the measurement of deprivation is desirable it is expensive to have a regular sequence of precisely targeted studies. An alternative is income surveys that explore the incidence of incomes that are significantly below average income levels. Taking their cue from deprivation studies, such surveys can arrive at regular estimates of the numbers likely to lack necessities. In the UK since 1979 there have been regular surveys that enable estimates to be made of the numbers of households with incomes below a specified percentage of the average income level. These surveys also offer some information on the household types with low incomes. Commonly used indices of poverty are, then, numbers of individuals living in households with incomes either 50 or 60 per cent below average incomes.

In a short account of data on poverty in the UK, it is not possible to go into the range of technical questions that arise in relation to this survey data: about the impact of differential housing costs, the impact of household size upon deprivation and the implications of changes over time within households. Readers should consult the writings on poverty recommended at the end of this chapter for discussions of these issues. What is crucial for the general picture of poverty in the UK is summarized below from an account of the findings of the official survey of household incomes (Department of Social Security, 2001) compiled by Howard et al. (2001, p. 30):

- in 1999/2000, 14 million people (25 per cent of the population) were living below 50 per cent of mean income after housing costs;
- about a third of those people were couples with children, and a further 21 per cent were lone parents with children;
- about 20 per cent were pensioners;
- about 63 per cent of these people were in households with no one in paid employment, in the remaining 37 per cent of households there was a member in full or part-time work.

Since, as noted above, surveys like this have been carried out since 1979, Howard and colleagues were able to compare contemporary data with data for that year. What this reveals is a dramatic increase in poverty as measured in this way. In 1979 only 5 million people (9 per cent of the population) were living below 50 per cent of mean income. It may be objected that the average has risen between the two dates, but that takes us back to the issue discussed above about the need to see poverty as an inability to share in generally accepted lifestyles. What is significant is that since 1979, benefit levels have risen in line with price inflation, and sometimes not even that, rather than wage inflation. Hence those out of work have not participated in the rise in the standard of living. At the same time the studies show an increase in people who are in work but who have very low incomes, suggesting a failure of the lowest earnings to move with the average. Additionally, a further feature of the change between 1979 and 1999 was a significant rise in benefit dependency on the part of single-parent families and of households where there is unemployment. The latter was starting to fall by the 1999 survey.

Hence, these poverty studies suggest concerns about benefit levels and about benefit dependence but also about the incomes of people in work. Since 1997 the government has addressed the issue of benefit levels only inasmuch as it has sought to raise the incomes of the poorest pensioners through the minimum-income guarantee (as illustrated above). It has seen it as very important to attack the issue of benefit dependency on the part of working-age people through measures to combat unemployment and to encourage labour-market participation. It has addressed the question of incomes in work both through the enactment of minimum-wage legislation and through the development of the various tax credits. Researchers have sought to measure the impact of these new measures upon poverty. The difficulty is that it takes time for new measures to have an impact and time for researchers to measure and report that impact. The judgement at the time of writing is that slow change is occurring (see Howard et al., 2001, pp. 63–72; also Piachaud and Sutherland, 2001). Alongside the need for further improvements to benefits and tax credits, effective poverty reduction will also depend upon the availability of employment.

Reference has been made to the relationship between social security incomes and average earned incomes over time. In many respects the key questions about social security policy concern not so much the setting of levels in the abstract as the need for, or the amount of, benefit increases. Pressure groups regularly draw politicians' attention to the ways in which, over a period of time, those whom they represent are losing ground. Two important alternative kinds of yardsticks are used for these judgements: indices of earnings and indices of prices. The plural form is used in both instances since there have been extensive arguments about the best ways of calculating these. In particular, it has been argued that a price index for the poor should be rather different from a more general one, since the poor spend their incomes in rather different ways.

Before 1973, there was no statutory requirement for government to take specific notice of wages or price movements in determining benefit levels. *Ad hoc* political judgements governed up-rating decisions. However, there was a tendency, over time, for the relationship between short-term benefit rates and wage rates to remain roughly the same (Barr, 1981). In the Social Security Act of 1973, the Conservatives provided a statutory link between benefits and prices. In 1975, an amendment to the Social Security Act committed the Labour government to up-rating long-term benefits in line with prices or earnings, whichever was greater, and most short-term benefits in line with prices. Heavy price inflation in the late 1970s did produce some relative gains for social security recipients. In 1979, the Conservatives amended the statutory requirement so that long-term benefits were to be linked only to prices. Also, short-term benefits might be increased by up to 5 per cent less than the inflation rate. These rules related only to the contributory benefits but, in most cases, means-tested benefit rates have been up-rated on a similar basis. The changes after 1979 led to a serious fall in the value of all benefits relative to average wages. Since 1997 the Labour government has shown little general inclination to rectify this position, except in respect of improvements to child benefit and to the application of means tests for benefits for the elderly. The latter was discussed above.

The relationship between social security incomes and low wages is clearly important. Several studies of poverty have related incomes to the level provided by the main means-tested scheme. Apart from drawing attention to the number of people falling below this level because of a failure to claim benefits, the studies have shown that there is a significant group who fall below that standard because of low wages. There are alternative ways of responding to this. One is to concentrate on raising wage levels; the introduction by the Blair government of a minimum wage is a modest move in this direction. Another is to argue not that something must be done to augment the earnings of the low-wage earner, but that means-tested benefit levels should be kept below the lowest wage levels. This view is linked with a concern to lower wage costs, expressed by those who see the only way forward for the UK economy to be for enterprises to have wage costs comparable to those of very much poorer countries. However, the main response has been to develop family benefits and housing benefits, which are available to low-income earners and are designed to tackle this problem. The universal child benefit significantly contributes to supporting low-income families, along with all other families with children. The other key policies all involve means-testing in some form, with now a strong shift towards the tax credit approach to the issue.

It has been argued that few of the unemployed are in fact deterred from obtaining work by benefit payments being above the levels they can obtain as earners. However, there is undoubtedly a relatively small gap between the benefits paid to some families, particularly large families, and the wages paid for low-skilled work. The deterrent effect of this will depend first on the actual costs of going to work, second on individual views of the psychological costs and benefits of work, and third on the benefits still obtainable when in work. However, there is a widespread public belief that this deterrent effect actually contributes to our high unemployment rates. Politicians share, or are sensitive to, this belief. It accordingly influences their attitudes to increases in the short-term benefits. However, the government sees the provision of in-work benefits to parents with dependent children whose net incomes are at, or below, the income support level, as dealing with this 'unemployment trap' problem. In practice, administrative problems associated with the shift from out-of-work benefits to in-work benefits complicate the situation for those trying to make the transition. That has an impact on take-up, as was discussed above.

As well as a concern about the relationship between benefits and other incomes, there is also a concern about relativities within the benefit system. The income support scheme rules make assumptions about the extent to which a couple may live more cheaply than a single person, about the extra needs of elderly and disabled people, about the different costs of providing for children at various ages, and about the lower needs of single adults under 25. Some of these judgements are clearly controversial. In particular, the low income support rate for single under-25s, and the particularly harsh treatment of 16- to 18-year-olds who have left school, seem to be related to an assumption that such people can live with their parents, and do not form separate households. The assumptions about the costs of bringing up children, made by the rules, have also been challenged as unrealistic regarding the costs of teenage children. It seems fair to suggest that considerations of the evidence on actual costs have been mixed, in the determination of some of these rules, with views about who are the most deserving among the poor.

We see then that there is a wide range of complicated issues about benefit levels and about their role in the eradication of poverty. In this discussion actual benefit rates are not given. These are changed every year, hence it would be confusing to cite them in a textbook designed to last for several years. Students who want to examine these rates in more detail will need to turn to some of the sources listed in the recommendations for further reading.

CONCLUSIONS

This chapter has shown that social security in the UK has diverged markedly from the model expected after the implementation of the Beveridge Report, in which a social insurance system (NI) was expected to be the dominant element, supported by a shrinking social assistance safety net and some private provision. Instead means-testing has become more and more important for the incomes of the poor, whilst the better off have generally looked to private pensions to provide security in their old age.

The replacement of the Department of Social Security by the Department for Work and Pensions in 2001 has underlined the Labour government's social security reform strategy – a strong emphasis upon work (and therefore on work-supporting benefits like the tax credits) for those under pension age, and some further privatization of the pensions system. In this context not only have the 'universalist' expectations of many on the Left been disappointed but serious concerns about the effectiveness of the system remain. Such issues have been highlighted here with reference to the problem of securing an effective framework of pensions for all, deficiencies in the means-testing approach to benefit provision, unsatisfactory features about the treatment of women, and evidence that poverty is still widespread in the UK.

SUGGESTIONS FOR FURTHER READING

The most up-to-date textbook on social security policy is *Social Security in Britain* by Mckay and Rowlingson (1999). Walker and Howard's *The Making of a Welfare Class?* (2000) also offers a good exploration of the way the social security system works. Another good overview of the issues discussed here is Alcock's *Understanding Poverty* (1997). Unfortunately all of these book have been slightly dated by the activities of the Blair government.

The Child Poverty Action Group's (CPAG) annual handbooks on means-tested and contributory benefits are the key sources for details, including benefit rates, which change at least annually (and have not therefore been quoted here). Other good, general, up-to-date sources are CPAG's journal *Poverty* and a journal called *Benefits*.

CPAG pamphlets are useful critical sources of information on the system. One of their books particularly recommended is Howard et al.'s *Poverty: The Facts* (2001). Gordon and Townsend's *Breadline Europe* (2000) also contains much of relevance to the UK.

The Department for Work and Pensions has a website which, in addition to providing most of the key publications, offers advice to claimants and job seekers at www.dwp.gov.uk. The Child Poverty Action Group's website is www.cpag.org.uk.

Chapter 6
Employment Policy

- Introduction
- Characteristics of the UK approach to employment policy
- The impact upon the UK of European Union membership
- The main employment policy measures
- Government regulation of work conditions and job security
- Reducing unemployment or stimulating employment?
- Employment and social policy: a European future?
- Conclusions
- Suggestions for further reading

Introduction

In chapter 1, it was pointed out that whilst government expenditure on explicit employment policy measures is very low by comparison with the other areas of social policy, consideration needs to be given to the role of intervention in the labour market as part of government management of the economy. Hence this chapter has the dual function of dealing both with these wider issues and with policies relating to job placement, training and employment protection. It has been placed immediately after the chapter on social security not simply because the same government department now administers that and employment policy but also because there are some important issues about the relationship between social security policy and the management of the labour market.

In considering the role of the government in relation to the management of the labour market, two extreme political positions may be contrasted. One of them sees the preservation of a market-based economic system as the main priority, and requires social policy to do as little as possible to interfere with the market. The other gives primacy to social goals and requires that market forces must be managed, and in certain cases eliminated, to ensure those goals are realized. If the former position is adopted, market forces impacting on individuals' prospects of finding and retaining work are to be left alone, the only concern is that those state interventions in society that are deemed to be unavoidable have a minimal impact on the labour market. The characteristic social policy of such a regime is the 'Poor Law' (see chapter 2, pp. 14–15), providing social aid in exceptional circumstances but designed to ensure that it has no adverse effect on labour-market participation. By contrast, the other extreme position sees the management of the labour market (and other markets) for social ends to be a perfectly legitimate concern; it therefore regards employment policy as a central concern of public social policy.

The actual political discourse, of course, lies between these polar positions. Hence, there are employment policies, which have social effects, to be studied. There are also issues to be considered regarding the employment effects of other social policies (particularly social security policies). However, it is also the case that there is considerable controversy about those effects, which needs to be seen in the context of different views about the extent to which the labour market can (or should) be subject to manipulation by governments. An analysis of social policy with a comparative perspective, Esping-Andersen (1996) has encapsulated the contemporary controversy about the appropriate relationship between social policy and the labour market (p. 10):

> Since the early 1970s, we can identify three distinct welfare state responses to economic and social change. Scandinavia followed until recently a strategy of welfare state employment expansion. The Anglo-Saxon countries . . . have favoured a strategy of deregulating wages and the labour market, combined with a certain degree of welfare state erosion. And the continental European nations . . . have induced labour supply reduction while basically maintaining existing social security standards. All three strategies were intimately related to the nature of their welfare states.

The UK is put by Esping-Andersen clearly into his Anglo-Saxon category, yet, as a member of the EU, it is confronted by the alternative models. Furthermore, within the EU, attempts are being made to develop active labour market policies, with social goals, despite different social security policies that cannot easily be harmonized. Hence, ever since the UK joined the EEC (now called the EU), there has been a political debate about the shape of employment policy, and the UK has had to respond to measures from that community which may have an impact on the working of the labour market.

There is a developing debate about the most appropriate response to what are seen as increasingly significant 'global' market forces. One side in that debate (what Esping-Andersen might call the Anglo-Saxon side) argues that the only way a nation can compete in the global economy is to adopt labour market deregulation, lowering wages and related employment costs. The other side either disputes the power of the so-called global forces or argues that a large economic bloc like the EU can resist or influence those forces. An in-between position involves the suggestion that an efficient, highly trained labour force can enable a nation to compete without at the same time necessarily lowering wages. It will be shown that some of the UK's employment-policy responses are premised on the possibility of this 'middle' course.

The discussion so far has sought to characterize employment policy in general terms. Once examined in more detail, employment policy is seen to have various aspects, each of which may be given more or less attention. In this sense, the overall perspectives, outlined above, can have various manifestations. Employment policy will be likely to involve attempts to influence:

- the overall level of labour-market participation;
- the characteristics of work;
- the nature of the supply of labour;
- the demand for labour.

First, then, government interventions may aim both to increase and to decrease the overall level of labour-market participation. The poor-law approach described above clearly aimed to maximize participation. Conversely, the introduction of pensions and sickness benefits may be seen as enabling some people to withdraw from having to try to participate. However, many other policies influence participation. Women have been explicitly excluded from some forms of labour-market participation in the past, whereas more recently efforts have been made to counter discrimination against women and to encourage them to enter the labour force. Education policies may offer opportunities for young people that keep them temporarily out of the labour market. Finally, emigration and immigration policies will have effects on the size of the labour force.

Secondly, governments may regulate work – influencing its hours, conditions and rates of pay, i.e. the characteristics of work. They may also enact measures, which influence the security of work. More indirectly they may influence the conditions under which employers and employees are able to bargain about these issues, through rules governing trade unions and collective bargaining.

The first point listed above dealt with the quantity of labour; the third one particularly concerns what may be called the 'quality' of labour. A government's education and training policies affect the nature of the supply of labour, so may measures designed to influence attitudes to work. In this category are also included measures (job centres etc.) which influence the rates at which employees and employers make contracts (inasmuch as these do not affect the level of labour-market participation *per se* but rather its working).

Lastly, governments influence the demand for labour in many different ways. In discussions of employment policy, attention tends to be focused on explicit job-creation measures, or explicit 'Keynesian' demand creating economic policies; but, in reality, work may be created by many government initiatives (sometimes without this being a specific intention). In this sense, many social policy innovations – to increase the availability of health or social care or education or to increase the supply of houses – will have employment-creating effects. So, of course, as was pointed out in chapter I, will a decision to wage war.

All of these themes occur in UK employment policy, but there has been a tendency for the first and third points to be more evident than the other two. For an understanding of contemporary policy there is a need to explore the way in which policy stances have evolved over quite a long period, with varying emphasis on the four themes. This is done in the next section.

Characteristics of the UK Approach to Employment Policy

Nineteenth-century governments paid little attention to managing the labour market, but they did adopt measures both to maximize the participation of adult males in the labour force and to restrict the participation of women and children. Alongside, and sometimes as part of, the latter measures, were efforts to control working conditions.

In the early twentieth century, UK governments gradually came to reject the view that the economy, and accordingly the labour market, should be left to work 'naturally'. At the end of the nineteenth century, adherents of 'classical' economic theory began to acknowledge that it was perhaps necessary for the government to play a role in assisting the market system to operate more smoothly. In particular, the problems of adjustment to changing economic situations in the short run began to be regarded as sufficiently serious to justify intervention. One such problem concerned the linking of 'sellers' of labour with 'buyers'. To this end, after 1908, systems of labour exchanges were created.

Around the turn of the century, attention was given to the existence of various 'sweated trades' in which marginal workers, often including large numbers of women, were exploited. A measure of protection was enacted for workers in the 1909 Trade Boards Act, and in moves towards the establishment of minimum wages in some industries during World War I. These might have been steps towards much greater regulation of employment. However, a bigger concern of the male-dominated working-class movement was to give greater legal protection to trade unions and for these to be the main protectors of wage levels and conditions of employment through negotiated agreements with employers. A voluntary approach to employment regulation became dominant.

Between the two World Wars, continuing evidence that the economy could not readily absorb all who wanted work kept the issue of unemployment on the political agenda. There were strong pressures that forced the erratic development of income maintenance measures for the unemployed (see discussion in chapter 2, pp. 22–3), but government employment policies evolved very little. A few limited job-creation and training schemes were developed, but economic orthodoxy was against the heavy public expenditure on the creation of work that, by the middle of the 1930s, began to characterize the policy response in the USA. Only as preparation for war began to alleviate unemployment did official thinking begin to come to terms with its structural character. This change of approach is primarily associated with the Keynesian revolution in economic thinking that linked unemployment with under-consumption and urged governments to spend, and, if necessary, to unbalance budgets, to pull out of a recession. The primary policy response required was, in this case, a macro-economic one, rather than a form of employment policy *per se*. However, at the same time, the special problems of certain regions, particularly those where employment had depended on declining heavy industries, also began to be recognized.

As indicated above, the two World Wars could be seen as massive labour-demand creation schemes! Indeed, so strong was the need for labour that measures were adopted to draw new participants, particularly women, into the labour force.

The unexpected low unemployment from 1945 to 1970 enabled UK governments to continue to adopt a comparatively passive stance on employment policies. The trade unions were broadly satisfied with this; full employment offered the ideal context for the continuation of male working-class advancement by way of collective action. The employment situation, initially at least, did not favour female interests. An expectation that the high female labour-market participation of the wartime period would come to an end was reinforced by neglect of attention to the prevention of discrimination against women and an absence of child care provisions. Full employment led, in the 1950s and 1960s, to official acceptance of the recruitment of labour from the countries of the former British Empire. Public employers, including the health service, sought workers from these countries. There were racist campaigns against open entry to the UK for immigrants from the Caribbean and the Indian subcontinent, and controlling legislation was enacted (a sequence of measures starting in 1962). These control measures used the need for labour as a crucial test for the grant of an entry permit. Since the enactment and subsequent tightening of immigration controls coincided with the beginning of a fall in labour demand, immigration very quickly ceased to have an impact on the growth of the labour force.

In 1970, the incoming Conservative government, led by Edward Heath, decided to restructure the public employment service as part of its effort to make public administration more dynamic. The consultative document *People and Jobs* (Department of Employment, 1971) declared that the employment service needed to be modernized. The employment exchanges were too readily identified with a limited service to the unemployed.

It is not irrelevant that this modernizing effort came at the time the UK entered the EEC. In modernizing the service, the government was clearly influenced by German and Swedish concepts of 'active manpower policy', in which the employment service was seen as playing a crucial role in preserving full employment without high inflation. The UK's own problem in swinging rapidly from economic stagnation, when unemployment began to rise, into situations of an 'overheated' economy, bringing inflation and balance of payments difficulties, was seen as, at least in part, attributable to problems of labour supply. Overheating was associated with difficulties in securing adequately trained skilled labour. It was felt that a more sophisticated employment service, dealing with a much higher proportion of job placements and able to give more expert attention to training problems, would much more effectively match supply and demand in the labour market, and thus contribute much better to the maintenance of a balanced economy. A new, active service would seek to have a real impact on the working of the labour market.

In practice, the UK's employment policy initiatives of the early 1970s were brought into operation in a context not just of high inflation but also of rapidly rising unemployment. The modernized employment services had to operate in an economy where many economists had abandoned the 'Keynesian' belief that there is a direct, simple relationship between unemployment and inflation.

While *People and Jobs* saw the future of the service in terms of a lesser concern with the unemployed and a greater degree of assistance to those who sought to move between jobs, in fact the stagnation that occurred in the labour market forced the system to give a great deal of attention to the issue of unemployment, and to develop a range of temporary special job-creation and training measures.

On coming to power in 1979, the Thatcher government inherited from its Labour predecessors various special measures to deal with the problem of unemployment. Its initial inclination was to curb these activities as part of its general attack on public expenditure. The main employment policies of the government involved an emphasis on reintroducing the full rigours of the market-place into the labour market. A succession of measures weakened trade unions. At the same time the government was eager to reduce the impact of the meagre employment-protection measures still on the statute book, such as the wage regulation which had survived since 1909 for a small number of trades.

It is difficult to separate the impact of Thatcherite measures designed to free the working of the labour market, from the changes in the labour market that had already started to occur in the 1970s. It seems likely that the former accelerated the rate at which the latter took effect. It is not appropriate here to go further into these issues. What is relevant, however, is that Margaret Thatcher's government soon decided that they could not entirely discard the special measures developed in the late 1970s. They quickly came to realize that the special programmes, particularly those for the young unemployed, offered the cheapest way of providing a response to the problem of growing unemployment. So, in fact, the early 1980s saw a growth of expenditure on special training schemes and temporary job-creation measures (Moon and Richardson, 1985).

Certainly some of the measures adopted – in particular, job creation and the use of subsidies – seem to have been influenced by the more active employment policies of countries like Sweden. Ironically, in Sweden in the 1950s and 1960s, such measures were seen as ways of helping the very small minority of the population unable to secure work on the open market when employment was as full as possible. These measures take on a rather different character in an economy characterized by a seriously deficient demand for labour. They were criticized as inadequate alternatives to the effective management of the economy. One distinguished economist, Lord Vaizey, argued (House of Commons, 1977, p. 147):

> The sum total of these schemes seems to me to be cosmetic rather than genuine in its economic consequences. What they do in effect is to push employment around a bit without much net effect. They are in no sense a substitute for the substantial regeneration of UK industry.

Politicians, when they justify special measures to provide employment, deliberately obfuscate these issues. They want to be able to claim jobs saved or created by government intervention as contributions to the alleviation of unemployment as a whole. The actual macro-economic effect of these interventions is, happily for them, profoundly obscure.

In economic terms, the official answer to Vaizey's argument was that these schemes provided jobs with minimal inflationary effects, by comparison with more direct ways in which the economy might be stimulated. Moreover, at a time when interventions affecting the demand for labour had become distrusted, because of their potential inflationary effects, measures affecting the supply of labour – moving workers more quickly between jobs – were seen to be beneficial. More recently this 'supply side' emphasis has become more explicit. It has led to an emphasis upon measures designed to reduce the costs and increase the efficiency of labour. This is discussed further below.

However, there is also another social policy issue here: such policies may be used to influence the impact of a recession on particular groups of people. While they may do little or nothing to change the overall level of employment, they may help to ensure that particular people – the young, the previously long-term unemployed, those resident in certain areas – experience the ill effects of being out of work rather less than other people.

Since 1980, programmes of training and of assistance to unemployed people have gone through a large number of changes. Students will find even quite recent books misleading on detailed schemes, and if they try to trace the changes over recent years, they will be bewildered by the 'alphabet soup' of different schemes each generally identified only by its initials. Undoubtedly this complex evolution – and perhaps, indeed, even the government's willingness to persist with such activities – has been influenced by the changing EU subsidies available from the European Social Fund.

In the early 1990s, the Conservative government's approach to job-creation and training measures became one in which the needs of the existing economic system were stressed, and control was firmly in the hands of private sector employers. There was a strong emphasis on the training of the young. For older, long-term unemployed people, there were special programmes, with an increasing requirement of activities as a condition of financial support (even if these did not readily help the individual back into the regular labour market). Conservative governments blew hot and cold about the desirability of measures of this last kind. One influence was the considerable sums the government was being forced, by the high level of unemployment, to spend on benefits. It spent with great reluctance, and increasingly found ways to reduce benefits and prevent individual access to such help.

Since 1997 the Labour government has placed a strong emphasis on employment policy but, in many respects, there is a high level of continuity with the policies of its predecessor. Examination of the history of employment policy suggests that Labour might have been expected to adopt a stance of stressing job-creation measures and strengthening the trade union role as the protector of the workforce. That has been rejected as very much an 'old Labour' strategy. Alternatively, Labour might have adopted some of the initiatives of the 1970s again and given them a more distinctly 'continental' European twist, with an emphasis on increasing employment security. That too has been rejected, with the partial exception of the acceptance of a need for a minimum wage. Instead the emphasis has been very much on measures to improve and increase the supply of labour. Labour's 1997 election manifesto emphasized its supply-side programme on youth unemployment and said: 'Labour's welfare-to-work programme will attack unemployment and break the spiral of escalating spending on social security.' Typical examples of this emphasis are given in the Green Paper on Welfare Reform (Department of Social Security, 1998a, p. 31):

> The Government's commitment to expand significantly the range of help available therefore alters the contract with those who are capable of work. It is the Government's responsibility to promote work opportunities and to help people take advantage of them. It is the responsibility of those who can take them up to do so.

The same theme is echoed in measures for disabled people and for single parents.

We thus see here supply-side measures that by putting pressure upon people to seek work, perhaps for less money than they want, or received before they became unemployed, reduce the cost of labour. These have been accompanied by the tax credits, discussed in the last chapter, which subsidize low wages. There are also related training measures that are expected to derive their supply-side effects by increasing the efficiency of this low-paid labour.

To sum up, the UK moved from a situation in which little was done to prevent unemployment in the 1930s, through an era when regional policies were quite prominent, but generally the health of the labour market seemed to make planning unnecessary, between 1945 and 1971, into a brief phase when it was recognized that part of the UK's economic problem stemmed from the lack of an 'active labour market policy'. The rise of unemployment from 1975 onwards then 'hijacked' active labour market policy, concentrating efforts on special measures for the unemployed. Responses to the problem of unemployment preoccupied the system from then on, but since 1997 (in a situation of falling unemployment) the government have added an increasing concern to encourage labour-market participation even by those not previously defined as unemployed.

The Impact upon the UK of European Union Membership

It was noted above that the development of an interest in active labour market policy coincided with the commencement of UK membership of the EEC. We will return at the end of the chapter to explore further the above observations about differences between UK and continental European attitudes to the management of employment. But what does need to be inserted before going on to the main employment policy measures is a brief discussion of the quite specific way in which European Union policy impacts upon UK employment policy.

It was noted in chapter 3 that the principal social policy interventions emanating from the European Union have been limited efforts to harmonize rules relating to employment, and the provision of funds to help to create work and aid training programmes. It needs to be noted that, in practice, the European Union has no resources of its own. Its budget is acquired by levies upon the member states. Consequently it is small, little over 1 per cent of European GDP. Historically it has been heavily oriented to agricultural support. While that has come down proportionately in recent years, it is still about 44 per cent of the total spending (Kleinman, 2002, p. 113). There is also inevitably a need for fairly heavy expenditure on simply running the Union as a whole (including a great deal that has to be spent on translation). Nevertheless, there is a significant budget of about 33 billion Euros (2000 figure quoted by Kleinman, p. 114) for what are called the Structural and Cohesion funds. These perform two functions in relation to employment policy: the provision of help to the more deprived European regions (principally through the European Regional Development Fund) and help towards the relief of long-term unemployment, youth unemployment and the problems of the 'socially excluded' (the Social Fund).

The politics of European Union expenditure is complicated. While efforts are being made to channel funds to those in greatest need it is inappropriate to see this as simply a process in which wise people in Brussels make rational expenditure decisions. Some readers may recall Margaret Thatcher going to a European meeting resolved to 'get our money back'. Clearly national governments try to maximize what they get back out of what they pay in. Arguments about the structural funds are therefore influenced by how the distribution of agricultural subsidies works out. Beyond that, governments stress national needs that the Structural and Cohesion Funds should consider. Moreover it is generally the case that where grants are made, matching contributions are expected from the receiving country. All this adds up to saying that there is a small budget from which the UK, as a relatively well-off member of the EU (relative for example to Greece, Spain or Portugal), cannot expect to get very much.

However, the presence of the EU funds described here does have an impact upon the orientation of national policy. In relation to support for the unemployed the EU's priorities influence national policies because they offer the possibility of some supplementary funding. Hence the emphases upon youth training and upon support for long-term unemployed people, in the EU's priorities, have been reflected in the UK. Similarly the fact that the EU identifies regions in need of some support tends to steer expenditure towards those parts of the UK where unemployment is high. This is, however, a complex matter since it is quite difficult to detect the impact of a small external addition to a much larger national budget. The real impact of Structural Fund additions in Wales has been the subject of dispute between the UK government and the Welsh Assembly.

Since the EU is a relatively small direct spender it will try to influence policy by the way it directs its grants. But probably more significant for the influence of the EU upon the UK is the stance it takes in relation to employment regulation. This subject is explored further in a later section.

The Main Employment Policy Measures

The UK's employment policies are the responsibility of the Department for Work and Pensions. Local services for job seekers have been managed by an agency called The Employment Service which is, at the time of writing being transformed, as was pointed out in the previous chapter (p. 103), into a new organization integrating employment services with benefit administration, called Jobcentre Plus. A range of training activities that used to be organized by the employment service now come under the Department for Education and Skills in England and related organizations in the other countries of the UK. They will only be mentioned here inasmuch as they form part of the battery of measures open to employment advisers.

'Job centres' are the modern successors to the labour exchanges which were set up in 1908 to do just what their name suggests, to link employers seeking workers with potential employees. In the 1970s, job centres were seen as replacing the large institutional exchanges with modern, shop-front offices in commercial and shopping centres. There was an emphasis on self-service, individuals being able to select jobs from open-display advertisements, turning to staff only when advice was necessary. The aim as expressed in 1971 was to counter the problem that 'the Service is regarded by many workers and employers as a service for the unemployed' (Department of Employment, 1971, p. 5). The hopes for this approach were dashed, however, by the rise in unemployment. The 1990s saw an explicit acceptance by the government that this is precisely who the service is for.

Accordingly, a visitor from the 1930s would find the modern job centre a puzzling place: on the one hand, all the apparatus of modern consumerism – a pleasant office, courteous staff, ample explanatory material – and on the other, a battery of questions and controls which would seem remarkably familiar.

During much of the twentieth century, as noted earlier in this chapter, policy for unemployed people involved principally the payment of benefit, with control measures to prevent voluntary unemployment. There has been extensive controversy about the impact of the social security system on the behaviour of the unemployed. This was discussed in chapter 5, where concern about disincentives was shown to be an important influence upon the development of in-work benefits.

Labour, in 1997, made the development of the existing measures to get people into work central to its social policy programme. It specifically pledged to give a quarter of a million young people (aged between 18 and 24) six months in either work or training. This was backed up by a further strengthening of the already strict system of benefit-withdrawal sanctions against those who did not accept places.

In chapter 5, it was shown that the state financial support for unemployed people is provided by the jobseeker's allowance. To qualify, a person has to make a clear undertaking, signing a jobseeker's agreement, on the steps he or she will take to try to find work. Even for those who have been contributing to the national insurance (NI) scheme, jobseeker's allowance is means-tested after six months. Benefit may also be stopped or reduced if individuals are found to have lost employment unnecessarily or to have failed to take employment opportunities.

The job centres play a central role in the surveillance of the behaviour of the unemployed. The initial jobseeker's agreement is subject to regular review. Particular attention is paid to those who have been out of work for six months or more. At the reviews, the individual's efforts to find work are examined, and a variety of other options are explored. In their literature the government refers to a variety of alternative strategies applied at this stage, according to the characteristics of the job seeker.

A job seeker who is aged between 18 and 24 will, after six months of unemployment, experience extensive consultation with a 'personal adviser' who may, alongside normal employment opportunities, consider referral to subsidized work, work in the voluntary sector, work with a specially set up 'environmental task force' or full-time education and training. Job seekers over 25 experience similar intensive examination of their situations, with referral to subsidized employment their main alternative to normal employment.

The special programme for over-50s, 'New Deal 50 Plus', includes the possibility of receipt of a tax-free employment credit for a year to top-up returns from low-paid or part-time work including self-employment. Presumably the introduction of the working tax credit (see p. 109) will lead to the termination of this measure.

The consultation or advice in these programmes may involve a requirement to attend a seminar or training course (there has been a variety of jargon names for these, which change from time to time: 'jobplan', 'workwise', 'restart', etc.) where attention will be on job-search strategies and personal attributes and attitudes.

The New Deal for Lone Parents is designed to help lone parents into work. This arose to fulfil a pledge in Labour's 1997 election manifesto:

> Today the main connection between unemployed lone parents and the state is their benefits. Most lone parents want to work, but are given no help to find it. . . . Once the youngest child is in the second term of full-time school, lone parents will be offered advice by a proactive Employment Service to develop a package of job search, training and after-school care to help them off benefit.

The advice programme for lone parents is a voluntary one, at the time of writing, but it may be that compulsory labour-market participation by single parents with children over school age will follow. On the other hand, childless wives of men who claim the jobseeker's allowance are being required to register for work, and a special advice programme has been developed for them.

There is a 'New Deal for Disabled People', rather like the New Deal 50 Plus, on offer to people on disability benefits as well as those registered as unemployed. Measures for disabled workers have evolved considerably in recent years. As far back as World War II a specialized advice service was set up for disabled workers. This measure was supported by a quota system to require a proportion of jobs to be available for disabled people. The Disability Discrimination Act of 1995 replaced the quota with procedures for the prevention of discrimination against disabled workers. These include a requirement that employers should make 'reasonable' adjustments to premises to overcome the disadvantages of disabled people. It is hard, so far, to assess the impact of the changes under the 1995 Act. The quota was poorly enforced, but the new law requires action against discrimination to be activated by disabled people themselves. This may be very difficult to do. It is difficult to assess whether there has been discrimination in a context of stiff competition for jobs.

Throughout the 1980s, the government tolerated – indeed, partly encouraged – a situation in which people with disabilities were able to leave the unemployment register and receive the long-term, higher-rated invalidity benefit. This contributed to a reduction in the apparent size of the unemployed population. There was a steady growth in the numbers on invalidity benefit, particularly men in their fifties and early sixties. Then, in the 1990s, the government became concerned about the cost of supporting this group. In 1995, invalidity benefit was replaced by incapacity benefit, with a much stricter test of fitness for work. The Labour government then followed up on that measure by further reducing the availability of incapacity benefit and by developing the arrangements for interviews with an employment adviser to explore work possibilities.

The evidence on the fall in the unemployment rate since 1997 (see p. 147), and particularly the fall in youth unemployment, seems to suggest that the efforts described above have born fruit. However, it is always difficult to separate the impact of specific schemes from other influences on the labour market. The Trades Union Congress (1999) suggested that 'the buoyant labour market was the main factor behind' the positive trend. Most measures seem premised on the view that work is available and that the problem lies in the attitudes and behaviour of unemployed people. An exception to this is the subsidies, which may create extra work. However, since these are time-limited and mostly funded from a one-off levy, the underlying assumption is therefore that they will not have a lasting effect on the level of demand. These measures give little or no attention to issues about the quality of work or the level of pay.

Of course, given that experience of unemployment is concentrated amongst low skilled workers (see p. 147) the emphasis in the New Deals (particularly that for the young) upon training is to be welcomed. However, in evaluating the real effect of such measures, there is a need to be aware of the phenomenon of 'positional competition' (Hirsch, 1976). If good job opportunities are in short supply the effect of additional training may be merely to increase the qualifications needed to get into such jobs. If that happens, additional training for the weakest competitors for those jobs may do very little to enhance their job prospects. Furthermore while enhancing skills levels is widely seen as desirable to increase the competitiveness of the nation as a whole, if what actually happens is that an increasing number of jobs are able to recruit overqualified new employees much of that effect may be dissipated.

Government Regulation of Work Conditions and Job Security

It was noted in the introduction that another approach to employment policy, comparatively neglected by UK governments, involves the regulation of work, influencing its character and its security. A closely related topic concerns the role of government as an influence upon the conditions under which employers and employees are able to negotiate on these issues, through rules about trade unions and collective bargaining. While the general stance adopted in the UK has been to see the work contract as a private deal between employer and employee in a free labour 'market', since the middle of the nineteenth century employment regulation has not been entirely absent in the UK. Moreover modern concerns about discrimination, and the influence of membership of the European Union, have both had some significant impact upon employment policy. It is therefore appropriate to look briefly at these issues, where government social policy involves not the provision of benefits or services but rather the regulation of private activities.

The earliest regulatory legislation was measures to prevent or restrict the employment of women and children, enacted in the middle of the nineteenth century. While from one perspective this legislation can be seen as designed to prevent exploitation of the vulnerable, from another it is recognizable as having the effect of protecting adult males from competition. To-day most of the measures affecting female labour-market participation have disappeared but limitations on child employment remain. To some extent men also gained indirect benefits from the early regulation, inasmuch as downward pressure on the hours of women and children had an impact on those of men.

A crucial related question, on the political agenda from the middle of the nineteenth century onward, concerned the right of collective organizations – trade unions – to bargain on behalf of employees. The history of this issue is a convoluted one, beyond the scope of this book, in which the main concern of the trade unions, and the political labour movement, was to secure legal protection for bargaining rights. What this implied, therefore, was that the UK followed a very different road from that of continental European countries where government became a crucial party to bargains between employees and employers, participating in and protecting the terms of agreements reached. To use a sporting analogy, in the continental model of industrial relations the government is often a player, in the UK it is at best a referee, and in fact often a reluctant one (or even one biased in favour of employers).

What has followed from this approach is that where the UK government has intervened, it has been to influence the terms under which employers and employees arrive at contracts of employment – determining what it sees as good employment practice in respect of working conditions and the way in which workers are hired or fired (more the latter than the former). In this respect an important government role has been to provide special 'courts' to settle disputes between individual employees and employers. These 'courts' comprise the Employment Tribunals (formerly Industrial Tribunals) set up in 1964 and the Employment Appeal Tribunal set up in 1975 to handle appeals, principally those coming from the Employment

Tribunals. These organizations originally had quite a minor role in respect of training matters. They became more important after the enactment of rights to redundancy payments in 1965; but their role particularly advanced after the enactment of legislation to deal with 'unfair dismissal', the Industrial Relations Act of 1971.

The emergence of legislation to curb discrimination in employment should be seen against this backcloth of government reluctance to be involved in more than a passive way in the protection of employment rights. The first measure directed against racial discrimination in employment, an Act passed in 1968, was very weak. In 1975 a measure to combat sexual discrimination in employment was passed, and a year later the legislation against racial discrimination was strengthened. These measures set up government-supported bodies to help to enforce the law, the Equal Opportunities Commission and the Commission for Racial Equality. The Equal Pay Act of 1970, updated by an amendment Act in 1984, also contributes to the reduction of discrimination against women in the labour market. Significantly, in its approach to the prevention of racial discrimination the government initially drew a clear line between race and religion, to avoid dealing with the widespread religious discrimination in Northern Ireland. Subsequently, Fair Employment Acts specific to Northern Ireland were passed in 1976 and 1989 to try to tackle that problem. At the time of writing, however, issues about religious discrimination seem to be emerging on the overall UK political agenda. Finally amongst the battery of anti-discrimination measures it is important to note the Disability Discrimination Act of 1995 and the Disability Rights Commission Act of 1999, which together establish a framework rather like those for combating racial and sexual discrimination, to deal with discrimination against disabled people. At the time of writing, concerns about discrimination against older workers are also appearing on the political agenda.

There is thus now a group of legislative measures, with supporting enforcement bodies, which extend government intervention into the labour contract – curbing unfair selection practices, harassment at work and unfair dismissal – on behalf of ethnic minorities, women and disabled people. But the process of rooting out deep-seated discriminatory practices is not an easy one. Reforming legislation has been brought in slowly and reluctantly, the enforcement bodies are still poorly funded and elimination of discrimination largely depends upon individual actions through the tribunal system.

One of the key driving forces towards measures to attack discrimination in employment in the UK has been initiatives emerging from the European Union and decisions by the European Court of Justice. It has been noted that European Union social policy consists primarily of a range of measures in the field of employment and that probably the primary impact of the European Union has arisen from efforts to harmonize employment conditions across the member nations. These efforts stem particularly from the fact that with the creation of a single market comes a need to ensure that – through the maintenance of inferior labour conditions – particular nations cannot compete unfairly with others. In this respect the relatively unregulated UK labour market has been viewed with some concern. Accompanying that overall economic concern has been the fact that within the notion of the single market is the idea that free movement of labour should be possible. That leads on to a trade union concern about the rights of workers who move to work in other member states.

The issues about the relationship between the UK's approach to labour market regulation and that of the rest of the Community came to a head in connection with the establishment of the Community Charter of the Fundamental Social Rights of Workers (often called simply 'the Social Charter') in 1989 and the negotiations over the Maastricht Treaty of 1993. That Treaty, crucial for the steps towards monetary union, contained a 'social chapter' endorsing most of the aspirations of the Social Charter. The UK government negotiated an arrangement under which the 'social chapter' should not apply to them. But that did not eliminate the general pressure towards increased recognition of workers' rights. On coming to power in 1997 Labour accepted the 'social chapter'.

Some recent developments flowing from European Union social policy have been:

- rights to parental leave to care for sick children (though significantly this does not mean a right to paid leave);
- a right to paternity leave;
- limitations upon working time – particularly a measure requiring the working week to be limited to 48 hours;
- extension of employment protection rights to part-time workers and temporary workers (though it should be noted that the UK government is resisting some of this).

Finally, it is important to mention one recent piece of legislation affecting employment which is not a response to European legislation: the National Minimum Wage Act of 1998. This specifies a minimum hourly rate for workers. The implementation of this measure is supervised by an appointed body, the Low Pay Commission. That body makes recommendations from time to time on the need to upgrade the minimum wage; there is no automatic inflation linking process. The minimum wage in October 2002 is only £4.20 an hour (£3.60 for people aged 18–21).

Reducing Unemployment or Stimulating Employment?

In much of this chapter the influence of levels of unemployment on the UK policy response has been highlighted. It is appropriate therefore to look a little at what is meant by unemployment. That issue is, moreover, made pertinent by new policies, which have been noted, which may be seen as having an impact upon labour-market participation rather than upon formal unemployment *per se*.

Comparison of unemployment levels is made notoriously difficult by the different ways these are measured. There has been a tendency for the published figures to be of those registering for employment, or receiving benefit. These ignore the unemployment of those without benefit entitlements, and can be subject to manipulation as registration and/or benefit systems change. An alternative is a labour-force survey, though even in this case it must be noted that variations in the way people are asked about their desire for work or their job-search behaviour influence the figures. According to official data, using a survey approach, about one and a half million people in the UK (roughly 5 per cent of the economically active population, see further discussion of this concept below) were unemployed and actively seeking work in spring 2002 (National Statistics, 2002a). There had been a substantial fall in unemployment over the second half of the 1990s. In 1993 the equivalent unemployment rate was over 10 per cent and in 1997 it was a little over 7 per cent.

There are considerable regional variations in unemployment levels, with significantly higher levels of unemployment recorded in Scotland, Wales, Northern Ireland and north-east England. Unemployment rates vary in terms of the skill levels of the unemployed. They also vary by age, with higher rates for young people, but withdrawal from labour-market participation by older people distorts this finding. The rates for men are higher than those for women but this is misleading because women are less likely to remain active labour-market participants when they are unemployed and are also much more likely to be found in the ranks of part-time workers. One particularly disturbing difference is that between rates for different ethnic groups. A calculation based upon data across 2000–1 shows an overall unemployment rate of 6 per cent but a rate for 'black' people of 15 per cent and for Pakistanis and Bangladeshis of 17 per cent (National Statistics, 2002b, table 4.21, p. 81).

The new concern to stimulate labour-force participation confuses the issue of unemployment still further by identifying a group of people who clearly choose to remain outside the labour force, some of whom the government think should be within it. It has been shown above that in the UK in spring 2001 about 1.5 million people were unemployed (National

Statistics, 2001). Yet at the same time there were about 7.7 million people aged between 16 and the retirement age who were not economically active. Within that 7.7 million there were:

- About 2.4 million females between 25 and 49 years of age – most of these of course had family responsibilities.
- About 0.8 million males between 25 and 49 – many of these sick or disabled.
- About 1.4 million males between 50 and 64 and 1.3 million females between 50 and 59 – in both these cases (and particularly the former) there has in the recent past been a great deal of early retirement mainly prompted by the unavailability of work.
- About 1.9 million men and women between 16 and 24 – most of these students.

We see therefore that there is a very large element in the population – much larger than the number who are formally counted as unemployed – who may enter the labour force in conditions of high labour demand (particularly if the government is seeking to encourage labour-force participation). In addition there are three other ways in which the size of the labour force may alter:

- Among the economically active there are around 7 million part-time workers, some of whom may want to change to full-time work.
- At the moment only 0.8 million (8%) of the population over pension age are economically active; much higher rates of work beyond pension age occurred in the labour-hungry days of the 1950s and 1960s. Given the much better levels of health amongst the young elderly, this could easily occur again.
- There will be changes in population composition as a result of immigration and emigration. Past evidence suggests that rising labour demand stimulates the former, but of course much depends upon entry controls.

Data about labour-force participation has been discussed at some length partly because of the way policies to stimulate participation are very much on the current agenda. But it has also been introduced because there is – on the part of politicians and journalists – much misleading talk about labour shortages. This kind of talk shifts dramatically, according to fashion, from expressions of worries about the emergence of a world in which there will be a permanent lack of work (many examples of this could be found in the 1980s) to concerns about a lack of people to do the necessary work to support an ageing population (this is the 'demographic time bomb' perspective set out regularly from the 1990s onward). In fact, as the data above show, there is a great deal of scope for variation in the size of the labour force according to the demand for labour. At the same time there is still little known about the factors that lead to long-term shifts in that demand.

The UK government has been prepared to countenance measures which will have the effect of increasing the pool of people seeking work. It has boldly characterized its own efforts in these terms (Department of Social Security, 1998a, p. 23):

> The Government's aim is to rebuild the welfare state around work. The skills and energies of the workforce are the UK's biggest economic asset. And for both individuals and families, paid work is the most secure means of averting poverty and dependence except, of course, for those who are retired or so sick or disabled, or so heavily engaged in caring activities, that they cannot realistically support themselves.

It will be evident, from some of the discussion in chapter 5 and in this one, that the driving force for current efforts to increase labour-force participation is the government's concern to reduce benefit dependency. But there are obvious difficulties about trying to drive single mothers or disabled people into the labour force if there is a lack of work for all who want it. Clearly, contemporary official thinking on this subject is that this is not the case, and that in the UK economic development can be stimulated by encouraging labour-force participation. There are two alternative expectations here. One goes back to the long-standing view that the market works best if public policies stimulate demand for work and drive down wages. The other rests upon a view that demographic changes are leading towards shortages of workers. There are some very complex economic questions that lie behind either of those propositions.

The very high premium placed upon employment in contemporary policy is open to four objections. First, it may be challenged as placing paid work on a pedestal, above all other means of sharing resources in society. That is a philosophical issue, which will not be examined here. Secondly, it disregards the very large amount of unpaid work carried out, particularly within the household and most of it by women. Thirdly, it presumes that the problems of supplying enough employment, for all who are to be forced to need it, can be solved. Fourthly, and closely related to that second point, is that it seems to be silent on the quality of employment opportunities on offer. If the government's initiatives increase the volume of employment available, what kind of work will that be?

A more gloomy assessment of this approach is based on the extent to which employment growth in the UK, as opposed to economic growth (these are issues that are not necessarily linked), has involved low-paid, insecure and often part-time work. Dex and McCulloch (1995) estimated that around half of all women and a quarter of all men were in what may be called 'non-standard work' contracts, i.e. part-time work, temporary work or self-employment. However, a much higher proportion of new work may be of that kind (Gregg and Wadsworth, 1995; Cousins 1999).

Many people, including the Prime Minister, Tony Blair, tell us we have to learn to live in a world in which working lives need to be more flexible. The crucial problem here is, as Wheelock (1999) suggests, whether we are on the 'high road' or the 'low road' to flexibility in the labour market. The low road means that:

> Global competition and the structural shift to services put downward press-
> ure on the wages of the unskilled, wages which are already at the lowest end
> of the market.   (pp. 79–80)

The high road, on the other hand:

> relies upon employment based on sophisticated technology and innovation to
> keep abreast of international competition. Those employed in this sector – in
> high tech industries such as petrochemicals, computing, biotechnology etc. –
> must be highly trained. They must be prepared to be 'functionally flexible' in
> the sense that they undertake a range of tasks and learn how to do new ones.
> (p. 80)

In fact, analyses of divisions in labour markets (Piore and Sabel, 1984) suggest that while a lucky minority may be on the 'high road', the majority, and particularly those people who are likely to have to apply for benefits and to use state services to help them in the labour market, are on the low road. This has serious long-term implications for other social policies, and particularly for contributory approaches to pension provision; these were discussed on pp. 115–16.

Employment and Social Policy: a European Future?

The previous section has explored the UK government's determination to stress the role of work in relation to social policy. It takes strong symbolic form in the departmental restructuring that occurred in 2001 and the creation of a Department for Work and Pensions. That new departmental title seems to tell us that unless we are pensioners, and thus allowed to be out of the workforce, our social security must be linked to labour-market participation. The government's slogan in the first line of the summary of the Green Paper on Welfare Reform (Department of Social Security, 1998a, p. 1) was 'work for those who can and security for those who cannot'.

To what extent does contemporary UK government policy prompt a rethink about what social policy is all about? It is useful to link that question to the issue of the relationship between UK social policy and

European social policy. To do so uncovers some paradoxes. On the face of it making a strong link between social security and work brings UK thinking more into line with European approaches to social policy. A recent textbook on European social policy suggests that:

> In the British empiricist tradition, social policy is identified closely with the collective provision of social services. . . . Elsewhere in Europe, the term 'social policy' has been identified more with institutions and relations pertaining to the labour market, and in particular with the rights of workers and the framework for agreements between employers, unions and government – the social partners. (Kleinman, 2002, p. 1)

But there are three different glosses that can be put on a statement like that:

1 As Kleinman shows very clearly in his book, employment issues have dominated the thinking about social policy in the European Community precisely because that community is primarily aiming at the creation of a single market in which economic institutions are shared between the constituent nations. In those circumstances, as noted above, issues about employment conditions are bound to be dominant.
2 Equally, as also mentioned above, if the notion of the relationship between workers and employers is a compact between them, setting out conditions for social protection guaranteed by government (sometimes described as a 'corporatist' social order), then this will be much more central for social policy than is the case in the UK.
3 This leads then to a third point, that in most of the continental European countries a key ingredient of this social compact has been a social insurance system guaranteeing much better income-replacement rates outside work than the UK's social security system. Furthermore, in many cases this social insurance deal extends to health care (and recently, in the German and Luxemburg cases, even to social care). In such circumstances the link between work and social security rights is much more explicit than in the UK.

What the three points made above add up to is a suggestion that the UK perspective on social policy is changing to resemble the European one only in respect of the first of the three considerations set out above. If, in the UK case, work is the key to 'security', we are individuals in the marketplace, *unaided* by constitutionally incorporated trade unions and required to buy pensions and other sources of future security.

But that brings us to what is identified as a crucial issue about where the European Union is going. Kleinman's analysis of this topic identifies the European Social Charter as the high point of the aspiration towards a Europe of shared collective social policy. Behind that Charter were people, in particular French socialists, with a vision of a Europe-wide society where social standards could be raised through collective action, bringing the laggard countries up to the standards of the leaders. But, in Kleinman's view, an even more important force in the development of European policy came from those who saw the achievement of monetary union as involving the establishment of an economic regime in which there would be strict controls over inflation and measures that prevented government use of deficit spending to solve social problems. It was, in other words, a 'monetarist' vision of strict fiscal control, to operate effectively in the global economy, as opposed to a Keynesian vision of a European society in which active economic policies could be adopted to combat unemployment.

Kleinman's prediction of the development path for Europe is reinforced by the new aspiration to enlarge the community. The inclusion of former Communist-bloc countries in Eastern Europe could make the achievement of rising social-policy standards even more difficult. However, Kleinman is talking about issues that are still very much contested within the European Union. At the time of writing, Germany is seeking to be allowed to develop a government deficit in excess of that allowed by the rules relating to membership of the Euro. Throughout the Union the arguments between those who want to see social policy advances and those who stress monetary 'rectitude' go on. As a prosperous community member that is at the same time something of a social-policy 'laggard' (see chapter 11), the UK's role in this argument may be crucial.

CONCLUSIONS

This chapter began by setting the issues about employment policy in their wider social-policy context and by emphasizing the wide range of ways in which governments may develop policies. Attention was drawn to the fact that employment policies may concern:

- the overall level of labour-market participation;
- the characteristics of work;
- the nature of the supply of labour; and
- the demand for labour.

It was then shown that these concerns have all appeared from time to time in UK employment policy but that the overall stance has been relatively *laissez-faire*, doing little to intervene directly in the labour market, leaving influences on labour demand to a combination of comparatively accidental effects stemming from other policy decisions and treating unemployment as an issue to be tackled largely through income-maintenance policies.

Then, the rise of unemployment in the 1970s was met by revitalized public agencies committed to 'active' employment policy. Initially, this led to exploration of the development of job-creation measures, but these measures were undermined by a reluctance to compete with the 'regular' labour market. This led to a concentration on intervention in the labour market on behalf of specific groups of the unemployed. Such intervention has a strong 'supply side' emphasis, the concern being with 'what is wrong with' the victims of unemployment, rather than on deficient demand. Workers who are either more highly skilled or more willing to work for very low rewards are seen as less likely to be unemployed. Concentration on these issues is expected to reduce unemployment.

When revising this chapter in the past, I said that my feeling grows, each time I revise it, that much UK employment policy is an exercise in rearranging the deckchairs on the *Titanic*, with an overriding concern to increase the discomfort of passengers. The Blair government strongly asserts this is not the case. However, I will not be convinced of this until there is better evidence from the government of three things:

- serious attention to issues about the quality of the supply of jobs as opposed to the deficiencies of the labour force;
- increased concern about job security;
- satisfactory recognition of the very complex relationship between labour-market participation and the others kinds of work carried out within households and the wider society.

Until that is evident, the suspicion will remain that the enormous emphasis on the future of welfare as lying in labour-market participation by all who can do so involves a sophisticated political exercise at 'blaming the victims', who are perceived as making insufficient efforts to secure paid work.

SUGGESTIONS FOR FURTHER READING

This is a topic on which recent policy change has rendered many books rather dated. There have been a large number of books on unemployment, but few have dealt with the measures for unemployed people in any depth. Two quite old books that nevertheless set out the issues about unemployment and policies for the unemployed very well are Sinfield's *What Unemployment Means* (1981) and White's *Against Unemployment* (1991). An examination of contemporary developments in the labour market, in the UK and elsewhere, can be found in Wheelock and Vail (1998). Christine

Cousins's *Society, Work and Welfare in Europe* (1999), while it is a comparative study, has a valuable discussion of contemporary UK developments.

An official publication from National Statistics called *Labour Market Trends* contains both statistical material and good articles on current issues.

Pitt's *Employment Law* (2000) is recommended on some aspects of employment regulation. Kleinman's book on European social policy (2002) recommended at the end of chapter 3 is a valuable source on the issues about the EU explored here.

The Department for Work and Pensions has a website: www.dwp.gov.uk. European Union publications can be located via www.europa.eu.int/index_en.htm.

A site that is a good source for recent studies of employment issues is that of the Institute for Employment Studies: www.employment-studies.co.uk.

Chapter 7

Health Policy

- Introduction
- The organization and management of the National Health Service
- Patients' access to health services
- The financing of the National Health Service
- Management and professional accountability
- Need and the rationing of the health service
- Equality of treatment: the impact of the private sector
- Equality of treatment: inequalities in health and medical treatment
- Health policy or illness policy?
- The representation and protection of the public
- Conclusions
- Suggestions for further reading

Introduction

Inevitably examination of the role and organization of the UK National Health Service (NHS) will be a central part of this chapter on health policy. But it is important to bear in mind that the health of the nation will be influenced by many factors either outside the remit of the NHS or given little attention by that organization. The NHS has been criticized as a 'national illness service', and while governments have attempted to address that problem it is inevitably the case that it is the treatment of identified health problems that is the central preoccupation of state health policy.

This chapter therefore starts by looking at the organizational arrange-

ments for the delivery of NHS services. The exploration of these goes to
the heart of contemporary controversy about the National Health Service,
leading on to issues about accountability and about the financing of the
service. Many of the concerns about need and rationing, and about the
extent to which the service deals effectively with health inequalities, which
the later parts of the chapter explore, have to be seen in the context of
the organizational complications in the NHS. Conversely, some of the
continuing search for the best organizational structure is motivated by a
view that this is the key to solving problems of equity. Sceptics may argue
that this search for an organizational 'fix' cannot solve a basic underlying
problem of underfunding, but the political imperative to seek to provide a
good health service at the lowest possible cost inevitably links these two
issues together.

The Organization and Management of the National Health Service

The ingredients of the NHS are hospitals, the family or primary-care
practitioners (doctors, dentists, pharmacists and opticians operating outside
the hospitals), and other community-based services (community nursing,
health visiting and preventive medicine).

The Secretary of State for Health is responsible for the NHS in England.
In Wales, Scotland and Northern Ireland, it is the responsibility of the
devolved governments. The Secretary of State is assisted by a policy board,
which he or she chairs. Then, to deal with operational matters, there is a
management executive chaired by a chief executive. While this seems to
involve a departure from the normal top civil service control structure
towards a system that mimics that of a private company, the NHS executive
is not a separate agency like the Benefits Agency.

Below the NHS executive, the structure is now really quite simple.
Accounts of the history of health policy – see, for example, Webster (2002)
– show how there has been a succession of alternative organizational
arrangements for the NHS of varying complexity. Now, many of the
complications have been swept away. There used to be quasi-independent
regional health authorities; now in England there is simply a limited
number of regional offices of the NHS executive. Then, at the local level,
there are Strategic Health Authorities, which have three functions:

- creating a coherent strategic framework;
- agreeing annual performance agreements and performance management;
- building capacity and supporting performance improvement (Department of
  Health, 2002b).

The next tier below the Strategic Health Authorities is a network of Primary Care Trusts. They have responsibilities both for the provision of all primary care and for the commissioning of 'secondary' care for the patients in their areas, that is acute and specialist services. These responsibilities are, at the time of writing, being transferred to them from health authorities. The main sources of 'secondary' care services are also called Trusts, organizations responsible for hospitals and other services.

The main providers of primary care remain medical practitioners (see the comments below on dentists, pharmacists and opticians) operating under contracts, provided now by Primary Care Trusts. Broadly speaking, they are free to decide how they will organize their practices, and are free to accept or reject patients. They are paid primarily on a 'capitation' basis: so much for each patient on their list, plus an allowance for practice expenses and special payments for various exceptional tasks undertaken. Ever since the introduction of the NHS, the system of payments has been the subject of regular negotiations and conflict between the doctors and the government, in the course of which the scheme has been elaborated in a variety of ways to include such things as additional fees for elderly people on doctors' lists and payments for night and weekend work. While the doctors have clearly been eager to secure maximum rewards but to remain within a system that preserves their freedom, the government's objectives in these negotiations have included the encouragement of forms of group practice, the development of health centres and an increase in the number of doctors practising in some areas. In the last few years, the GP (general practitioner) service has become much more sophisticated. Isolated independent practice has declined, and group practices, providing a wide range of medical services, have multiplied. In 1997, legislation even provided for the possibility of the direct employment of GPs by Trusts.

Some of the issues about the current relationship between primary and secondary care services, and thus that between the two types of Trusts, can be better understood if we take a brief excursion back into the reorganization carried out by the Conservatives in the early 1990s. This split purchasing of services from their provision. The health authorities were purchasers, but only exceptionally were they direct providers. What this meant was that the health authorities were required to enter into specific contracts to secure the services needed for the patients in their area. The providers engaged in this way did not necessarily need to be in the health authority's geographical patch. The providers were organized into 'Trusts'. These Trusts remain the key elements in the secondary care service. Providers can, however, be private organizations (see p. 170).

The changes created what was often described as an 'internal market' or 'quasi-market' system of purchasers of services and providers. This arrangement generated considerable controversy. The case for the internal market was that the separation of purchasers and providers helped to undermine the tendency for those who provide services to exaggerate their value and hide their inefficient aspects. Bureaucratic allocation procedures had been replaced by a system of contracts, allowing purchasers to make choices between providers and to change them if they did not deliver what was required.

The system that actually developed did not measure up to the aspirations of the market advocates. Political and managerial interventions sought to allay some of the anxieties expressed by the opponents of the internal market. It proved to be very much a managed market, with its potential effects on some hospitals and some services damped down (Le Grand et al., 1998).

When Labour came to power it declared, at the outset, that it wanted to end the 'internal market'. However, in changes enacted in 1999, it accepted the idea of a purchaser/provider split but set out to operate it in a way which would have more stability. It also accepted the idea of GP involvement in secondary-care purchase, but was unhappy about the way in which this had been developed as a 'GP fundholder' system operated in parallel with the health authority purchase arrangements. It therefore initiated a process, which the reforms of 2002 completed, in which Primary Care Groups (then later Primary Care Trusts) would commission services for their area, supplying them with the necessary resources and ultimately 'holding them to account' (Department of Health, 2002b, para. 4.3). Note the use of the word 'commission' rather than purchase. Reflecting this, arrangements are expected to run for longer periods than the 'contracts' they replaced – up to five years.

The government indicated it wanted a flexible approach, taking into account arrangements previously adopted in each area. There are requirements of the Primary Care Trusts, however:

- to be representative of all GP practices in their area;
- to have a governing body which includes community nursing and social services as well as GPs;
- to promote integration of health and personal social services;
- to ensure that appropriate dental, optical and pharmaceutical services are available in their district;
- to help patients to obtain practitioners and to deal with complaints;
- to have clear arrangements for public involvement.

Patients' Access to Health Services

Access of patients to the health service, except in emergencies, is by way of the primary-care practitioners. These practitioners are thus the 'gatekeepers' of the service, making judgements about when referral to the more specialized secondary services is appropriate. Direct self-referral is accepted in the event of accidents and emergencies. This tends to increase, therefore, when primary care services are slow to react or when waiting lists for hospital consultations impose unacceptable delays.

It is an inevitable feature of a managed and non-marketized service that difficulties will arise about swiftly matching supply to demand. The main manifestation of an emergent problem of this kind will be the development of a queue, or waiting list. If that queue then persists there are grounds for regarding the service, or part of it, as under-resourced. This issue has been a consistent source of concern for governments for a long while.

In the late 1980s the Conservatives saw the development of an 'internal market' as a way to respond to this problem. Then, once they concluded that this would not solve the problem, they shifted attention to the management of the most obvious index of unmet need, waiting lists. Specific pledges were made to reduce waiting lists, which were inevitably echoed by the Labour opposition. Pledges in the Labour election manifesto for 1997 included a commitment to remove 100,000 people from waiting lists and to end waiting for cancer surgery. Those pledges were repeated again once Labour was in power. There are, however, problems about a political emphasis on waiting-list reduction. Waiting lists are, in many respects, merely a function of administrative practice. There is an easy way to shorten waiting lists, by refraining from putting people on them. Another approach is to terminate an initial wait by a consultation, but that does not necessarily lead immediately on to effective treatment. Using waiting lists as a general index of unmet need will not take into account the fact that some needs are more serious than others. It may be desirable that some people are kept waiting for minor surgery in the interests of securing more rapid responses to life-threatening conditions. Simply concentrating effort on shortening waiting lists may distort the overall service provided

The government has been concerned about the growth of self-referral to hospitals and the difficulties some people have in securing access to general practitioner services. They have established an organization called 'NHS Direct' to enable people to telephone for medical advice from a team of nurses, who may in emergency be able to activate other services.

Once under hospital care, individuals may be treated as in-patients or out-patients. The general notion here is of a hospital-based service for problems that are beyond either the expertise or the resources of GPs and other primary-care staff. However, the lines are sometimes blurred. Modern health centres can often provide services that are elsewhere provided by hospitals. The strong emphasis upon the provision of services as cheaply as possible means that governments have encouraged this development. Moreover even when people are treated in hospital, stays are nowadays very short, with many minor operations being carried out without an overnight stay.

Patients have a free choice of dentists and opticians, whom they approach directly. Dentists and opticians are paid on a fee-for-service basis. However, there have been problems, particularly as far as dentists are concerned, about the setting up of a system of remuneration that rewards most adequately the best practice, that is administratively straightforward and that can be supervised without detailed surveillance of day-to-day activities. The consequence is that it is hard to obtain NHS-supported dental services in many areas.

When patients are in hospital necessary drugs will be dispensed there. Outside hospitals, prescriptions for medicines normally have to be taken to pharmacists working in private shops, who are remunerated for this work. Exceptionally, in rural areas where shops are hard to access, doctors' surgeries may be allowed to provide medicines.

Charges cover much of the cost of spectacles and dental treatment and part of the cost of the supply of drugs and medical appliances. Prescription charges do not have to be paid by hospital in-patients, persons with specified chronic illnesses, children or the elderly. There are means tests that enable people on a low income to secure remission of charges. In the cases of dentistry and optical services these charges are sufficiently high now to mean that those who have to pay the full charges enjoy little benefit from the NHS. Opticians have always been largely private practitioners mixing private with NHS-subsidized work, but now much dentistry is also private.

Patients may receive a range of community health services. These include community nursing services, maternity clinics, preventive services offered by doctors and health visitors and measures to prevent the spread of infectious diseases. These are sometimes run by separate Trusts, sometimes organized as part of the work of hospital-based Trusts and sometimes organized by GPs. There is a particular need for these services to work closely with local authorities. There are clear overlaps between the concerns of health authorities and those of social services authorities (we return to this in chapter 8, pp. 191–4). Education authorities and schools have concerns about the services they offer to children. There is also a need for liaison with local government services to deal with environmental hazards and community health services (see pp. 174–5).

The Financing of the National Health Service

The NHS is financed out of national taxation. In 2000–1, in the UK, it cost £59 billion (this figure does not include any income offsets, which are in any case quite small) (National Statistics, 2002b, p. 137). Nearly three-quarters of its expenditure is on hospital and community health services, much of the rest is on family health services.

Throughout the history of the health service, the growth of its cost to the Exchequer has been a matter of political concern. Demographic changes affecting need, technological changes affecting the quality of treatment, and rising staff costs mean that the cost of the NHS increases without there necessarily being any improvement in the service it provides. Attempts have been made to estimate how much expenditure has to grow each year merely to maintain a consistent level of services to the public. A conservative estimate puts it at 2 per cent, but many suggest that it is nearer 4 or 5 per cent (Robinson and Judge, 1987; see also the discussion of this difficult, controversial subject in Glennerster and Hills, 1998, ch. 4). This is important in explaining why both the public and NHS practitioners regularly complain about falling standards, supported by concrete evidence from increasing waiting lists for operations, while governments claim they are spending more, in real terms, than ever before on the health service.

Public investment in new hospitals and other health care facilities is kept under strict control by central government, with the Treasury eager to ensure that public sector debt is kept down. The Conservatives developed a device to try to deal with the lack of investment that followed from this control. It allowed Trusts to bring forward, for approval, plans for privately financed developments. What this implied was new capital investment by the private sector providing facilities then leased to the NHS. In addition, support services such as portering, catering and cleaning (but not professional services) might also be leased. Such ventures would be interested in linking other money-making activities with hospital building, for example the inclusion of shops within a hospital complex. Objectors to this 'private finance initiative' were concerned that health policy priorities might be distorted by these ventures, and even that this might be the 'thin end of a wedge' that would lead to health service privatization. Perhaps a more cogent concern still was that this approach to capital underfunding merely shifted costs forward, since health service budgets would become increasingly encumbered by leasing commitments. It might have been expected that a new Labour government would abandon the private finance initiative. This has been far from the case. Its commitment to continue to keep down public sector borrowing coupled with its desire to be seen as the party of health service development has led it to approve a number of new ventures under the initiative.

At the 1997 election the Labour Party committed itself to maintaining the levels of spending on public services that had been set by their Conservative predecessors. They continued to expect deficiencies in health services to be met by greater efficiency and set a variety of targets for reducing waiting times. Gradually it became evident that under-funding had to be addressed. Glennerster portrays the change of attitude as coming in the following way:

> It was the flu epidemic of Christmas 1999 that triggered an explosion that was really inevitable at some point. Blair presumably saw this. His pledge to raise UK health spending to that of the rest of Europe in January 2000 was highly significant as are the detailed plans for spending the increment that followed in July 2000.   (Glennerster, 2001, p. 401)

The detailed plans Glennerster mentions were both a comprehensive spending review by the Chancellor, providing for a 27.3 per cent cash increase over three years, and a document called *The NHS Plan* (Department of Health, 2000), which set out in detail a range of ways the new money would be spent (including, particularly, marked improvements in staffing levels), a variety of performance targets and new endeavours to increase efficiency. The restructuring described above represents aspects of the latter, being seen in the plan as 'redesigning' to ensure the enforcement of 'national standards combined with far greater local autonomy', objectives that in the context of a very prescriptive plan may be contradictory. The Secretary of State made clear his commitment to breaking down barriers to service efficiency, including, controversially, using resources from the private sector where necessary 'to provide NHS patients with the operations they need' (ibid., p. 15).

The commitment to increased spending on the NHS was an important pledge in the general election of 2001. One key event during the campaign was a confrontation about inadequate cancer care, which clearly embarrassed the Prime Minister. The opposition warned that the spending increases could not come without tax increases yet such was the public recognition of the need for NHS improvements that this did no apparent electoral damage to the Labour Party. This is perhaps a turning point for the obsession of the Labour Party, after its defeats in the late 1980s and early 1990s, that it should not be seen as a 'tax and spend' party. In the budget of 2002 the Chancellor made a further commitment to continuing the increases in NHS funding. To do this he raised National Insurance contributions (a further indication of the way governments see these as simply another tax, see pp. 103–4). He linked this with some measures of further reform of the mechanisms to control the operation of the NHS, a topic to which we now turn.

Management and Professional Accountability

All over the world, health services have largely been set up on terms dictated by doctors. Doctors have been closely involved in the politics of the creation of state health care systems, often securing organizational arrangements that suited them as a profession. They have acquired high financial rewards and they have secured positions of power from which to influence the day-to-day running of services. In doing all this, they have defined good health, health care needs and the responsibilities of health services in ways which put them in a central and indispensable role (Friedson, 1970; Moran and Wood, 1993; Harrison and Pollitt, 1994; Ham, 1999). As people and politicians have begun to demand more control over health services, and as it has become increasingly recognized that it is difficult to control the costs of 'provider-led' services, so efforts to curb medical power have assumed a central place on health-policy reform agendas.

Until the 1980s, the managerial arrangements for the NHS could have been described as broadly 'collegial': that is, the various professionals within the service were represented in the management structure. Then, after 1983, each administrative unit was required to appoint a general manager, on a fixed-term contract. Many of these general managers were already health service administrators, but there were appointments from outside and, in a few cases, senior professionals, particularly doctors, but occasionally nurses, received these posts. These managers were accountable to the relevant appointed authorities. Then, under the changes enacted in 1990, the health authorities were restructured to comprise up to five 'executive members' (to include the chief executive and the finance director), and five non-executive members (including a non-executive chairman). Non-executive members were appointed by the Secretary of State. Trusts are required to have similar management structures.

Hospital doctors have traditionally exercised a considerable degree of autonomy. Crucial for this is the concept of clinical freedom, which can be effectively extended from a right to determine the treatment of individual patients to a right to plan the pattern of care as a whole. The managerial arrangements adopted in the 1990s, and the significance of the contracting system for patterns of work, have been seen by some to threaten that freedom (Harrison and Pollitt, 1994). It is difficult to say how significant that threat is, since much depends on the internal management arrangements made within the Trusts. There is a requirement for the hospital Trust executive to have a medical member. This may place one doctor in a strong position; but alternatively, he or she may be seen merely as a figurehead to represent the consultant group as a whole, without disturbing individual autonomy.

Hospital consultants may be part-time appointees, who combine private practice with NHS work. Junior hospital doctors, below consultant status, are organized in consultant-led teams. Most of them are in short-term appointments, which are seen as building blocks of trainee experience leading to consultant status. There are problems of relatively low pay, heavy duties and insecurity for junior doctors, enhanced by difficulties in advancing to consultancies.

The last Conservative government placed, briefly, some faith in the feasibility of the internal market as a device to control doctors. The Labour government has developed alternative ways to increase the public account-ability of doctors, and other professional staff. It sees a need to do this by involving these people in the managerial and monitoring arrangements for the service rather than by simply imposing hierarchical controls. Key aspects of its strategy are itemized in a list by the Department of Health (1998a, para. 6.4):

- to involve Trusts in the shaping of their local Health Improvement Programmes;
- to ensure that explicit quality standards are set in local agreements;
- to involve professional staff in the design of service agreements;
- to develop a system of 'clinical governance'.

The concept of 'clinical governance' requires that the processes that are currently used in the NHS to try to improve the quality of clinical work are integrated with quality planning for the Trusts (and ultimately the NHS) as a whole. An earlier measure was a requirement that systems of 'clinical audit' should be set up in each Trust to review clinical work, but this was criticized as being a private review process within the medical profession, which individual doctors do not always take seriously and for which there is no system of external accountability. This is now tied in much more to the system of clinical governance. There are also require-ments that better use should be made of what the profession calls 'evidence-based practice', with wider dissemination of new examples of good practice. A National Institute of Clinical Excellence has been set up to promote clinical effectiveness and to produce and disseminate clinical guidelines.

Clinical governance is another attempt by government to bring about significant shifts in the way medical staff conceive of their work and hence to bring about substantial change in relations within clinical settings. For it to be successful there will need to be major investments in information systems, and programmes to increase clinical effectiveness. The government describe it as 'a partnership between the Government and the clinical professions. In that partnership, the Government does what only the

Government can do and the professions do what only they can do' (Department of Health, 1998a, para. 1.13). It goes on to argue (para. 3.9):

> Clinical governance requires partnerships within health care teams, between health professionals (including academic staff) and managers, between individuals and the organizations in which they work and between the NHS, patients and the public.

Sceptics may feel that this is merely another attempt by the government to convince the public that it has clinical autonomy under control. However, it does seem to involve a much more explicit attempt to integrate professional accountability with managerial accountability in the NHS. The whole issue was given a greater degree of urgency by the emergence into the public arena in the summer of 1998 of a scandal at the United Bristol Healthcare Trust. At that time, the doctors' disciplinary body, the General Medical Council (GMC), found three senior hospital consultants guilty of serious professional misconduct. The three included a former Medical Director of the Trust and the Trust's medically qualified Chief Executive. There had been serious problems about the way heart operations had been carried out on children, leading to deaths that could have been prevented. The evidence on this problem had been suppressed for quite a long while (though quite widely suspected within informed medical circles). Clearly, the direct involvement of some very senior doctors, whose patronage would be important for more junior staff, contributed to this. It was eventually brought to light by an anaesthetist, who was sacked for his 'whistleblowing' activities and who emigrated to Australia before being eventually vindicated. The Secretary of State reacted angrily to the disciplinary body's report, setting up an inquiry and stressing that the new accountability measures must bring to light deficiencies in medical practice. At the time of writing, that inquiry has reported and changes to the NHS complaints system are expected (see pp. 177–8).

In 1999 the government established the Commission for Health Improvement to provide an independent scrutiny of clinical governance arrangements in England and Wales. This body, managed by an appointed board, carries out a rolling programme of reviews of the quality of patient care in every health authority and Trust. It also conducts studies of specific parts of the health service's work (its first being a study of cancer services, which was published in 2001) and responds to requests for investigations of services that are causing concern.

On top of all this, immediately after the 2002 budget the Secretary of State announced that he was setting up a new health care inspectorate. He also indicated that trusts that proved to be efficient might secure a new more autonomous status, as 'foundation hospitals'. These measures emerged whilst the NHS was still dealing with the restructuring described earlier (p. 158), and just as this book was being completed. It will be some time before their full implications can be assessed.

This section has explored some of the efforts being made to deal with the extent to which it has been seen as problematical that the NHS tends to be 'provider-led'. Central to this activity has been a search by governments for ways to provide better value for the public whilst minimizing increases in costs. But perhaps they have expected too much, perhaps the central problem is that the UK has an underfunded health service.

Need and the Rationing of the Health Service

The main medical services provided by British health services are, broadly speaking, free and universally available. The general issues raised by the absence of a price mechanism to convert needs into effective demands will be discussed in the next chapter (pp. 195–7). One of the political preoccupations ever since the founding of the NHS has been the difficult question of how to respond to need.

There seem to be two crucial problems that were given insufficient attention by those, in the 1940s, who forecasted a decline in need for health services once the NHS was in place. One is that everyone whose life is saved, lives on to become ill again. More precisely, increases in life expectancy bring with them the likelihood of increased work for the service in dealing with chronic illnesses. Such illness is concentrated amongst the elderly. Over-65s were only about 11 per cent of the population in 1951; they now constitute 16 per cent. About 7 per cent of the population are over 75 (calculated from data in National Statistics, 2002b, pp. 29–30). The growth in the proportion of elderly people has temporarily stopped, but will start again just after 2010, as the post-World War II baby-boom population begins to reach 65. However, it is important not to exaggerate the implications of this – the fact that older people are living longer is an indicator that they are healthier and most critical health-care episodes are concentrated at the very end of life, at whatever age that occurs.

The other problem in predicting the need for health services arises from difficulties in defining need. There is a growing understanding that the relationship between having a medical need and seeking medical attention is complex and obscure. Individuals may experience considerable suffering from a condition that manifests no pathological abnormality. Conversely, they may have serious medical problems, yet experience little suffering. Perhaps more significantly in quantitative terms, minor deviations from 'good health' are tolerated by many people for long periods of time without medical attention being sought. This applies, for example, to problems like indigestion, recurrent headaches and skin complaints. It is important to recognize that 'Illness is the subjective state that is experienced by an individual, a feeling of ill-being. Disease is a pathological condition recognized by indications agreed among biomedical practitioners' (Stacey, 1988, p. 171).

The definitions of 'biomedical practitioners' are no more valid than people's subjective judgements. They are subject to variation over time and between 'experts', and are conditional on the dominant paradigms in medical knowledge. They are, however, crucial in influencing demand for health services. This is the sense in which there may be a problem for health services about 'producer'-determined demand, deriving from biomedical practitioners' claims to competence and, in some circumstances, their tendency – encouraged by public faith in medicine – to 'medicalize' social problems.

There is a choice of policy conclusions to be drawn from these findings. One is that a great deal more should be spent on the health service, and, in particular, that many more efforts should be made to screen for unidentified illness in the population at large. The quite opposite view is that the fact that many people manage without medical treatment for many complaints suggests that those who do 'bother' doctors with similar problems should be encouraged to become more self-reliant and to make more use of self-medication. A less extreme version of this view suggests that, since medical resources are clearly limited, it is important to control access to the services in such a way that the more serious complaints are treated, while doctors are not overburdened with the trivial. The development of NHS Direct (see p. 159) is a step towards the examination of the idea that access to health services may be channelled, and implicitly controlled, in other ways. Increasing attention is being given, as with NHS Direct, to the use of nurses rather than doctors as 'gatekeepers' for the service as a whole, engaging in initial diagnosis and authorized to provide or prescribe various medicines and treatments.

Another issue on the agenda is the exclusion of some kinds of treatments from the NHS; for example, one much-debated example is the treatment of infertility. Attention is also being given to issues about the use of medicines, limiting the use of expensive drugs when there are cheaper equivalents or where their therapeutic properties are not regarded as having been clearly established.

There have been suggestions that there are ways of controlling demand by pushing the responsibility for it back to the patients. This provides one argument for the exploration of the case for 'cost-sharing' charging systems, to control demands on the service. One possibility that has been debated is the introduction of 'hotel charges' for hospital stays. The problem with this is that stays are becoming shorter. The administrative costs of billing and collecting charges for the many very short stays would be considerable. Further complications would be introduced if, as with prescriptions, some patients were not required to pay. Similarly considerations apply to another idea: flat rate charges for consultations with GPs.

A case for health service charges is also argued in terms of the desirability of choice and competition. This case has been made most cogently in the USA by Friedson (1970), who sees the power of the consumer as enhanced by a relationship with the doctor in which he or she has the capacity to 'hire or fire'. In Friedson's view, the British model of health service organization places individuals in a very weak position in dealing with doctors, and provides the community at large with an absence of weapons for bargaining with a medical profession that would not be so united were doctors in competition with each other.

The fundamental point in favour of a free service is that charges may deter people from seeking necessary help (Abel-Smith, 1976). This is particularly likely to be the case with people on low incomes. Moreover, the effects of ill health will often naturally include a reduced income and an increase in other costs. Clearly also, while in other areas of life people may be expected to make choices between different ways of spending money, serious illness leaves little choice. Individuals will bankrupt themselves to save their lives and those of their loved ones.

Where much of the health service is still 'in the market-place', as, for example, in the USA, the issues are rarely actually as stark as these. There are two reasons for this. One is that many people insure themselves against sickness. The other is that a 'safety net' means-tested medical system exists for the poor. Arguments in favour of a free service must therefore deal with the weaknesses of these two alternative forms of provision.

The key problems with private insurance schemes are that they will not insure the 'bad risks'; they often exclude some conditions (especially preventable ones – for example, pregnancy); and they may collapse. These schemes may reduce the powers of doctors, making them dependent on the patronage of the insurance agencies; but the latter often encounter the same problems of provider-determined need as the British system has been alleged to suffer from. Moreover, they do not necessarily curb trivial demands, since subscribers may be determined to obtain their money's worth. In the 1980s, the case for an insurance-based approach to health care re-emerged on the British political agenda. Private insurance schemes had grown rapidly, facilitating the growth of private hospitals (Higgins, 1988). Debate developed, therefore, about the extension of such schemes nation-wide. Those advocating such an approach argue that individuals should be required to insure themselves privately, and that the state should underwrite such schemes and make special means-tested provision for those for whom they cannot cater. This approach was given serious attention by the Conservatives in their review of policy before their 1990 changes to the system. The creation of a tier of potentially autonomous providers (the Trusts) opened the way for such a development.

The problems with a means-tested health service are the requirement of a test of means before treatment, the likelihood of situations in which individuals will have to abandon resources – or wait to 'hit the bottom' – before they can ask for treatment, and the probability that (as was the case in the UK when such a system operated) two classes of health service will result. In the last resort, as implied above, the case for a free service is not that it helps to distribute resources from the rich to the poor, but that it enables the healthy to support the sick. If it is believed, on the other hand, that it is in the interests of the evolution of society that the 'weak should go to the wall', it will of course be comparatively easy to take an alternative view.

Whilst arguments for a shift towards a system of wholly or partly private health insurance are now less widely heard in the UK, another idea that has gained ground as a response to the problem of under-funding has been that the NHS should be specifically funded out of a health tax (Le Grand, 2001). It is suggested that whilst people are resistant to general tax rises they may accept them when they see them as clearly linked to service improvement. The problem with this argument is that it would then encourage those who have private insurance or purchase private health care to argue that they should not pay the tax, thereby opening the door to a greater drift towards privatization and a two-tier health system. Also, if there is a case for earmarked funding for health then why not for other public services, such as education, opening up much more complicated issues about the relationship between taxation and public spending.

Hence the debate about the level of funding needed to sustain a satisfactory NHS runs on. As noted above, at the time of writing, the injection of new money has been quite considerable. Whether it is enough remains to be seen. Meanwhile improvements to the service as a consequence of that new money may be quite slow to emerge. Inasmuch as staff shortages are a central part of the problem, it will take a long while to see a change since many of the key people (this is particularly true of doctors) take a long time to train. At the same time cynics argue that much of the new money may simply contribute to pay increases for the current staff, without necessarily increasing recruitment.

Equality of Treatment: The Impact of the Private Sector

In the atmosphere of concern about rising health service costs and advocacy of privatization by the Right, there is considerable concern in Britain about two related issues: the most appropriate relationship between the health service and the residual private medical sector, and the extent to which the health service provides equality of treatment to all the population.

These two issues are related, since the diversion of medical resources into a private sector, largely accessible only to the better off, reduces the resources available to other sectors of the population. However, the defenders of private medicine argue that the resources involved are, in a sense, extra ones, which would not necessarily be diverted into public medicine in an entirely nationalized sector. Particular bones of contention, however, have been not so much the right of the private sector to exist, as the support the sector receives from a variety of special links with the health service.

It is difficult to achieve a precise estimate of the size of the private sector. Nearly 7 million people in the UK have private health insurance (National Statistics, 2002b, p. 143), but this does not mean they will not also be users of the public sector. Most people have public-sector GPs, using insurance to secure themselves easier access to secondary services.

Both GPs and consultants are able to take on private patients as well as health service ones, and NHS Trusts may offer private services for patients from home or abroad. The private finance initiative, discussed on p. 161, may further encourage this. Similarly it has been noted (see p. 162) that the government is encouraging the purchase of services from private providers as a way of reducing pressure on public services. While the government argues that this is just enabling the NHS to obtain services – at lower cost or where public providers are unavailable – such arrangements may implicitly subsidize the private sector, and may be the thin end of a wedge leading to the transformation of the free health service.

In these situations, health service resources are likely to be used in various ways in support of private medicine. They facilitate the undertaking of public and private work side-by-side, the use of public resources (such as expensive equipment) for private patients, and 'queue-jumping' when public beds are scarce. The way in which doctors with both public and private work distribute their time between the two may result in subsidy to the latter, in that they may neglect NHS duties to enhance fee earning. Also, situations arise in which it is possible for doctors to say to people that, whereas health service treatment will be inadequate or long delayed, they may secure a better deal by becoming private patients. There is a substantial hidden subsidy from public to private medicine because doctors are trained in the NHS, and much medical research is publicly funded. Furthermore, private hospitals are able to turn to the public sector in emergencies.

The growth of private insurance raises the question of the overall impact on the state service of alternative ones. Is there scope here for desirable competition? Is it a valuable addition to consumer choice, enabling people who are so inclined to pay a little extra for a superior service? Or does it threaten the basic service, and reduce its capacity to meet the needs of all?

Equality of Treatment: Inequalities in Health and Medical Treatment

The health service's capacity to meet need has been subjected to extensive scrutiny. Epidemiological studies of the differential impact of mortality and morbidity have been of importance here. These show considerable differences in the experience of ill health between different regions of the country, between different social classes and between different ethnic groups (Townsend et al., 1988; Acheson, 1998). More challengingly for the NHS, as mortality rates have declined overall, these differences have not decreased; indeed, in many cases, they have increased. Particular attention has been given to what is termed 'premature' mortality. While five out of every thousand babies with parents in the Registrar General's 'social classes' I and II died in the first year of life in 1994–6, the corresponding death rates for those with parents in classes IV and V was seven out of a thousand (Acheson, 1998, p. 14). Similarly it has been shown that there are substantial mortality differences between different social classes in mid-life, providing similar evidence of social class contrasts (ibid., p. 12). A disturbing aspect of this data is the evidence it provided on a widening gap between the 'classes' when 1991–3 data were compared with those for 1970–2. If we judge these mortality rates by giving those for class I an index of 100 then the relative mortality rate of class V was 179 in 1970–2 but 287 in 1991–3.

There is similar evidence of health disadvantages amongst minority ethnic groups. One very disturbing statistic reported by *The NHS Plan* (Department of Health, 2000) is that 'children of women born in Pakistan are twice as likely to die in their first year of life than children of women born in the UK' (p. 108). Such indices in many respects reflect socio-economic differences between ethnic groups, but there are also issues about the quality of service minorities receive. A report on *The Future of Multi-Ethnic Britain* speaks of a 'striking paradox':

The NHS depends, and for several decades has depended, on the contributions of Asian, black and Irish doctors, nurses, managers and ancillary staff. At the same time, patterns of mortality and morbidity are more serious in Asian, black and Irish communities than in the population as a whole, and there is much insensitivity in the NHS to the distinctive experiences, situations and requirements of these communities. (Parekh, 2000, p. xix)

Regional differences will also to a large extent reflect social class differences. Inequalities of health have been found between different localities, down to quite small areas. Such work has shown (a) differences which it is possible to correlate with other indices of deprivation (including environmental factors) and (b) a tendency for these differences to widen at the end of the last century (Phillimore et al., 1994).

The policy questions this evidence raises obviously concern the extent to which these differentials are attributable to differences in the availability of health services. But it must also be asked, inasmuch as they are attributable to other factors (low income, poor housing and so on), to what extent better health services can offset these disadvantages.

The Acheson committee, in its examination of these issues, suggests that the key questions that remain are about the extent to which sufficient services are available to those groups particularly likely to have poor health. It notes (Acheson, 1998, p. 112):

> Access to effective primary care is influenced by several supply factors: the geographical distribution and availability of primary care staff, the range and quality of primary care facilities, levels of training, education and recruitment of primary care staff, cultural sensitivity, timing and organization of services to the communities served, distance and the affordability of safe means of transport.

The Acheson committee argues that many deprived areas have difficulty in recruiting GPs and other primary-care staff, and that there are many poorly equipped primary-care practices in deprived areas, particularly in parts of inner London (Acheson, 1998, p. 116). In *The NHS Plan* (Department of Health, 2000, p. 107) the government points out that primary-care service inequities have been excluded from attention in the formulae governing NHS resource allocation (see the discussion below):

> Instead, the Medical Practices Committee (MPC) has sought to ensure the fair distribution of GPs across the NHS, with only limited success. For example there are 50% more GPs in Kingston and Richmond or Oxfordshire than there are in Barnsley or Sunderland after adjusting for the age and needs of their respective populations.

They promise action to deal with this, seeing it as one of the issues to be tackled with the abolition of the MPC and the setting up of a new Medical Education Standards Board.

Overall the Acheson committee suggests (p. 112) that 'Communities most at risk of ill health tend to experience the least satisfactory access to the full range of preventative services, the so-called "inverse care law".' It suggests that evidence on secondary services is more difficult to interpret, indicating a need for better monitoring (p. 112), but it also notes continuing inequalities in the allocation of funds for hospital and community health services. This emphasis is echoed by *The NHS Plan* (Department of Health, 2000, p. 107).

Back in 1974, the government set up a Resource Allocation Working Party (RAWP) to develop a formula to facilitate comparisons between the resource needs of different regions. This used population estimates, weighted to take into account differential mortality, and different utilization rates based on differences in the age and the structure of the population (Department of Health and Social Security, 1976). Allocation of new money to the regions was based on the RAWP formula, and allocations by regions to districts were based on similar principles. This proved a difficult, controversial exercise in light of the inadequacy of the statistics available, the difficulties in relating such data to needs, and the uncertainty about the relationship between costs and effectiveness. The 1990 changes brought the RAWP procedure to an end; some of the problems that it had had to deal with in relation to 'flows' of patients across boundaries were solved by the contracting procedure. The allocation of money to health authorities was then based on population numbers weighted to take into account some of the considerations about differential needs. The government is reviewing this. In *The New NHS* it says (Department of Health, 1997, para. 9.6):

> The Government will put in place new mechanisms to distribute NHS cash more fairly. A new Advisory Committee on Resource Allocation will further improve the arrangements for distributing resources for both primary and secondary care. The healthcare needs of populations, including the impact of deprivation, will be the driving force in determining where cash goes.

The NHS Plan (Department of Health, 2000, p. 107) promises the completion of this review by 2003, linking it with the government's wider concerns to reduce health inequalities.

In 1998 the government set up 26 Health Action Zones in England to try to develop partnerships that would help to tackle health inequalities in deprived areas. There is little clear evidence yet that these have had a significant impact (Powell, Exworthy and Berney, 2001).

While efforts to tackle some of the problems of 'territorial injustice' that have beset the NHS since its foundation have been widely welcomed, there are some other issues about the availability of services that require attention. As suggested in the references to the Acheson Report quoted above, social class differentials in the use of health services suggest that efforts need to be made not only to ensure that adequate resources are available in underprivileged areas, but also to facilitate access to the use of those resources by all in need. This raises policy questions about the siting of surgeries and hospitals, the arrangements made by doctors to enable patients to secure appointments, the extent of the use of health service personnel – such as health visitors – who actively seek out those in need of health care, the amount of health education, and the significance of screening services.

Finally, these questions lead on to the other question raised: how far there might be an expectation that health services should be better in some areas, or for some people, to help to compensate for other social disadvantages. Alternatively, to what extent should the concept of a state health service embrace a responsibility to point out how other social factors contribute to ill health? The Acheson Report, as a product of an independent inquiry commissioned by the Secretary of State for Health, is an important step forward in indicating the wide policy agenda that has to be addressed if health inequalities are to be reduced. The issues considered in chapter 5 on the growth of poverty at the end of the last century, and the slow progress being made in efforts to reverse that trend, are clearly enormously relevant here. So are the issues about the prevention of unemployment, considered in chapter 6. The same is true of the incidence of homelessness and poor housing, to be considered in chapter 10.

Other aspects of this topic are explored further in the next section.

Health Policy or Illness Policy?

At the very beginning of this chapter it was stated that it is important to bear in mind that the health of the nation will be influenced by many factors which may not be given attention by the NHS. Reference was made to the criticism of the NHS as a 'national illness service'. *The NHS Plan* (Department of Health, 2000, ch. 13) examines this aspect, stressing the government's concerns about inequalities in health and its commitment to the prevention of ill health. It is fair to say that these issues have been given increased attention by the NHS in recent years. GPs have been encouraged to provide health checks for their patients and to develop health advice programmes.

There are a number of interrelated approaches to the prevention of ill health, many of them going beyond the simple questions about the provision of health services. As was shown in chapter 2 (see pp. 15–16), this is one of the oldest issues on the social policy agenda. Ever since it was recognized that uncontrolled effluents from domestic and industrial premises could be a cause of ill health there have been governmental responses to these problems. In the nineteenth century local authorities were pioneers of measures to improve the environment, their efforts reinforced by a range of public-health legislation. When direct responsibilities for health services were taken away from local government, a process finally completed in 1974, a split system was developed to deal with public-health issues. Local authorities remained responsible for inspection, data collection and basic preventative action against public-health nuisances, and were able to draw upon the services of medical public-health specialists employed by the health authorities. The environmental health officers of the unitary and lower-tier local authorities remain the lynchpins of the system, with powers to inspect shops and restaurants, regulate markets, take preventative actions against the spread of infections and deal with effluents from some industrial processes. At the same time the more complex forms of pollution from industry and agriculture are regulated by central government through agencies answerable to the Department for Environment, Food and Rural Affairs, in particular the Environment Agency and the Food Standards Agency. There is a large and complex body of legislation dealing with these issues, which cannot be examined in any detail here. Nowadays the European Union also plays a key role in the advancement of the environmental health agenda. The approach to these issues in the UK obviously requires collaboration between central and local government and the NHS. Characteristically it involves a combination of powers to deal swiftly with the most obvious abuses and a rather more cautious, often essentially educative, approach to emergent problems. The system is often seen as too slow, and too ready to see the point of view of the producer.

In many respects the traditional approach was to see public-health concerns as dealing only with serious dangers. A liberal ideology saw many matters of consumption to be matters for free choice. Note, for example, the slow and still limited official responses to evidence on health hazards from smoking and drinking. A recognition of the nation's economic dependence upon manufacturing and commerce inhibited drastic action. In any case, the health of the nation steadily improved over the twentieth century. There are good grounds for regarding growing national prosperity as more important for health improvement than medical development (McKeown, 1980). It is only over the past twenty to thirty years that many of the more subtle and complex dangers to human health have begun to be recognized. Health improvement has been seen to be less than it could have been. Unexpected health hazards have emerged, from pesticides or from food additives for example. Accordingly a 'green' agenda has emerged, challenging complacency about the institutions ostensibly there to protect us, and showing the need to improve the capacity to identify risks for current and future generations. That agenda recognizes the need both for individual action in respect of consumption choices and for official action to curb health hazards and to try to modify behaviour (Huby, 1998; Cahill, 2002).

Governments have responded to the public-health implications of this new agenda with a combination of tightened regulation, increased recognition of a role for the NHS in relation to health improvement, and an emphasis upon health education. It is very difficult to measure the impact of government interventions: while some regulatory measures have been adopted, much government action has consisted of providing information and advice, and making health checks easier to obtain from GPs. Yet lifestyle options are influenced by income and environment, constraining choices. They may also be influenced by the practices of the food and drink industry, the additives they use and the things their advertisements promote. Other aspects of our living and working environments may be quite outside our control. It may be argued that governments could embrace more boldly their regulatory responsibilities to help to protect our health.

The Representation and Protection of the Public

When the formation of the NHS was debated in the years before 1948, many doctors made clear their opposition to local government control. While some community services were kept within local government between 1948 and 1974, the main forms chosen for the local control of the health service were hybrid organizations in which ministerial appointees served alongside local authority nominees. Since 1991, the arrangements for direct local government representation on health service governing bodies have disappeared. Elected public representation is therefore only at the national government level.

An interesting innovation in 1974 was the setting up of locally based community health councils (CHCs) to enable the public viewpoint to be expressed. However, the status of these bodies was that of officially recognized and subsidized pressure groups, with rights to make representations and to seek information. Such power as they had primarily rested on their capacity to embarrass health authorities. Even in relation to this weapon, they had an awkward choice to make between seeking a close day-to-day working relationship, which might inhibit its use, and remaining more aloof, but thereby losing opportunities to secure information and to make informal representations. They also had difficult choices to make between concentration on individual grievances, the passing on of views of all kinds from the local groups which formed their 'constituency', and the development of a carefully documented, informed critique of the service. Their low resources exacerbated these problems of choice.

CHCs were not themselves representative bodies in any of the senses in which that term is used in democratic theory. Half their members were appointed by local authorities, one-sixth by the Department of Health; the remainder were elected by relevant voluntary organizations (by means of rather haphazard election processes which did nothing to ensure that they were representative of the patients in their areas).

Legislation to abolish community health councils will almost certainly be on the statute book by the time this book is published. The legislation setting up the new organizational arrangements for the NHS (see p. 158) includes replacing them by more complicated arrangements for the consultation of the public and support for patients with grievances against the NHS. There is to be a central Commission for Patient and Public Involvement in Health and a requirement that every Trust (that is, both every Primary Care Trust and every provider Trust) should set up a Patients' Forum. There are to be separate arrangements to assist people with complaints about services, a Patients' Advocacy and Liaison Service. The tentative note in this paragraph arises because these changes are encountering opposition in the House of Lords. There do seem to be good grounds for arguing that a relatively simple system for patient consultation and support is being replaced by very complex arrangements that may baffle patients.

The separation of commissioning and providing could facilitate the development of a new approach to the issue of democratic control. However, the decision by the government to give the commissioning role to Primary Care Trusts, which it significantly describes in one of its news releases as 'run by family doctors and nurses' (Government Press Release, 2001), means that suggestions that there could be democratic control of commissioning have been ignored.

For many members of the public, what matters more than representation is protection from abuse and malpractice, and the chance to be heard when dissatisfied with the service provided. Apart from the general opportunities to make representations, which apply to all the public services, there are, for the health service, a number of special procedures available. Practitioners and hospitals may be sued for tort damages, and professional malpractice may result in debarment from practice by the relevant professional organization. Complaints against health service Trusts have to be formally investigated, using a procedure that may give the complainant an opportunity to give evidence to a committee headed by a lay chairperson. Finally, a patient may complain to the Health Service Commissioner, though the powers of this official broadly preclude investigations in areas where other forms of investigation or litigation are available. There is thus no absence of avenues for further action by individuals with grievances, but the multiplicity of procedures is confusing to patients; and all involve formal approaches that deter action. At the time of writing, these issues are also under review. Matters needing attention include the fact that the expensive and draconian solution to grievances involved in litigation tends to inhibit open examination of problems, and encourage the professions to close ranks in the face of a problem. At the same time there are grounds for doubt about the independence of the normal complaints procedure.

CONCLUSIONS

Long ago, an American student of the British NHS (Lindsey, 1962) described it as 'something magnificent in scope and breathtaking in its implications'. He went on to say (p. 474):

> In the light of past accomplishments and future goals, the Health Service cannot very well be excluded from any list of notable achievements of the twentieth century. So much has it become a part of the British way of life, it is difficult for the average Englishman to imagine what it would be like without those services that have contributed so much to his physical and mental well-being.

That expresses rather well the peculiar mixture of utopian expectations and of taking the service for granted that gives a slightly exaggerated quality to British discussions of policy issues in the health service.

We have expectations of the service that often go quite beyond any capacity to deliver results. We oscillate wildly, therefore, between pride in our system and disquiet about its waiting lists and overcrowded wards. We put doctors on a pedestal as the experts who dominate the system, and we are angry about their arrogant presumptions. We demand more and more from the service, and we worry that we are perhaps becoming a nation of hypochondriacs who can too easily make demands on it. These mixed emotions colour the reactions of both politicians and the public to the main policy dilemmas that inevitably confront the service.

Undoubtedly, a public approach to medicine involving disproportionate expectations about its capacity to solve the problems of suffering and death lies at the root of some of our difficulties in putting health policies in context and coming to terms with the strengths and weaknesses of our health service. There are signs, however, that a 'demystification of medicine' is beginning to occur. This is helping us to assess, much more realistically, decisions about the allocation of resources between the hospital service and the community services, and between the health service and other public policies. Some of these issues have been considered in this chapter.

We are beginning to ask whether we have not so far been too ready to delegate decisions involving moral questions as well as medical questions to professional practitioners. We are beginning to achieve a better understanding that many of the determinants of the health of the nation have little to do with the quality and nature of its clinical medical services. Yet the debate about these issues is inevitably conducted in the shadow of concerns about the continuing rise of health care costs. Questions about what the NHS is able to achieve cannot be, and should not have to be, considered in a context dominated by questions about what the NHS can afford to do.

It is all too easy to pillory the NHS for its shortcomings; of course it is in need of improvement but it remains a surviving monument to its socialist founder, Aneurin Bevan, who said 'A free health service is a triumphant example of the superiority of collective action and public initiative applied to a segment of society where commercial principles are seen at their worst' (1952, p. 85). That 'superiority' can only be sustained if the NHS is adequately funded.

SUGGESTIONS FOR FURTHER READING

Wendy Ranade's *A Future for the NHS* (1997) offers a review of aspects of health policy in the period before the change of government in 1997. Two long-lasting textbooks are Christopher Ham's *Health Policy in Britain* (1999) and Rudolph Klein's *The Politics of the NHS* (1995). Hopefully they will be updated before long, meanwhile Webster has updated his history of the NHS to include contemporary developments (2002). The government's *NHS Plan* (Department of Health, 2000) is a good source for many of the recent developments, but this is another policy area where it is important to follow matters by consulting the official website (www.doh.gov.uk). The website of King's Fund (www.kingsfund.org.uk.) is also a useful source for discussions of contemporary health policy issues.

Issues about finance and performance are well examined in the relevant chapter of Glennerster and Hills (1998) and Glennerster, Hills and Travers (2000). The Acheson Report on *Inequalities and Health* (1998) is a vital source on the evidence about health inequalities. Stacey's (1988) exploration of the wider sociological issues which need to be taken into account in any evaluation of health policy is still very relevant.

Chapter 8

The Personal Social Services

Introduction

Policy for the personal social services is, at the central government level, the responsibility of the Department of Health in England and of the respective devolved authorities in Wales, Scotland and Northern Ireland. This division of responsibility, accompanied by some legal differences in Scotland, makes the assembly of statistical material for the UK difficult. In this chapter most of the statistics quoted will be for England only.

Except in Northern Ireland, where they are integrated with health services under Health and Social Services Boards, the provision of social services is the responsibility of local government. Local authorities are experiencing increasing regulation of their social services work by central government. There is an Inspectorate within the Department of Health that advises and inspects the work of local authority social services in England and similar arrangements elsewhere.

In earlier versions of this book, the personal social services were defined as the responsibility of the social services *departments* in England

and Wales (social work departments in Scotland). While that is still very often true there are now local authorities which are organizing their services rather differently, so these services are not now always within a department with exclusive social services' responsibilities; they may be linked with other local government functions or, exceptionally, split between departments. Furthermore, there are in some areas Care Trusts (not to be confused with the Primary Care Trusts discussed in the previous chapter) where some or all social care for adults is linked together with community-based health care activities in a jointly managed organization (this development will be discussed further on pp. 293–4).

One way of classifying the personal social services is in terms of their contributions to the needs of specific groups in the population: elderly people, physically handicapped people, mentally ill people, people with learning difficulties (a group which used to be called 'mentally handicapped'), and children. An alternative classification is in terms of kinds of services: residential care, day care, domiciliary services etc. These two modes of classification can, of course, be related to each other. A two-dimensional table can be drawn up, relating kinds of clients to kinds of services. The data on personal social services expenditure is set out in this way in table 8.1, which gives figures for England in 1999–2000.

Table 8.1 highlights how much residential care is for elderly people, and how much child care is outside residential settings.

Table 8.1 Local authority personal social services gross expenditure by client group, 1999–2000

	Elderly	Children	Learning disability	Physical disability	Mental health	Total (includes other items)
HQ costs						161
Area officers/ senior managers	102	188	28	29	33	380
Care management/ assessment	369	567	78	107	145	1,265
Residential care	3,453	792	922	242	242	5,651
Non-residential care	1,719	1,259	605	454	213	4,252
Total	**5,644**	**2,807**	**1,633**	**832**	**633**	**11,887**

Source: Data based on statistics in Department of Health (2002a), table E5.

Alternatively, services may be seen in two distinct groups: those for children (broadly governed by the Children Act of 1989) and those for adults (broadly governed by the National Health Service and Community Care Act 1990). This legislation, particularly the latter, has largely undermined the aspirations towards an integrated service with general commitments to families, embodied in the legislation which set up the social services authorities in England and Wales and the social work departments in Scotland. In recognition of the fundamental importance of this new divide in the services, the first part of this chapter looks separately at these two groups of services.

Child Protection

A distinction may be made between the issues about 'child protection' and those about 'child care in general'. This distinction is made because it is appropriate to separate the specific measures that may be brought into operation in respect of the relatively small number of children who are seen as 'at risk' of ill-treatment, neglect or abuse and the wider issues of child care policy which may be applicable to all children. In theory, of course, the child protection system protects all children; in practice most children and their parents will have no encounters with any part of that system. It is hard to provide precise figures to back up this distinction, but it has been estimated that perhaps about 600,000 children in England (5 per cent of the child population) may be in need of some attention from the child protection system (Department of Health, 1995). Figures quoted below will show that far fewer than this are actually directly affected by child protection measures at any time.

Whether it is desirable to make the distinction between child protection policy and other child care policy is a matter for debate. It may be argued that much more public-policy attention should be given to the welfare of all or most children, and in particular that it is undesirable to have special measures that focus upon a limited number of ill-functioning families whilst disregarding the many problems of child poverty and deprivation. It is also sometimes contended that child protection policies are too intrusive, stigmatizing and controlling the lives of many families who do not need this intervention. Nevertheless it does seem important to recognize that on the one hand the child protection system is not a 'child care' system affecting most families and that on the other there are some policies in respect of child care in general, particularly with regard to pre-school children, which are much wider in their impact.

Contemporary government policy encourages the distinction made here because much of the responsibility for both child-care policy and the regulation of child care has been moved to the education system. In order to relate the discussion in this book to that development this chapter will only deal with what was described above as child protection – readers will find the rest of the discussion on child care in chapter 9 (pp. 207–10).

The Children Act of 1989 (and a Scottish Act passed in 1995) consolidated previous legislation on the protection of children. The complex legal framework in this Act tries to ensure that children are protected while at the same time recognizing that the level of public interventions into family life should be kept as low as possible. It carries forward a long-standing concern to minimize the likelihood of the removal of children from their family of origin. The Act identifies a wide range of ways in which authorities may spend money to try to avoid taking children into direct care.

Social workers in the social services authorities have a crucial role to play in situations in which evidence comes to light that children may be at risk of ill treatment, abuse or neglect. Their authorities are required to maintain 'child protection registers' of children 'at risk' and offer appropriate supportive services to these children and their families. There were about 26,800 children on these registers in England in 2001, that is about 24 children per 10,000 children in the population (Department of Health, 2002a, table C2). Only a small proportion of children at risk are taken away from their families.

The most draconian powers available to childcare workers are those which enable them to activate procedures under which children may be 'looked after'. The rather confusing expression 'looked after' is now used in describing situations in which children are taken into the 'legal' care of a local authority. To avoid ambiguity it will be put in inverted commas in this discussion. Children become formally 'looked after' when their parents are unable to care for them or are providing care that is deemed to be placing the child seriously 'at risk'. Decisions on this are the responsibility of the courts, but most action to 'look after' children will have been initiated by social workers in the social services authorities. Once a child is 'looked after', the local authority will seek to ensure a settled future for him or her. In some cases, this will mean return to parental care under supervision. Where this is not possible, foster care is widely used. Institutional care is likely to be regarded as a temporary expedient in many cases, while the situation is assessed and longer-term plans are made.

There were about 58,900 thousand 'looked after' children in England in March 2001 (Department of Health, 2002a, table C1). Of these, 65 per cent were boarded out with foster parents, 11 per cent were 'placed' with their own parents, and there were 12 per cent 'other placements' (generally with a friend or relative). Only about 11 per cent were in some kind of institutionalized care. There has been a slight tendency for the number of 'looked after' children to increase in recent years, but the proportion in institutional care has declined.

Among the children who may be deemed in need of this form of statutory care is a group of generally older children who are considered to be out of parental control. Under the 1969 Children and Young Persons Act, local authorities acquired increased responsibilities for the care of children brought before the courts for delinquent acts. The object of this legislation was to move away from labelling young offenders as criminals, and to make the issue for decision by the juvenile courts one about responsibility for care rather than punishment for crime. Social services authorities may now have to undertake the 'supervision' of such children, or they may be given legal custody of them. They may fulfil the parental responsibilities entailed in a variety of ways, including the supervision of a child within a residential institution. The former remand homes and approved schools became specially staffed 'community homes' under this legislation. Since many local authorities do not possess the residential resources to fulfil responsibilities of this kind on their own and, in particular, lack the necessary range of resources, which must include (exceptionally) a 'secure' institution, regional planning committees have been set up to facilitate the use of homes by authorities other than those responsible for their management.

Where the responsibilities of local authorities to 'look after' children are discharged through the use of foster parents, payment will be made, and the arrangements will be supervised by social workers. Some 'looked after' children may eventually be legally adopted into another family. Social services authorities are responsible for organizing and supervising adoption procedures, but these may sometimes be sub-contracted to private agencies. It is, however, important to bear in mind how low the level of adoptions is in Britain today; there were just 4,800 in England in 1999–2000 compared with 21,000 in 1969–70 (Department of Health, 2001, p. 95).

A little over half of all children adopted were 'looked after' prior to adoption. The government is putting pressure on local authorities to try to ensure that they consider the possibility of adoption when they are 'looking after' children. But there is a need to be sceptical about suggestions that there are large numbers of unwanted young children who could be adopted. As was shown above, many children are in care in ordinary homes. Many are away from the care of their parents for relatively short periods. More than half of 'looked after' children are over ten years of age, and only about 2300 are under a year old (Department of Health, 2002a, table C1).

In many cases, prevention of child abuse or neglect requires activities other than the institution of legal procedures to transfer formal responsibility for the care of children. Social workers have a number of ways in which they may try to do this. They may themselves try to offer support to families – visiting regularly, making suggestions about how to deal with stresses in the household, listening and counselling, and generally responding to cries for help from families under pressure. In doing this, they may be able to mobilize resources: domestic help, day care for children, grants or loans, help in kind. They may also try to secure help for the family from other statutory organizations: for example, better housing or attention to educational or health problems. There may also be voluntary organizations that they can mobilize to help: providing charitable help in cash or kind.

In recent years, there has been a succession of very disturbing incidents. Children have been seriously ill treated and even killed by parents or stepparents. Typically these cases do not come 'out of the blue'. The families have been known to social services authorities beforehand and the case for the removal of the children has been considered. Social services authorities have been criticized for a lack of decisive action, but there has also been criticism of authorities for over-reacting. Furthermore, worrying cases have come to light in which children have been abused while 'looked after'. In sum, while various public inquiries and central government have, from time to time, been very critical of social services authorities, there are no easy formulae to guide authorities on when to act and when not to act.

Social Care for Adults

It should be noted that the group of services for adults is sometimes called 'community care', and that this title is used regardless of whether the care is residential or domiciliary. This was the conventional terminology at the time the National Health Service and Community Care Act of 1990 was passed. It is falling out of use, with the generic expression 'adult social care' being preferred. The White Paper which preceded the 1990 Act started by saying:

> Community care means providing the services and support which people who are affected by problems of ageing, mental illness, mental handicap or physical or sensory disability need to be able to live in their own homes, or in 'homely' settings in the community. (HMSO, 1989, para. 1.1)

The fact that the last part of that definition includes 'homely settings in the community' and that it has long been the aspiration that all adult social care institutions should be 'homely' means that this definition embraces all care except that provided by hospitals.

It is reasonable also to ask what is implied by 'services and support' in that definition. There are two points about this. At the margins, health and social care services tasks may be difficult to distinguish, and it is certainly widely recognized that effective community care depends on close liaison between the providers of health care and the providers of social care. These issues are taken up later in this chapter (see pp. 191–4).

The second problem embedded in the reference to 'services and support' is that it is not clear who is to provide or pay for these. An outsider reading that definition may jump to the incorrect conclusion that it is the state which is the sole provider and carrier of the costs of community or social care. That is very definitely not the case. In reality, anyone who seeks any form of care has to go through rigorous tests of need and means before help is available from the public sector. Many who are clearly 'affected by problems of ageing, mental illness etc.' (as in the above definition) fail those tests and have either to go without services and support, or pay for them or receive them from their family and neighbours. The thresholds used in tests of need are inevitably influenced by the levels of resources available.

Social services authorities have a wide range of responsibilities for the social care of adults. Their predecessor departments (local authority welfare or health and welfare departments) inherited residential care responsibilities from the Poor Law in 1948. To these were added a range of domiciliary services, as it became recognized that care concerns might be better met in this way rather than by admission to an institution. The restructuring of both social services and health services in the early 1970s brought further developments: the evolution of services outside health service institutions for mentally ill people and for adults with learning difficulties, and the aspiration to use skilled social work services effectively in the care of adults.

In the early 1980s, while the public residential-care sector was continuing to contract and hospitals were increasingly reluctant to become involved in long-term care, the number of private, voluntary residential-care facilities began to increase rapidly. This growth in independent (that is, both private and voluntary) care was stimulated by an increase in availability of social security benefits to enable people (in particular, elderly people) to pay independent home charges. This came about during the early 1980s as a result of the relaxing of some of the rules relating to the means-testing of applicants from private residential homes by the social security authority. To keep the story short, this can only in retrospect be described as a 'mistake'; the government seemed to have thought it a good idea to subsidize private care without accurately forecasting the implications for the social security budget.

The growth of private residential care was uneven. In some areas, it dramatically reduced the demand for local authority care; in others, its impact was quite slight. An Audit Commission report on this issue in 1986 described this growth as a 'perverse effect of social security policies', distorting efforts to create the right balance between care inside and outside institutions. People might be given social security subsidies for residential care in circumstances in which social services authorities would not regard them as in need of such care. The social security authorities were not concerned with this issue; they merely carried out a test of means. This development increased regional inequalities. The greatest growth of independent care was in the south and west of England, particularly in seaside areas (Audit Commission, 1986).

An odd situation had thus developed by the end of the 1980s, to which it was necessary for the government to give attention. Local authorities had been seeking to extend forms of care outside institutions. The local authority burden had been reduced, relatively, by the growth of an independent sector. Yet this was a substantial charge on the social security budget, unconstrained by public authorities' concerns regarding the importance of maintaining people in their own homes and confining the use of residential places to the most needy. The government's response to this was contained in its White Paper entitled *Caring for People* (HMSO, 1989), and legislation was enacted in 1990 to try to deal with the situation. What was decided was that local authorities should be responsible for assessing need for care (for all who sought publicly supported care), and should then purchase that care. Hence, they would be responsible for determining whether residential care was necessary or, alternatively, whether some form of domiciliary care should be provided (or, of course, nothing), and also for determining who should be the provider.

This transferring of responsibility was a complicated process. It involved mechanisms to shift resources from the social security budget to local authority social services budgets over a period of time, leaving arrangements for people already in independent care undisturbed. The new system came into full force in April 1993.

This account of events has laid a strong emphasis on the anomaly that developed because of the social security subsidy of the independent care system. I believe that the government's concern to reform the system of care stemmed particularly from the problem it had in controlling the growth of social security expenditure on independent care for elderly people. However, the case for reform was expressed in wider terms, which suggested that there was a need for the rationalization of social care as a whole. It was proposed that there were problems to be resolved concerning the boundaries between health and social care. It was argued that there was a need for better planning, to maximize care in the community and participant involvement in decision making. It was even suggested, though there is little evidence that what was enacted achieves this, that there was a need for the system to be more responsive to the wishes of the consumer. Hence, it was possible for practitioners to try to seize on the 'community care reforms' as an opportunity to give those in need of care and their carers a better deal.

All this occurred against a background of growth in the numbers of those in need of social care (particularly among elderly people), a search for economies in the health service which contributed to reducing that system's contribution to care, and a central attack on local government expenditure. The specific proposals for change were laced with new pro-market language. Social services authorities were to become 'purchasers', making contracts for the supply of services ideally (from the government's point of view) with 'providers' from the private and voluntary sectors but, if not, then from separate units in their own authority. The government's aim was to increase the role of the independent sector. Not surprisingly, therefore, the process of change was a complex one.

In England, in March 2001, there were about 255,000 people in local authority supported residential and nursing places for elderly people and other adults in need of care (Department of Health, 2002a, table C7). 'Supported' in that statement will, in practice, mean 'partly supported', because all these places were means-tested. Residents are required to contribute to their care costs from their income and capital. About 17 per cent of these places were in local authority homes. The rest were in independent care and nursing homes. These independent institutions have contracts with local authorities to take people who are judged by a social services authority to be in need of care.

The registration and regular inspection of all care homes and nursing homes, including those owned by local authorities, is the responsibility of an independent National Care Standards Commission set up by the Care Standards Act 2000, to take over the inspection task and to regulate all homes (including those for children) and adult domiciliary care providers. This started work in April 2002, but in that same month the government also announced it wanted to develop a new inspection system to operate alongside the new health inspection system it proposed (see p. 165).

Note the distinction above between 'residential' (sometimes called 'care') homes and nursing homes. About 28 per cent of residents cited above are in nursing homes. Nursing homes offer high levels of support for those needing intensive nursing care, and were formerly the responsibility of health authorities. Now the support of residents in them is the responsibility of the local authorities and the distinction between the two types of homes is increasingly blurred. Some homes are explicitly recognized as 'dual purpose' and a significant proportion of the residents of care homes are in need of some nursing care. In the old public sector, before the community care legislation, there had been a problem with maintaining a distinction between the population of local authority homes and the patients of the overburdened geriatric wards of hospitals. Long-stay hospitals have now largely disappeared, being replaced by independent-sector nursing homes for elderly people and by a variety of forms of community care for those who are mentally ill, physically handicapped or with serious learning difficulties.

A Royal Commission on Long-Term Care set up to examine options for a sustainable system of funding of long-term care reported in March 1999. Its central concern was the arrangements made to pay for residential care. The main problem with much of the care system is that the means tests force large numbers to contribute substantial sums towards their own costs. This is a particular problem as far as residential care is concerned, where home charges may absorb large parts of the savings of elderly people. Where an owner-occupied house has been left, its sale will be expected to contribute to these charges. There is therefore resentment that assets which a next generation expected to inherit may be used up to meet care costs. This problem has risen on the political agenda as more and more people survive into very old age, with a significant percentage of them becoming severely dependent. The issue has been further highlighted by the fact that whereas, in the past, many highly dependent elderly people occupied free beds in NHS hospitals, they are now expected instead to seek the 'care in the community' to which these charging rules apply.

The Royal Commission recommended:

> The costs of long-term care should be split between living costs, housing costs and personal care. Personal care should be available after assessment, according to need: the rest should be subject to a co-payment according to means. (Royal Commission on Long-Term Care, 1999, p. xvii)

It justified this split in terms of the fact that people being cared for in their own homes expect to meet living and housing costs, and was obviously forced by this logic to argue that the more intensive forms of domiciliary care should be free too.

In support of its recommendation, the Royal Commission criticizes some of the exaggerations of the future burden of care, arguing that the risk of long-term care is appropriately covered by some kind of 'risk pooling' but that private insurance cannot deliver at an acceptable cost, and that (p. xvii):

> A hypothecated *unfunded* social insurance fund would not be appropriate for the UK system. A *prefunded* scheme would constitute a significant lifetime burden for young people and could create an uncertain and inappropriate call on future consumption.

That last comment seems justifiable in the British context, where the NHS is tax-funded and the NI system has largely collapsed. Hence the

Royal Commission offers a classic justification for a universalist approach (p. xvii):

> The most efficient way of pooling risk, giving the best value to the nation as a whole, is through services underwritten by general taxation, based on need rather than wealth.

The Royal Commission was not unanimous. Two members appended a note of dissent, arguing against the central proposal. The government's response was to draw a distinction within personal care between social care and nursing care, making only the latter free. Clearly the government's response was influenced by the cost of the Royal Commission's proposal. Yet failure to enact it leaves very high costs for many old people. Means and asset tests remain therefore still very significant in relation to residential care, with strong incentives to hide or pass on assets. It may be doubted whether a satisfactory distinction can be drawn between nursing care and social care when people are so handicapped as to need residential care. There is considerable pressure on the government to think again on this issue. In this respect, pressure groups have been encouraged by the fact that the government of Scotland has accepted the Royal Commission's recommendation.

After this diversion to mention the Royal Commission's report, there is a need, before leaving this section, to say more about other care services. Social services authorities organize, or purchase from independent providers, a variety of day care services. For elderly people, there may be day centres where they can go for company, social activities, occupational therapy, perhaps cheap mid-day meals, and perhaps some aid or advice. Similar facilities are often provided for handicapped people. For younger handicapped people, and particularly for people with learning difficulties, there are centres where company and therapy may be accompanied by productive activities. In some cases, these are more or less sheltered workshops, doing commercially sponsored work and paying pocket money to handicapped people. There are some difficult distinctions to be drawn here between sheltered work, therapy, and provision for some daytime life outside the home. Under the community care legislation, the government's expectation is that local authorities will become more flexible about the range of help they provide 'in the community' and, of course, that they will make use of an increasingly wide range of non-statutory providers.

The primary form of domiciliary care supported or provided by social services authorities is home-help services. These have developed remarkably from a service conceived primarily to help in maternity cases to large enterprises serving predominantly elderly people, and thus playing an important part in helping them manage in their own homes. Local authorities in England provide, directly or through independent agencies, about 416,000 households with some form of home care (Department of Health, 2002a, table C5). Of course, people may purchase their own domestic help unaided by a local authority, and where services are inadequate, the gap is likely to be filled by large amounts of unpaid work by relatives and neighbours. Local authorities may charge for home-help services, and may use means tests to determine the level of the charge.

Local authorities may also support the provision of meals, taken to people in their own homes. These 'meals on wheels' services are often provided through a voluntary or private organization. Again, the extent of coverage varies widely from area to area, from, at one extreme, a 'token' meal a week to, at the other, the provision of a comprehensive, seven-days-a-week service. Local authorities may set charges for this service, and the extent to which they subsidize it is variable.

Local authorities provide a range of other 'benefits in kind' to assist with the care of people within the community. The Chronically Sick and Disabled Persons Act of 1970 suggests a wide range of services that local authorities may offer to handicapped people. Despite the emphasis in that Act on local authority duties, the word 'may' in the last sentence is appropriate. There are wide variations in the adequacy of the help provided. Authorities may provide, and pay the rental costs of, telephones; they may adapt houses to meet the needs of disabled people; and they are able to provide a variety of aids to daily living. They tend, however, to impose budgetary limits that ration quite severely the money available for such benefits. However, a further piece of legislation, the Disabled Persons (Services, Consultation and Representation) Act of 1986, increases the rights of disabled people to be informed about provisions and consulted about their needs. Additionally, the Carers (Recognition and Services) Act of 1995 is designed to facilitate the consultation of carers, and attention to their needs.

The administration of these diverse mixes of services requires social services authorities to have a large workforce. The purchaser–provider split means that the purchaser role in social services authorities has to be undertaken by 'care managers', who assess needs and commission services from the available providers.

The Relationship between Personal Social Services and the Health Service

In many respects, the concerns of the health service and those of the social services authorities overlap. People are likely to need mixtures of health care and social care. Increasingly, the NHS is trying to limit its care to what may be described as 'treatment'. Where possible, also, in-patient treatment is being replaced by out-patient treatment. Hospital stays are becoming shorter, the aim being to send patients 'home' as soon as high inputs of specialized treatment are no longer necessary. Mentally ill people are hospitalized as little as possible. It is broadly accepted that there is only very exceptionally a case for hospital care for those with severe learning difficulties. In general, there is a concern to maximize care 'within the community' rather than in hospitals.

Many people are in receipt of a combination of health treatment from GPs and community-based nursing staff, on the one hand, and social care, on the other. Deficiencies on either side may have to be made up by extra services on the other.

The discharge of patients from hospital, in itself, has substantial implications for personal social services provision. It is important that social support services are readily available at this stage. Hence day-to-day co-ordination between the two services is crucial.

In this context, there is a special problem when residential (including nursing home) care may be necessary. As was noted in the discussion about the Royal Commission on Long-Term Care (see pp. 189–90) hospital care is still free, whereas residential care deemed necessary by social services authorities is not. The increasing unwillingness of the health service to keep people in hospital is creating situations in which people are discovering that they have to pay substantial amounts for social care in situations in which, in the past, they might have expected free hospital care. Furthermore the supply of residential care, and the local authority budgets to support such care, are limited. The consequence is the unnecessary retention of people in hospital, thereby limiting the capacity of the health service to respond to emergent need. The government has had to recognize that one of the responses needed to deal with the lack of hospital beds is enhanced funding for local authorities.

Another, very different example of the need for inter-service co-ordination and co-operation is supplied by the problem of child abuse. Doctors and health visitors frequently discover non-accidental injury to children; yet it is the social services authorities that have the responsibility for preventative and legal action in these circumstances. Conversely, where social workers suspect child abuse, they may need medical confirmation of their suspicions. Once child abuse is suspected, continued vigilance is necessary. Sometimes it is a health service worker who is best placed to maintain a watching brief; sometimes it is a social worker. In many cases, both authorities accumulate evidence on the problem; it is important that they share that evidence both formally through case conferences and informally.

The importance of the overlap between health and social services has led the Department of Health to encourage, and the local agencies to adopt, a variety of means of developing links. At the service planning level, the Department of Health has led the way by emphasizing the need to look at the health service and personal social services together. Within individual localities, they have encouraged the development of formal joint planning activities. A particular stimulus to this has been provided by 'joint financing'. Money from the health service budget is made available to help to finance projects within the social services authorities to meet needs that might otherwise have to be met by the health service. In the long run, social services authorities are expected to take over the full cost of these ventures.

The restructuring of arrangements for the delivery of both health services and local authority social services at the end of the 1980s brought issues about collaboration into sharper focus. The 1989 White Paper on community care (HMSO, 1989), which preceded the 1990 legislation, devoted a chapter to 'collaborative working'. In that chapter, it was argued (p. 49):

> For the past 15 years policies designed to promote effective collaboration between health and local authorities have focused mainly on the mechanics of joint planning and joint finance. Significant progress has been made but this approach no longer fits well with the Government's aims for the NHS . . . nor with its proposals for community care.

The document went on to stress the government's concerns to have 'strengthened incentives and clearer responsibilities'.

In the ferment after the 1990 Act, collaboration between the health service and the local authority social services was given a new impetus. Then, after the election of a Labour government in 1997, the White Paper *The New NHS* (Department of Health, 1997) made a commitment to consulting on ways to encourage further joint working between health and social services. A later ministerial commitment, set out in the foreword of *Partnership in Action* (Department of Health, 1998c) expressed the view that 'all too often when people have complex needs spanning both health and social care good quality services are sacrificed for sterile arguments about boundaries'.

Partnership in Action set out a range of proposals to enhance joint working, required at three levels: strategic planning, service commissioning, and service provision. The Health Act 1999 was then enacted to make joint working easier through arrangements whereby health and social services authorities can:

- operate 'pooled budgets' (putting a proportion of their funds into a mutually accessible joint budget to enable more integrated care);
- lead commissioning arrangements with one authority transferring funds to the

other, which can then take responsibility for purchasing both health and social care;

- integrate provision so that one service-providing organization can provide both health and social care.

This flexibility was designed to allow National Health Service organizations greater freedom to provide social care and to allow social services authorities to provide some community health services on behalf of the National Health Service. These new measures were accompanied by a new statutory duty of partnership on all local bodies in the health service, and on local authorities, to work together to promote the well-being of their local communities.

It should also be noted that as Primary Care Trusts were developed (see p. 158), local authorities were given formal positions to ensure that local policy making was co-ordinated and that they were involved in health care commissioning. One direction in which all this could be leading is the shift of adult care services out of local government into the NHS. While official statements deny this intention there is a distinct shift in this direction, perhaps enhanced by the development, noted at the beginning of this chapter, of separation of adult social care from child care in some local authorities. Also significant is the development in some areas of Care Trusts (bear in mind that, as was pointed out in the chapter introduction, these are not the same as Primary Care Trusts). These are explicit joint bodies delivering social services 'under delegated authority from local councils' and thus 'able to commission and deliver primary and community health-care as well as social care for older people and other client groups' (Department of Health, 2000, p. 73). The development of these has been slow, and most are specific to the needs of particular groups of people – mentally ill people, people with learning difficulties or older people. One Trust currently developing in Brighton and Hove aims to cover services for all adults.

Hudson and Henwood (2002) provide a good overview of these developments, suggesting that despite the fact that *Partnership in Action* rejected structural change as the solution to these boundary issues this now seems to be the way the system is moving. Drawing on evidence from Northern Ireland, where there are combined Health and Social Services Boards, they argue that this is not the best way forward, the issues about collaboration are essentially about behaviour at the 'street-level' and are not necessarily solved by large structures.

Needs and Priorities

The increased recognition in the 1980s of the limited funds available for public services, and the relationship between this and the growing need for social care (as a result, for example, of the growing numbers of very elderly people), have sharpened concern to find ways of balancing the respective contributions to what is called the 'mixed economy of welfare'. While this is sometimes presented as a new issue, social care has always involved some combination of care within the family and community, care which is bought, care which is provided by voluntary and charitable agencies, and care which is provided by public agencies. What is perhaps new is acceptance that the contribution from the last source is inherently limited – hence the development of a lively debate about the roles of the other forms of care.

An important part of that debate concerns the search for ways of defining need, and identifying how public agencies should respond to it. Economists have a distinctive approach to this issue. Instead of attempting to tackle the concept of 'need', they emphasize the concept of demand, which they define as a willingness to buy at a given price. This approach emphasizes the price mechanism as a means of adjusting services to demands. If there is a high demand for a particular thing, then this will be reflected in a willingness to pay higher prices. Higher rewards will attract more suppliers, and may ultimately bring down the price. Always, however, an equilibrium is maintained in which supply and demand are balanced by the price mechanism. To what extent does this offer a solution to the problem of needs in the social services? Clearly, it does not if the local authority is the only supplier of a particular service or controls access to that service. Equally it does not if that authority is the funder of the service for people on a low income without the resources to purchase it themselves. Conditions of monopoly or near monopoly then exist, in which, in theory, the supplier can determine the price, and those unable to pay must go without. The attempt to identify real needs regardless of ability to pay is the hallmark of the public service here. Rationing according to the capacity to pay is quite widely regarded as an inferior way of distributing many such services. The price-mechanism solution is also inappropriate where it is arguable that people who need particular services are unlikely either to recognize the need or to translate it into an effective, money-backed demand. Social work services designed primarily to protect children from their parents fall into this category. There remain, however, services like the home-care service that are provided both by the statutory authorities and by the private market. In some sense, the need for these services can be regarded as fairly limitless – many of us would like our domestic chores to be done by someone else. The price mechanism seems to offer a basis for distinguishing absolute need from effective demand, and to allow for the existence, side by side, of a public and a private sector.

The use of the price mechanism may be fair enough in theory, but what happens to those with high needs, in some absolute sense, but a low capacity to pay? There are two possible answers to this objection to the use of the price mechanism. One is that social affairs should be arranged in such a way that what are really income-maintenance problems do not have to be solved by the provision of subsidized services. This is an attractive argument, but one that matches poorly the real world. The other is that means tests should be devised to enable cheaper services to be given in some cases. The trouble with this latter solution is that it can cope with situations in which only a minority has to be helped outside the market-place, but it quite destroys the market concept when it has to be wide-spread. The reality is that for many of the personal social services (including the home-care service) some more fundamental way of defining need is required: a minority can buy the services on the open market; but there remains a large group who appear to need them free or at a reduced price, only some of whom actually receive them. The problem remains of determining how much the service should expand to meet the unmet needs (Judge, 1987; for a strong pro-pricing line see Harris and Seldon, 1976).

This digression into the market approach to need was necessary, first because it has significant advocates, and secondly because it offers a challenge to the definition of need. The alternative is some more absolute way of determining need. In some cases this does not seem too problematic; in relation to some diseases, for example, there may be a finite group who, it is generally agreed, are in need of treatment. In other cases, however, the problem is one of making a distinction between 'absolute need' and some more limited concept. While I may contend that I need my house cleaned to free me to write books, you may argue that I am still physically capable of doing this work while others are not. They, you will say, are the ones really in need. So, would this be a disagreement about needs or about priorities?

For the personal social services, then, the determination of needs is complicated first by the fact that the authorities do not have the sole responsibility to meet certain kinds of needs, and secondly because their views of needs must be determined by their views of priorities. With an ageing population and limited funding growth, the level at which need is being acknowledged is getting steadily more stringent. There is some evidence that this is beginning to be recognized and that some of the new money for the Department of Health's activities (see p. 162) will be passed on to the local authorities.

Theoretically, the purchaser–provider split in social care requires the care managers to take decisions about need, based on some of the ideal considerations set out above. They must then commission the services they regard as appropriate. At that stage, means-testing is likely to occur. However, it is doubtful whether this split system operates in this way in reality. The author's own experience, when seeking care for elderly relatives, is that once social services staff gather that people are unlikely to qualify for subsidized care they leave them to find their own way around the 'market'.

Social Work in Social Services Authorities

The social work aspect of local authority field-work is often emphasized; in Scotland the authorities are called 'social work departments', while in England and Wales social workers occupy many senior management roles. However, it is important to recognize two things: first, that the support of people in their own homes is carried out by a variety of workers, not all of whom are, or should be regarded as, social workers; and secondly, that the coming of the care-management task has led to a challenge to social workers as front-line case-workers. The practical tasks of identifying what are often straightforward, readily identifiable needs and securing the services required to meet those needs may be performed by workers without the specific training given to social workers. Local authorities may find it more practical, and cheaper, to use other staff in these roles.

In general, the distinction here between the social work task and other tasks is a difficult one. The public often makes no distinction between social work and many other caring activities. This has implications not only for social workers' 'professional' aspirations, but also for the costs of various services, since trained social workers are relatively expensive.

The roots of contemporary British social work are diverse. In the nineteenth century, charities employed case-workers to help them discriminate between the deserving and undeserving poor, and to ensure that the alms that were provided were used efficiently. Charitable hospitals particularly needed staff to assess the extent to which people could pay for their services. Early in the twentieth century, the development of psychiatry and psychotherapy stimulated the development of some forms of case-work for people who were mentally ill, but social work in its modern form did not really take off until the setting up of Children Departments in local authorities in the 1940s (Packman, 1975). Even after that, there was still very little conception of a specific social work task in relation to other clients until the 1970s, when a notion that there could be a generic social work skill applicable to a wide range of problems was an important influence on the legislation which created the local authority social services function as we understand it today (Hall, 1976).

During the 1970s, the numbers of trained social workers in local authority employment increased rapidly. The advocates of genericism made some progress, and trained social workers became involved in activities in which they had hitherto been rare – such as the care of elderly people. Then there were setbacks for the profession: in particular, the concepts of care management and care assessment embodied in the 1990 Health Services and Community Care Act do not presuppose that the key workers will be formally trained social workers.

There are some forms of field-work which are seen as needing social work skills. Attention has already been drawn, in the section on children's services, to the special skills needed to determine whether children are at risk and to engage in preventative work in these circumstances. There has been a general tendency for workers in this field – other than residential workers – to have social work qualifications. Social workers have statutory duties under the 1983 Mental Health Act to assess and take appropriate action when mentally ill people appear to require compulsory hospitalization. It is perhaps anomalous that this is the only area of social services activity for which a specific qualification is mandatory. In the Care Standards Act 2000, the government has replaced the training body for social work (the Central Council for Education and Training in Social Work) with a General Social Care Council, which sets conduct and practice standards for social services of all kinds and has powers to 'register those in the most sensitive areas' (Department of Health, 1998b, para. 5.6). While this may in the long run imply specific training and other requirements for many areas of social care work, the White Paper preceding the legislation made it clear that early attention would be given to issues about the staffing of homes (ibid., para. 5.27) and about the operation of services for children (ibid., para. 5.28).

What is clear, however, is that while there is consensus about the need for more training, there is still going to be extensive controversy about what that training should be. The model of training espoused by social work academics, based in universities and colleges, is not altogether shared by many of the decision makers in central and local government. There has been an extensive debate about what social work is, and a related one about whether it can be practised within local authority social services authorities. That debate is clearly unhelpful to those who would seek to establish unambiguous roles for social workers. Significantly, in a compendium, *The Blackwell Companion to Social Work* (Davies, 1997), which contains extensive discussions of many controversial issues about social work, the reader will not find a concise account of *what social work is*.

Many of the needs for social work help are seldom expressed – at least not in any straightforward sense. The pressures that lead to calls for more social work come from the anxieties of the public and politicians about child abuse, the deterioration of old people who live alone, or the disturbance caused by aggressive, mentally ill people, for example. These are issues of social control as much as of service. Pressure also results from the many requests that come to social services authorities that are not so much for specific services as for help with a wide range of problems of poverty and deprivation. Social work is seen as having a contribution to make to addressing the problems of underprivileged communities in many different ways; indeed, these expectations often go way beyond the profession's capacities, particularly when political and economic problems are perceived as social or individual ones.

CONCLUSIONS

The responsibilities of the social services authorities in England and Wales, and the social work departments in Scotland, involve a wide range of activities. These extend from the provision or commissioning of relatively precise benefits and services, through a variety of residential and day care facilities, to a number of very personal, individualized services. They include a high proportion of the social work practised in these countries.

This mixture of activities has grown rapidly. The growth is perceived with quite considerable anxiety by the public, since most of the activities were hitherto undertaken outside the statutory sector, within the family and the community. One interpretation of this growth is that public services can now be provided to help to strengthen family and community life. If this view is taken, then residential care replaces the neglect of the isolated old, and social work helps families to cope with crises that would hitherto have destroyed them, and so on. However, there is an alternative view, that the growth in these services is itself an index of social pathology, that people are not coping so well with aspects of life that in the past were of little concern to public services. This ambivalence is compounded by widespread uncertainty about what social services authorities do (indeed, they are often confused with social security departments), a vague conception of the social worker's role, and a deep uncertainty about the circumstances under which help may be sought from the various specific services.

Social services in Britain are going through an intense period of change, which it is difficult to portray accurately. Government surveillance of social services is increasing. Best-value indicators (see pp. 63–4) specify objectives for social services in local government. An increasing range of specific grants are adding to the capacity of the centre to prescribe local responses.

Inspection of services is becoming more rigorous, and the government has made it very clear that it will not hesitate to use legislation that enables it to take social services functions away from local government where it is dissatisfied with performance.

Different authorities are changing at different rates. Two new fissures are occurring in the authorities which many tried to integrate in the late 1970s and early 1980s: between children's services and adult services, and between those given purchaser roles and those given provider roles. The discussion of the relationship between health and personal social services has shown how adult social care is being pulled away from its previous organizational connections with child care and towards the NHS. Child care may become again, as before the Seebohm legislation in 1970, a relatively free-standing element in local government. Or it may be pulled towards integration with the education service, a trend being encouraged by developments in provisions for pre-school children. In the next edition of this book the subject matter of this chapter may need to be dispersed into the 'health' and 'education' chapters.

SUGGESTIONS FOR FURTHER READING

My edited book *Local Authority Social Services* (Hill, 2000) is the sole recent attempt to produce a textbook covering this changing field as a whole. For updating, the best source is probably an official one, the report the Chief Social Services Inspector for England publishes every year.

There are a number of accounts of social care policies. Means and Smith's *Community Care: Policy and Practice* (1994) is particularly recommended; a new edition is expected in 2003. Readers should also note Hudson's edited volume *The Changing Role of Social Care* (2000). Aspects of the development of the care system are examined in Knapp et al. (2001) and in Hudson and Henwood (2002).

The Blackwell Companion to Social Work edited by Davies (1997) offers commentaries on many of the issues concerning social work, but little on the organizational context. Issues about children's services are explored in Aldgate and Hill (1996) and Tunstill and Aldgate (1999).

For social services in England the Department of Health website (www.doh.gov.uk) is a key source for current policy. Readers may also find the website for the Joseph Rowntree Foundation (www.jrf.org.uk) useful, since that is an organization that funds social care research and has an active dissemination policy.

Chapter 9
Education

- Introduction
- The main features of the school system
- Higher and further education
- Child care and pre-school education
- Control over the education system
- The government and the curriculum
- Diversity and selectivity in the education system
- Education and the disadvantaged
- The education of ethnic minorities
- Special education and other welfare measures
- Conclusions
- Suggestions for further reading

Introduction

The state's role in education is a dual one; it is the major provider of education, and has also assumed a responsibility to supervise education and child care in the sectors for which it is not directly responsible. About 6 per cent of the UK's schoolchildren are in private schools. Much pre-school child care and education is privately provided.

Historically, the public sector has been seen as involving a partnership between central and local government, yet recent years have seen a shift towards much greater dominance by the centre and a readiness to reduce the role of, or even discard, local government as a partner. Issues to do with the changing nature of the central–local relationship in respect of the control of education will arise at many points in this chapter.

In Scotland, Wales and Northern Ireland, education is the responsibility of the devolved governments. In England, the relevant central government department is the Department for Education and Skills.

The Main Features of the School System

Public education in state schools in the UK is free. Even from the political Right, there has been little challenge to that principle. There have been some attempts on the Right to make a case for education vouchers, which could be cashed at both state and private schools. Only in the area of nursery schooling did this movement have some temporary success, until the fall of the Conservative government in 1997.

The majority of schools are, as has long been the case, the responsibility of local government in the UK. They come under the counties, the metropolitan and other single-tier districts, and the London boroughs. In Northern Ireland, they come under appointed Education and Libraries Boards. However, legislation forces local authorities to fund schools on the basis of a centrally determined formula and to delegate significant management responsibilities to the schools' own governing bodies.

Under the 1988 Education Act, the Conservative government opened up the possibility for schools to be directly funded by central government, through funding agencies. They might apply (with the agreement of a majority of parents) to become 'grant-maintained'. In the School Standards and Framework Act of 1998 the Labour government abolished this grant-maintained status for schools. Instead these schools have been allowed to apply to become 'foundation' schools under the overall supervision of their relevant local authority but with a status that enables them to retain special arrangements for their government and a substantial measure of autonomous control over their land and property. At the same time another kind of school, deriving from another Conservative innovation, partly privatized City Technology Colleges, has been allowed to survive. Moreover, other kinds of partial autonomy have been encouraged, particularly schools managed by specific religious groups, both Christian and non-Christian.

The School Standards and Framework Act made it clear that the government accepts diverse managements for schools, particularly if the local authority's record as a manager has not been good. Under the Act it has assumed powers to intervene where it considers that a local education authority has failed to carry out its duties adequately. This may involve making alternative arrangements for the management of specific parts of a local authority's service including, therefore, the management of particular schools.

Tomlinson (2001, p. 98) sums up the effect of all this diversification by pointing out that what has been produced is a hierarchy of kinds of mainstream state schooling (excluding special schools for children with learning difficulties and units for excluded children), as follows:

- city technology colleges;
- grammar schools (that have 'survived' local ballots, see below);
- foundation specialist schools;
- community specialist schools;
- foundation schools;
- voluntary-aided or controlled schools;
- city academies;
- community schools.

The school system can be seen as involving three sectors: pre-school education, primary education and secondary education. In most cases, these sectors can be identified respectively with the education of children under five, between five and eleven, and between eleven and the school-leaving age of sixteen (with many pupils continuing at school until eighteen). However, some authorities have developed systems that deviate from the strict break between primary and secondary education at 11-plus. These have generally introduced an intermediate, middle-school system, for children in two or three of the year bands between nine and thirteen years old. Another innovation has been the introduction of 'sixth form colleges' for the over-sixteens. The educational arrangements for those over the minimum school-leaving age is further complicated by the fact that further education colleges offer both practical and academic courses for people in the sixteen to eighteen age bracket.

The arrangement for the starting of compulsory education at the age of five differentiates Britain from many other countries, which do not make it compulsory until six or seven. However, the concomitant has been that public pre-school education was, until recently, ill developed. This began to change in the 1990s, so that by the end of the decade nearly two-thirds of children in the UK aged three and four were attending nursery schools.

The main point of note about policies for primary education has been the ferment of experimentation through the last forty years. Initially, change took the form of diverse, often locally inspired, innovation. Primary schools were transformed from formal institutions in which uniformed children sat in straight rows in classes streamed on the basis of tests of educational ability, to very informal places where pupils moved about freely to work together in little clusters drawn from mixed-ability classes. The gradual elimination of selection at 11-plus clearly contributed to this 'liberation' of primary schools. It was an interesting example of a change that developed from the bottom, and never required any formal recognition in legislation, but which may nevertheless be regarded as a major policy development. However, in the late 1970s and early 1980s, its implications began to receive attention. Voices began to be raised questioning whether this largely professionally driven innovation had gone too far. There was a growing concern about levels of literacy and numeracy, with responsibility for their alleged inadequacy sometimes attributed to this educational revolution. Increased controls, involving a national curriculum, testing and more rigorous inspection under the 1988 Education Act, were a response to this concern. These developments are discussed further on pp. 210–13. Diversity ceased to be celebrated and there were pressures against the more extreme examples of informality. Under the Labour government this reversal has been continued, with quite explicit central prescriptions about the amounts of time to be devoted to formal teaching, designed to increase literacy and numeracy, and even recommendations about amounts of homework to be done by children (Department for Education and Employment, 1997).

Chapter 2 (p. 34) described how the idea of the comprehensive secondary school gradually replaced the bipartite or tripartite system envisaged at the time of the passing of the 1944 Education Act. By 1979, the development of comprehensive education was nearing completion. The Labour government had, in the 1976 Education Act, required local authorities to develop plans for comprehensivization. A minority of authorities were holding out on this. On coming to power, the Conservatives repealed this law; this had the effect of stemming the tide, but not reversing it. In 2000–1 about 85 per cent of secondary school children in the public sector in the UK were in comprehensive schools (National Statistics, 2002b, p. 54). However, that statistic may be rather misleading. In the mid-1990s, the Conservative government had encouraged a partial return to selectivity, mainly by enabling schools to reserve a small proportion of their places for pupils with identified higher abilities in general or in specific subjects such as music. Labour, on return to power, in 1997, decided not to revert to its 1970s aim of pushing through to total comprehensivization, without reference to local opinion. On the other hand, in a move characteristic of its stance on the powers of local government, it did not simply leave the veto power in the hands of elected local authorities but decided instead that pro-comprehensive campaigners should be able (if they could secure the signatures of 20 per cent of eligible parents) to secure local ballots of parents on the issue, in the areas where selection was still in use. At the same time the government has encouraged a variety of forms of school specialization that is probably undermining the comprehensive principle. This will be discussed further below (see pp. 213–15).

Paradoxically, the change to the education system for those over eleven years of age, in most areas, did not have as dramatic an effect on teaching for children over eleven as it did on that for children under eleven. The continued importance of examinations towards the end of the school years meant that, in many subjects, the comprehensive schools had to have ability divisions and different programmes of instruction for the differing levels of ability.

Higher and Further Education

Higher education and further education are outside local authority control. Higher education involves a network of quasi-autonomous universities and related bodies funded and supervised through funding councils. A Learning and Schools Council in England and a National Council for Education and Training in Wales have responsibility both for further education and to some extent also for post-16 education in schools. They direct the work of a network of local Learning and Skills Councils.

The concepts of further and higher education embrace a number of different activities: vocational education, further academic education (both of a kind provided generally in schools, and at higher levels) and non-vocational adult education. Education for degrees and for post-graduate qualifications is provided in universities and in colleges of higher education. Amongst 16- to 18-year-olds, 78 per cent are in education and training. These are divided between those still in schools, those in further education colleges, those on specific training schemes and a few already in higher education. Beyond 18 years of age further education serves a diverse mix of full- and part-time students of all ages.

Young people aged 16 or 17 who have left school but not obtained work are expected to participate in a system called 'work-based training for young people' (replacing what was called 'youth training'). There is a system of qualifications, known as NVQs (national vocational qualifications), which may be acquired while participating in this training. In March 2001 there were about 266,000 young people on these schemes in England (National Statistics, 2002b, p. 65). Many of these are what are called 'modern apprenticeships'.

These training programmes involve public subsidy to a wide range of schemes – provided by private employers, voluntary organizations and public bodies – offering a mixture of work experience and training. The achievement of qualifications is now strongly emphasized. However, these schemes vary enormously in quality, from elaborate skill training at one extreme to what are little more than 'make work' schemes for lower-ability young people in high-unemployment areas at the other. The better the local demand for young workers, the better the quality of the schemes, in terms of both the training they offer and the real labour-market opportunities they lead on to. However, three points must be recognized:

- The UK has (by contrast with most of continental Europe) a very high proportion of young people ending their full-time education and training at the age of sixteen.
- The UK used to have a strong pattern of apprenticeship into skilled work in industry, which has now collapsed.
- Before the rise of unemployment in the mid-1970s, the labour market for young people aged sixteen to eighteen was a thriving one, which has now more or less disappeared.

Youth training may be seen as a necessary means of filling a vacuum in the UK education and training system, but it has also contributed to the creation of that vacuum by undermining the incentives to employers to provide work or training for young people at their own expense. The state now pays for most of this, through youth training.

There is a system of allowances for young people in youth training, and in addition the government is now operating a means-tested scheme to assist 16–18-years-olds from low-income homes who remain in schools and colleges.

There are a little over 2 million students in higher education, but it must be noted that this figure includes both overseas students and part-time students. There are about a quarter of a million of the latter. Since people go into higher education at various ages, it is difficult to calculate a participation rate for a generation as a whole, but it is estimated that about 37 per cent of the young adult population now obtain first degrees (National Statistics, 2002b, p. 63).

At the time of writing there is in England, Wales and Northern Ireland a unitary system of tuition fees for first degrees in higher education, and students may obtain loans to help with the payment of these and of their maintenance costs. Students have to pay a fixed fee unless their parents or they (if they are 'mature students') have very low incomes. A challenge to this by the Scottish government (see p. 62) has, at the time of writing, led to a review of the policy as yet unfinished.

Post-graduate education is subsidized for some through grants from research councils. There is considerable competition for these; conse-quently, many students (or their parents) are paying for post-graduate education. Some further, non-vocational education has to be paid for by students, but generally the fees are subsidized.

As noted above, the issues about fees are closely connected to issues about maintenance costs. The former system of means-tested grants for these has been replaced by a loan system (which applies to all except young students whose parents have very low incomes and mature students with low incomes). Loans have to be repaid once students are in work and have incomes beyond a defined threshold.

It is argued in justification of the heavy costs imposed upon students and their parents that they receive public funds while delaying starting to make a contribution to national income. Nevertheless, by studying, they enhance their own future earning potential. It is therefore argued to be reasonable to expect students to repay all or some of the benefit bestowed on them in this way. Critics of loan schemes point to the benefit the nation gains from its educated people, and warn that loan schemes may deter some people, particularly people from low-income families, from entering higher education.

Child Care and Pre-School Education

Readers may have noted that in chapter 8 a distinction was made between the aspects of the child care system designed to protect children at risk, and child care in general, noting that the government has moved much of the responsibility for the latter to the education system. A discussion of this issue was promised in this chapter.

As a prelude to looking at contemporary child care policy it is appropriate to identify three separate policy issues that are complicatedly intertwined in practice. Child care policy may be seen as about:

- Provision of care which will supplement the care provided by parents – simply as something that reduces stresses and pressures, particularly in the early years of a child's life.
- Activities for children, particularly pre-school children, that will supplement the normal education system.
- Care in order to facilitate labour-market participation on the part of parents.

In each of these cases it may be argued that such activities cannot, or even should not, be the concern of the state, except perhaps as activities to be regulated as part of the child protection system. They may be seen as supplements to family life, which may be purchased or provided through reciprocal community and extended family networks.

Alternatively it may be argued that there is a need for public policies to provide these forms of child care, at full or partial public expense. But then there are rather different arguments for each and rather different rationales for public subsidy.

In the first category – simple supplementary care – the case for state provision is likely to be seen as very similar to that for the child protection system discussed in chapter 8. Such care may reduce family stress and it may be appropriate to develop it where that is particularly likely or where others – families or neighbours, for example – cannot provide it. The justification for public subsidy will be much the same as that for the child protection system.

The second category – child care as a form of supplementary education – arises particularly with regard to provision for pre-school children (but may also apply to after-school and holiday activities). Justifications for such activities in general would seem to be based upon a view that what is provided by the regular education system does not start soon enough or is not enough. Then, if the regular education system is provided free by the state, surely there is a case for this education to be free too? An argument against that view will be that it is an inessential extra, in that sense it may be regarded as being much like post-school education. In practice we find an official view being taken which stands somewhere between those two positions: that it is an extra that some may purchase, but that the resulting inequality requires subsidy on behalf of low-income families. That argument of course is particularly relevant where this additional education is seen as 'compensatory', providing extra for those who may otherwise not take full advantage of the regular education system.

Attitudes towards the third category are of course closely linked to views about the desirability of labour-market participation. The central issue is of course labour-market participation by women. Closely connected with this is the issue about such participation by single parents, most of who are women. Those who regard this as unnecessary, or simply a matter of private choice, will equally see child care provision as a private matter. If, on the contrary, it is seen as every parent's right then there will be a case for state provision of child care. But even here it may be regarded as a matter for attention by employers rather than the state. Again, there is a middle position, which sees a need to subsidize child care to facilitate employment where the rewards from work are low. At the same time the issues about labour-market participation by single parents are very bound up, as was shown in chapter 5, with the fact that the alternative may be another cost for the state (a social security benefit).

The reason for this long prelude is that the arguments for and against public child care provisions in the UK, and about which part of the government system should pay for anything provided, have been complex precisely because of the alternative positions taken in relation to the three justifications outlined above. The Second World War saw the development of subsidized child care provisions to facilitate female employment. After the war there was a dramatic decline in this; the dominant view was that labour-market participation by mothers was not desirable. The publicly subsidized child care system shrank to a small local authority-provided sector, seen as an essential supplement to the child protection system. Then there was a growth of provision by the education system, 'nursery education' for under-5s. In the 1960s and 1970s, developing interest in compensatory education stimulated that growth, particularly in deprived areas. Evidence suggested that pre-school education might offset disadvantages that were contributing to educational under-achievement (Halsey, 1972). Later, demand grew for pre-school education for all and a wide range of private nursery schools and playgroups emerged. In the 1990s the government developed a voucher system that would extend subsidy to all pre-school education, a measure repealed by Labour at the end of the decade in favour of the extension of public provision. But alongside the growth of pre-school education more and more parents were making arrangements for pre-school (and after-school) care to facilitate labour-market participation by mothers. The state recognized this as a phenomenon in need of regulation through a registration system but was reluctant to subsidise it. Eventually some subsidy arrived through the child care tax credit (see p. 109).

Some new money has been put into public provisions, particularly in deprived areas. In these there has been strong emphasis upon the setting up of partnerships of statutory and voluntary organizations. Notable here has been 'Sure Start': the funding of local partnerships in deprived areas to improve the early learning experiences of pre-school children, improve child care and offer a range of support to parents. The government aims to be supporting about 500 programmes by 2004 and to be spending £500 million a year on this initiative (Department for Education and Employment, 1999).

The end result of the developments described above is a confusing mixture of activities with limited state support, except in the forms of extensive pre-school education provision and now some tax-credit subsidy for lower income parents. In the UK today 63 per cent of children aged three and four are attending nursery schools, many on a part-time basis, but then a further 28 per cent are attending what are described as 'non-school education settings in the private and voluntary sector, such as local playgroups' (National Statistics, 2002b, p. 54). A different set of statistics can be found on day care places. These show that there are very few publicly provided day care places – 18,000 in England and Wales – but over a quarter of a million private day nursery places and even more registered child-minders. These statistics are a product of official registration arrangements, now the responsibility of local education authorities under the supervision of a branch of the school inspection system. In addition there will still be a range of private child-minding arrangements that have not been registered.

While this may be confusing to the reader, what is even more important is that it is confusing to a parent who wants to make satisfactory care arrangements for a child. What this is likely to involve is a progression through from a child-minding arrangement to some nursery education by the age of three (which has to be supplemented by continuing child-minding to cover all working hours and school holidays), and then on to a similar hodgepodge of measures (child-minding, after-school clubs, holiday play schemes) for the early school years. Very little of the non-education provision gets public subsidy. Hence doubts are being expressed about the government's objective to stimulate labour-market participation by women who can expect relatively low rewards from employment.

Control over the Education System

The control of education in Britain involves what has been described as a 'partnership' between central and local government. Yet, clearly, that partnership has been largely undermined. Since central government exercises strict control over local government expenditure, the fact that education accounts for around half of this expenditure inevitably puts it in the spotlight. Furthermore, politicians at national level take a great interest in the way education is organized and conducted. The development of comprehensive education was an issue that fundamentally divided the parties. Governments have also felt it important to take stands on such matters as literacy, the core content of the curriculum, the role of nursery education and the future of higher education. Concern about 'failing schools' has led, as was shown above, to a willingness to replace local authority control in some cases.

The uneasy relationship between central and local government is not the only area in which there is a power struggle within the British educational system. At the local level, the running of the system involves a number of different groups that are contending for influence or protecting their prerogatives. Local authorities have powers to influence the character of the school system in their area, and employ a chief education officer, who leads a team of officials who generally have teaching qualifications. There is thus a strong professionally oriented administrative group at this level.

Schools are required to have governing bodies. These are required to consist of parents, teachers, co-opted members and local education authority nominees. As pointed out above, these bodies are now responsible for delegated budgets partly guaranteed by the central government. They have significant control over appointments.

An issue that has received considerable attention has been parental choice of schools for their children. While there were high pupil–teacher ratios and pressure on school numbers in many parts of the country, the scope for parental choice was fairly limited. As school rolls have fallen, though, the situation has changed. In urban areas, in particular, variations in the popularity of schools have often become very clear. In the Education Act of 1980, the government tried to provide parents with some measure of choice over schools. Local authorities are required to give information that will help parents to choose schools, and there is an appeal procedure available for those whose wishes are not granted. Parental choice seems to be operating as a curb on innovation by teachers; it may also be helping to determine where cuts will be made. Inasmuch as choice is more likely to be exercised by middle-class parents, it may be enhancing the tendency for there to be a hierarchy of schools, under the influence of geographical location. Patterns of social and ethnic segregation may thereby be enhanced (Gewirtz et al., 1995). We return to that subject on pp. 213–15.

In the schools themselves, head teachers expect a considerable measure of freedom in determining how their school is run and the way in which subjects are taught. They operate, of course, in consultation with their teachers, but vary extensively in the degree to which they allow staff participation in decision making. In the last resort, however, the class teacher clearly has some autonomy in determining his or her input, and relationship to pupils.

However, contemporary political developments have influenced these relationships. The next section will look at the ways in which central control over the curriculum has increased. That has been accompanied by the elaboration of the long-standing system of school inspection, now run by a quasi-autonomous agency – the Office for Standards in Education (Ofsted) – which regularly produces reports, some of which are highly critical both of the way schools are managed and of the effectiveness of individual teachers. On top of this, now, teachers have been put even more directly under the government spotlight. The government has been developing a new career structure for teachers involving a rigorous appraisal and assessment system and a salary structure that gives extra rewards for good teachers (Department for Education and Employment, 1998).

The further and higher education systems have experienced parallel developments under the supervision of their funding councils. In higher education, the expectation that staff will be researchers as well as teachers has involved the development of a 'research assessment exercise' in which research and publications are assessed by an expert panel drawn from within the profession. Part of the funding formula for universities and colleges is based on this exercise.

All of the education system has experienced the development of a control system in which the activities of teachers are increasingly under scrutiny. Under the Conservatives, there was some attempt to make the crucial control devices market-based. The success or failure of schools and colleges were to depend on their success in attracting students (and, in higher education, research funds). The Labour government is less happy with the use of such devices, but we therefore see, instead, further prescriptions about how activities should be carried out and the strengthening of methods of checking that the instructions given are followed. In the next section, this theme is explored further, with reference to the national curriculum.

The Government and the Curriculum

The 1988 Act introduced a requirement that a national curriculum should be developed for use in all state-financed schools in England and Wales. That curriculum has been elaborated since the original legislation. It consists of three core subjects (English, maths and science, plus Welsh in Welsh-speaking areas) and seven foundation subjects (history, geography, design and technology, information and communications technology, music, art and design, physical education), and for the over-11s citizenship and another modern language. There is also a requirement to provide a programme of religious education, which reflects the 'dominance' of Christianity in Britain. Curriculum councils have been set up to keep these developments under review.

Linked to that curriculum is the testing of children at 7, 11, and 14 years of age. The testing system involves the setting of attainment targets, and is carried out under the supervision of a central curriculum and assessment body. This testing supplements the longer standing arrangements for examinations at the end of the school years, between 16 and 18.

These measures represent a marked departure from the philosophy of the 1944 Education Act, which left most education under local government control and issues about the determination of the curriculum largely in the hands of teachers, operating with an eye on the entrance requirements for higher education and the expectations of employers.

A comment is appropriate here about religion in the curriculum. The British Social Attitudes survey showed that only 60 per cent of the population claimed to belong to a specific religion, with 55 per cent being Christian (quoted in National Statistics, 2002b, p. 220). A much lower percentage actually practise their religion through regular attendance at a place of worship. It may seem strange that the state education system should take on a role as the propagator of religious belief. Historically the arrangements for religion in schools originated from a compromise between the government and the religious bodies in the 1940s, providing both for religion in state schools and the possibility of participation by religious bodies in the provision of schools given state funding.

A feature of education policy under the Blair government is that the government has been happy to reinforce religious participation in the provision of publicly funded education. Where before most 'single faith' schools were Anglican or Roman Catholic, with a very small number of Jewish schools, now Muslim and Sikh schools have been set up. Furthermore, there have also been some schools set up by smaller Christian groups. At the time of writing controversy has developed about teaching at a City Technology College run by a fundamentalist Christian group that challenges evolutionary theory in biology. But perhaps a more serious worry about the encouragement of diversity in religious participation in education is that it may undermine efforts to eliminate discrimination and racism. We will return to this theme.

Diversity and Selectivity in the Education System

Results of the statutory tests required by the National Curriculum are published, providing data on the 'achievements' of individual schools in a form which encourages their presentation by the media in 'league tables'. Since much educational attainment is determined by factors outside the control of the schools, these can be very misleading. Some schools may be securing a considerable 'value-added' element in enhancing the achievements of children. Others may be doing very little for pupils who, by virtue of their socio-economic backgrounds, are likely to score well in tests in any case. Schools in the former group may be unfairly perceived as achieving little, while those in the latter group win unwarranted esteem. These comparisons encourage schools to try to recruit pupils with a high academic potential. Middle-class children, Asian children and girls have been regarded in some places as the pupils to attract (Gewirtz et al., 1995).

Sociological studies of education have suggested that as pupils approach school-leaving age, there are many factors, often beyond the control of the schools, that contribute to divisions between school-oriented 'academic' pupils and an anti-school group who increasingly see their education as irrelevant and who drop out of participation in all school activities (Ford, 1969; Willis, 1977). A relevant concern in secondary education, therefore, is not so much the fate of the brighter pupils – the comprehensive schools have been eager to 'prove themselves' by doing justice to the needs of this group – as the difficulties entailed in providing a relevant education for those at the other end of the ability range. There are related problems here, of course, of absenteeism and delinquency.

Overall, this issue concerns the relationship of the education system to the needs of underprivileged groups in our society – for example, low-skilled workers and some ethnic minorities. Since, moreover, such groups are located in specific areas, there is a geographical dimension to this problem. One of the arguments advanced in favour of the comprehensive school is that it is able to take all the children of a limited geographical community. But suppose such a 'community' is manifestly not truly 'comprehensive', and, worse still, suppose atypical residents in that community take steps to educate their children elsewhere, then new distinctions arise between schools. This is a significant problem for comprehensive secondary education in Britain. It is one that has been intensified by government efforts to ensure that parents have maximum opportunities to choose schools for their children.

The Conservative governments of the 1980s and 1990s seemed prepared to disregard these issues in favour of an approach to education which emphasized the raising of standards through competition between schools. The rhetoric of the Labour politicians suggests a commitment to changing this. In its 1997 manifesto, Labour argued that 'far too many children are denied the opportunity to succeed', spoke of 'zero tolerance of underperformance' and said 'no matter where a school is, Labour will not tolerate under-achievement'. Labour has given a high priority to education. It headlined the education section in its 'annual report' for 1997–8 (HMSO, 1998, p. 30):

> The Government's aim is to build a world-class education system by taking excellence wherever it is found and spreading it widely. We want every school to be a good school so that parents know that wherever they send their children they will get a decent education.

The underlying question here is whether a search for 'excellence' throughout the education system, with a strong emphasis on standards, can be sustained without, in the process, creating winners and losers. In the last analysis, an education system channels people towards the limited opportunities that exist in the wider society. In aiming to raise education standards for all, the government has an obvious political need to reassure parents whose children are already benefiting from the best the system has to offer that the process is one, to borrow other words from the Labour manifesto, of 'levelling up, not levelling down'. Yet any emphasis on reducing educational disadvantage must imply, in a race that all cannot win, advancing some at the expense of others. Perhaps a shift of attention away from crude competition between schools, in which those with the right social catchment areas must inevitably win, towards a more egalitarian system is occurring, under the camouflage of an 'all can win' rhetoric designed to reassure anxious middle-class parents. The author will begin to be more convinced of that possibility when school tests results are published with an emphasis on 'value added' as opposed to the crude data on proportions of children at each level, as is the case at the time of writing.

Doubts about the reality of the government's egalitarianism are, however, reinforced by its willingness to allow greater diversity in schools, particularly secondary schools, and its willingness to countenance the reintroduction of some forms of selection. Conservative legislation in 1993 allowed schools to become 'specialist' and to practise limited forms of selection. It was argued that this implied specialization in technology (as in the City Technology Colleges) or in the arts or sports. Labour's 1998 legislation permitted specialist schools to admit up to 10 per cent of children on the basis of aptitude. The question is: what does such a measure do to the character of the school as a whole and the way it is regarded by parents? Tomlinson concludes:

> The Conservatives promised *Choice and Diversity*, New Labour promised *Diversity and Excellence*. The reality was that structural differentiation was ensuring a hierarchical pecking order of schools, which unsurprisingly, given the history of English schooling, continued to mirror the social class structure. (Tomlinson, 2001, p. 99)

The issues about educational disadvantage are explored further in the next three sections.

Education and the Disadvantaged

In the previous section the Labour government's commitment to education improvement for all was quoted, but reservations were expressed about how this is being translated into action. In fairness it is important to acknowledge other aspects of the government's strategy. Key measures towards the improvement of education, with an eye on educational disadvantage, include:

- the establishment of Education Action Zones in deprived areas, where public/private partnerships have been set up to try to secure additional investment and to encourage innovation;
- setting improvement targets for schools and assuming government powers to intervene in failing schools (including the power to impose an alternative management system, as described above);

- establishing a network of the best performing schools as 'beacon schools' which may play a role in disseminating best practice to others;
- new investments to reduce class sizes.

The discussion in the previous section highlighted the role education plays in relation to the distribution of occupational opportunities in our society. On the Left, there has traditionally been considerable concern about the extent to which education contributes to upward mobility. There are two versions of this preoccupation. One of these involves a commitment to equality of opportunity, and therefore a demand that all able children of whatever social background should have access to educational openings. The other is a concern about equality in a more absolute sense. A naive version of this places faith in the possibility of an education system that can help to create a more equal society. A more sophisticated approach recognizes that education cannot be, by itself, an engine of social change, but stresses that it must play a part by ensuring that children are not socially segregated and that schools attempt to compensate for other sources of inequality.

These issues have been explored in relation to socio-economic status (or social class), ethnicity and gender. This section will concentrate on the first of these. The next section explores some of the issues about ethnicity. As far as gender is concerned, most explicit discrimination against females has now disappeared. In fact, there is now a female majority in higher education (55 per cent of higher education students are female; National Statistics, 2002b, p. 60). There have nevertheless been concerns about the extent to which there is within the education system a 'hidden curriculum' which socializes males and females differently – inculcating separate gender roles and influencing the subjects chosen in the later years in schools and in universities. This may have indirect implications for women's treatment in the labour force, where inequality is still very evident.

Male under-achievement has begun to secure attention, with suggestions that the culture of primary schools is largely feminine. This is a complex subject which will not be explored further here. It is perhaps symptomatic of continued male dominance in society that, as soon as most discrimination against females has been eliminated, concern about male under-achievement is leading to calls for explicit interventions!

As far as the issues about socio-economic class are concerned, 'equality of opportunity' is a slogan that finds quite wide political support. Differential educational opportunity and achievement have been extensively studied by sociologists and psychologists. The evidence accumulated by research in the 1950s and early 1960s (Floud et al., 1956; Jackson and Marsden, 1962; Douglas, 1964) was used in making the case for comprehensive education and for the abandonment of streaming. Later, attention shifted to those problems of under-achievement in the education system that cannot be directly attributed to the way that system is structured. Two particular themes were emphasized: the significance of home background for educational success and the extent to which the 'culture' of the school system is alien to some children.

It has been shown that poverty and poor housing conditions militate against educational success (Douglas, 1964; Central Advisory Council for Education, 1967). There is little the education system can do about these problems, but it can try to compensate for them with extra efforts to help deprived children. Home backgrounds are relevant in another sense, too. There are wide variations in the extent to which parents help with the education of their children. Such help takes many forms, involving not only the more obvious forms of encouragement and the provision of books and study facilities, but also a great deal of implicit 'teaching' through interaction with children. The latter starts when babies are very tiny, and one of its most significant ingredients is the learning of language. The children who are most deprived in these respects are often those who are also most deprived in a material sense. However, parental educational levels and abilities are also relevant. The education system may help to compensate for these less straightforwardly material disadvantages in a variety of practical ways, both before and after children reach compulsory school age (Halsey, 1972).

The issue with regard to the culture of the schools is a more difficult one. In part, the problem is one of identification of the needs and special interests of children whose backgrounds differ from that of the white, educated middle-class whose needs have dominated the values of the system. There is a variety of ways in which stories, educational situations and examples can be devised that seem relevant to these children. Hence there is ample scope for change here.

However, as far as social class disadvantages are concerned, there are limits to how far this issue can be fully met, if only because of the extent to which it implies a conflict with the objective of facilitating social mobility through education. If a key concern of education is to prepare children to operate in a middle-class world, even perhaps to join that world, then it may not be particularly functional for it to be concerned to relate to working-class culture. There is a great dilemma here, which is relevant to the alienation of some children from an education system in which they are becoming the 'failures'. You cannot eliminate the concept of failure as long as you have the objective of enabling some to 'succeed' through the education system. It may be desirable to eliminate the more invidious aspects of competition within the system – to recognize, for example, that progress relative to ability may be as important as the easy success of the advantaged and talented – but notions of achievement, and consequently non-achievement, are fundamental to the role of education in our kind of society.

Tomlinson (2001, p. 160) quotes research by Killeen et al. (1999) showing young people's views of education to be very instrumental, with 'qualifications . . . a paper currency that could be exchanged for work opportunities' and a low opinion of vocational courses. At the time of writing, the government is trying to address issues about the relevance of education for under-achievers by giving more attention to vocationally relevant courses in secondary schools. They face a dilemma in that there is an inherent conflict between this objective and a truly comprehensive approach to education.

The idea of attempting to compensate for disadvantage by providing special resources for the schools in some areas was suggested in a report of the Plowden committee (Central Advisory Council for Education, 1967). Many of the measures adopted did no more than attempt to redress the imbalance of educational resources between run-down inner-city areas, where the schools were old and facilities were limited, and newer suburban areas. Additional money was made available for capital projects and current expenditure in areas where there were high levels of deprivation. In addition, the government provided for extra teachers, above the normal quotas, and special additional allowances for teachers in those areas. Areas were designated on the basis of statistics on the socio-economic status of parents, the extent or absence of housing amenities, the number of children receiving free school meals, and the proportion of schoolchildren with serious language difficulties. In 1998 this was replaced by an 'ethnic minority achievement grant'.

The Education Action Zones, listed above as one of the post-1997 policies, involve a return to interventions of this kind. They are expected to offer a range of innovations and experiments including the development of specialist centres and the employment of teachers with special roles, family literacy schemes and literacy summer schools, and the exploration of new forms of work-related learning. The government has expressed a willingness to adapt the national curriculum to meet specific local needs. The sums of public money going into these zones are quite slight, but the government is seeking partnership arrangements with local firms and other organizations to try to increase the resources available.

The Education of Ethnic Minorities

Britain has a non-white population of over three million. Around half of these are British-born. The remainder are predominantly immigrants from the West Indies and the Indian subcontinent. There is thus a substantial non-white school population, concentrated in urban areas. Most of these youngsters are the British-born children of immigrants, since immigration has been tightly controlled since the 1960s. Over 94 per cent of Afro-Caribbean children under fifteen years of age and about 92 per cent of children under fifteen whose parents originate from the Indian subcontinent were born in Britain (figures calculated from 1991 census data).

The Parekh Report summarizes the evidence on the educational performance of ethnic minority children as showing that Afro-Caribbean children start school 'at much the same standard as the national average' but have fallen behind by the age of ten, Indian pupils achieve above the national average and Pakistani and Bangladeshi children achieve below average but 'steadily close the gap between themselves and others in the course of their education' (Parekh, 2000, p. 146). All those statements should of course be read as being about British children with these different ethnic backgrounds.

In the period when many non-white children were themselves immigrants, the system saw their language problems and cultural differences as the main issue. Some of these are still evident. However, many Asian children are encouraged by parents to make the most of educational opportunities, and many have made remarkable progress within the British system. They may face problems, however, in coming to terms with strong contrasts between patterns of home life and those of school life.

Some Asian groups have begun either to make demands for new developments in the education system in tune with their cultural needs (e.g. appropriate religious education and courses in Asian languages) or to call for separate state-subsidized schools for their children. It has been noted above that the government has been prepared to respond to this demand (see p. 213). A look across to Northern Ireland, where a division in education along religious lines has many of the characteristics of a division along cultural lines, and contributes to the division of that community, gives pause for thought regarding this model of education for a culturally diverse society. Such misgivings are reinforced by the extent to which there has also been interest in independence expressed by white parents eager to minimize the Asian influence on certain schools.

At one time in the late 1960s and early 1970s, a number of education authorities bussed children to other areas, to try to prevent certain schools from having high concentrations of Asian children. Since this bussing was a one-way process, applied only to Asians, it was rightly abandoned as discriminatory. Now, the imposition of rules about regard for parental choice means that local authorities cannot even manipulate catchment areas in the interests of any kind of ethnic 'balance'. Parental choices may enhance tendencies towards segregation.

West Indian immigrants come from a society in which European cultural models have a strong influence, and are reinforced through the education process. It is precisely this bias in West Indian society, and in American Negro society, that has been attacked by those concerned about the development of black consciousness. It is argued that this dominance of a white cultural model contributes to the maintenance of a subordinate self-image. Black leaders in Britain have become deeply concerned about the under-achievement of children of West Indian origin. They attribute this to a variety of factors, but see the white ethnic and cultural bias in the education system as reinforcing other aspects of disadvantage.

Hence, while the education system continues to see the issues regarding non-white children as issues about their characteristics, it may alternatively be suggested that the central issue is its ethnic and cultural assumptions, the phenomenon described as 'institutional racism'. An official committee, chaired by Lord Swann, reported on its 'Inquiry into the Education of Children from Ethnic Minority Groups' in 1985. In a brief guide to the report, Lord Swann, while not using the expression 'institutional racism', made it very clear that the issue of the response of society and of the education system was of central importance in explaining the problem of under-achievement by non-whites. He argued (Department of Education and Science, 1985, p. 9):

> on the evidence so far there is at least a dual problem. On the one hand, society must not, through prejudice and discrimination, increase the social and economic deprivation of ethnic minority families. On the other, schools must respond with greater sensitivity, and without any trace of prejudice, to the needs of ethnic minority children.

Lord Swann saw the latter as to be achieved through the concept of 'Education for All'. This meant that (p. 10):

> [t]he fundamental change needed is a recognition that the problem facing the educational system is not just how to educate the children of ethnic minorities, but how to educate all children. Britain has long been an ethnically diverse society, and is now, mainly because of her imperial past, much more obviously one. All pupils must be brought to an understanding of what is entailed if such a society is to become a fair and harmonious entity.

A later report by the Office for Standards in Education (Ofsted, 1999) indicated the need for continued attention to 'institutional racism' in schools. It spoke of a lack of attention to explicit strategies to attack these issues and of an absence of monitoring.

Clearly, the central issues now concern the culture of the education system. There is a need to tackle the biases in the system through the encouragement of culturally relevant studies and action to combat ethnocentric biases in the curriculum. This last problem, about the education of black children, is very closely linked with the issue of the place that disadvantaged white children find themselves occupying within the system – as discussed in the previous section – and with the quite concrete disadvantages of children from lower-income homes. Inasmuch as black entrants to Britain have generally been forced to accept many of the poorest jobs and some of the worst housing, children find that the 'inferior' stereotype of the black person seems to be reinforced by their, and their parents', experience. Moreover, the fact that many black parents have had relatively little education themselves, and use a dialect form of English very different from that used in the schools, means that, like comparable lower-class white parents, they are ill-equipped to help their children to tackle the education system. There is a web of reinforcing disadvantages here.

Many of the points made here are relevant to other policy areas. In particular, the chapter on the personal social services might have discussed some of the issues about the inadequacies of services for minorities, and explored, in terms not unlike those used about educational separation, the issue of trans-racial adoption, for example. Similarly, the chapter on the health service could have dealt more with the extent to which there is an ethnic dimension to inequalities in health, and explored some of the communication difficulties which arise when white health professionals pay insufficient regard to cultural and language problems. Lack of space prevented those discussions; the subject has been interposed here because of the particular salience of the issue for education. Readers are urged to think about the relevance of the points made here for those other policy areas. We will return to this subject in chapter 12.

Special Education and other Welfare Measures

The education of handicapped children requires the system to develop certain special resources. However, the trend is to try to integrate the education of handicapped children as far as possible into the ordinary system. There is a significant group of children in each authority who are classified as experiencing 'learning difficulties', as a result of the possession of various kinds of physical or intellectual handicaps. They are required to be carefully tested, and a 'statement' has to be prepared setting out their needs. Parents have a right of appeal to an independent tribunal if they are dissatisfied with the statement. On the basis of the statement, children with learning difficulties will either secure some extra teaching or support in an ordinary school (for which school budgets are enhanced) or be sent to a school where there are special facilities and staffing arrangements. There is a variety of special schools. In most authorities, there are separate ones designed for children with 'moderate' or 'severe' learning difficulties. There are also some specialized schools, run by private or voluntary bodies, at which local authorities may buy places. But there is a strong emphasis upon efforts to integrate as many children with learning difficulties as possible into mainstream schools.

There are a number of non-teaching activities that contribute to the overall performance of the education system. Schools may provide meals and milk to children. The former may be available free to pupils whose parents are on income support. The extent to which they should be subsidized for others has been something of a political football, and extensive cuts have been made to these services. Means-tested grants may also be available towards the cost of school clothing, and towards support of pupils in the 16–18-age group who are still at school.

The welfare of schoolchildren is also given attention through the school health service and the education welfare service. Historically, the main concern of this service has been truancy. Today, its objectives have been widened to embrace a whole range of problems that may affect educational performance. In this, it has the support of child guidance services.

There are growing concerns about the tendency for schools to use their formal powers to exclude disruptive children. This seems to have been stimulated by the development of competition between schools encouraged by parental choice and the publication of performance data.

CONCLUSIONS

The state system of education had roots in a mid-nineteenth-century concern with the training of an effective workforce able to operate in an increasingly complex industrial system and society. Its growth has been inextricably entwined with the development of a democratic society. The original view that the newly enfranchised should be literate has been answered by a belief on the part of the electorate that education holds the key to social advancement. Such a view is certainly encouraged by the enormous emphasis put on education by the political parties, particularly Labour and the Liberals. This may be, in part, an illusion. The opportunity structure is determined by the economy and by the political system. Increased education does not, in itself, increase the supply of 'top jobs'; it merely increases the competition for them. The fact that educational qualifications are widely used as a basis for discrimination between applicants for jobs emphasizes the link between education and social and economic advancement, regardless of whether those jobs require education at the level, or of the kind, possessed by those deemed best suited to fill them. Hence, the nature of the education system and the opportunities it provides are of central political importance in Britain.

As job opportunities for young people diminished in Britain in the 1980s and 1990s, a debate about the role of the education system was stimulated. This was linked to a long-standing controversy about how far British economic under-achievement can be attributed to defects in the education system – insufficient emphasis on science and engineering, high esteem for a cultural education that has no immediate practical use, and so on. This is a complex issue, involving propositions that are difficult to test empirically. What it does involve is a tendency to assign too much importance to the role of the education system, disregarding the extent to which it has to respond to social and political demands on it. More immediately, this debate seems to encourage a tendency to attribute the shortage of jobs not to deficiencies in the demand for labour but to inadequacies in the supply of labour – to see the education system as failing the youth of this country. This flies in the face of the evidence that competition for jobs is stimulating 'qualification inflation', that the qualifications needed for many jobs are being increased because of the stiff competition for them. It is leading, however, to an ever-increasing demand for vocationally relevant education (particularly for the vast majority of publicly educated boys and girls unlikely to move easily into elite jobs).

The emphasis in political rhetoric about education as a preparation for work – both in discussions of individual under-achievement and in evaluations of the role of the education system as a contributor to global economic competition – exacerbates the difficulties in developing an egalitarian education that can offer a preparation for life for all children.

Education has become perhaps more politicized than ever before. Governments are now very clearly unwilling to leave education to the educationalists, or to delegate responsibility for education policy to local authorities or the governors of schools and colleges.

SUGGESTIONS FOR FURTHER READING

Tomlinson's *Education in a Post-Welfare Society* (2001) provides an excellent, more or less up-to-date account of this area of policy. Examination of some of the key modern developments can be found in Ball's *Politics and Policy Making in Education* (1990), Bowe and Ball's *Reforming Education and Changing Schools* (1992) and Gewirtz et al.'s *Markets Choice and Equity in Education* (1995).

Liu (2001) provides a good exploration of the complex evolution of child care and nursery school policy.

Much of the sociological literature on social class and education is now very dated, but a formidable modern overview of this subject is available in Halsey et al. (1997). Law's *Racism, Ethnicity and Social Policy* (1996) explores the issues about education, among other topics, as does the Parekh Report (2000), while Gillborn's *Race, Ethnicity and Education* (1992) is a rather older examination of these issues.

The official website for education policy in England is www.dfes.gov.uk.

Chapter 10
Housing

Introduction

In the UK in 2001, the housing stock comprised a little over 25 million dwellings. About two-thirds of these were owner-occupied, the remainder rented (National Statistics, 2002b, p. 166). Within England 70 per cent were owner-occupied, 13 per cent rented from a local authority, 7 per cent rented from a non-profit-making 'social landlord' and 10 per cent rented from a private landlord. In the other countries of the UK the owner-occupied proportion was a little lower and within the rented sector the proportion renting from a private landlord was also lower.

It will be shown in this chapter that public policies have influenced all these sectors, if not directly through public provision, then indirectly through tax subsidies (in the case of the owner-occupied sector) or rent support for tenants (in the privately rented sector).

From the end of World War I until 1979, the owner-occupier and publicly provided sectors grew dramatically at the expense of the private rented sector. Since 1979, the growth of owner-occupation has continued, but the public rented sector has declined in size as a result of the sale of council houses to their occupiers. Moreover, many council houses have been transferred into housing association ownership. Hence, it is appropriate to talk about a 'social housing' sector distinguishable from privately rented housing, consisting of rented housing under a mixture of local authority and housing association ownership. Much of the subsidy for this sector now comes directly to tenants, in the form of housing benefit. This benefit is also available to private tenants, further blurring the private–public distinction.

Developments in the UK housing system have been enormously influenced by government intervention. The department directly responsible for housing policy in England is the Department for Local Government and the Regions (DLR). In the other countries of the UK, housing policy is one of the devolved responsibilities.

To understand housing policy, there is a need to look at issues about all the housing sectors. There are complex interactions between them; a change in one sector has implications for others. For example, during much of the twentieth century increased opportunities for owner-occupation both diminished the demand for private rented accommodation, and were partly created by landlords' desires to sell houses that seemed no longer to offer a satisfactory return if they were let. At the time of writing, there are signs that increased difficulties about getting into owner-occupation, because of the cost of houses, have correspondingly increased the profitability of providing housing to rent, bringing to an end, and even perhaps slightly reversing the growth of owner occupation. Later in this chapter, fuller attention will be given to some of the interactions of this kind that have policy implications. However, it is clearly simplest to introduce this discussion of policies by examining each sector separately.

The Social Housing Sector

While a small amount of public housing was built earlier, the effective growth of the social housing sector dates from the enactment of legislation after World War I to enable local authorities to receive central government subsidies towards the provision of housing 'for the working classes' (now often called 'council houses'). A long succession of subsequent Acts of Parliament elaborated this initiative, encouraging both the building of large estates designed to meet basic housing needs and the adoption of substantial slum clearance schemes. This sector became the main provider of houses for those unable to buy their own.

The history of the subsidy system developed in this sector is complicated. There is a need to look at it briefly so as to understand the contemporary situation. For many years the government used, but regularly changed, a system whereby local authorities secured a fixed sum per dwelling annually over a fixed period of years. In the 1960s, the Labour government adopted a new approach, without terminating the older subsidies, whereby percentage subsidies were paid, effectively to subsidize the rate at which authorities borrowed money. However, in the 1972 Housing Finance Act, the Conservatives sought to sweep away all the continuing older systems of subsidy. The objective was to move to a system in which general-purpose subsidies would eventually be eliminated. They recognized the need to continue to subsidize certain particularly expensive forms of development, in particular slum clearance. They also acknowledged a case for subsidizing low-income tenants by requiring authorities to operate rent-rebate schemes, which received an element of national subsidy. Otherwise, they expected local authorities to move towards balanced housing budgets by raising rents. A national system of 'fair rents', at higher levels than existing rents, was to be developed, which might leave some authorities, those whose housing commitments were particularly costly, with deficits, but these would be met partly out of central government grants. However, most authorities were expected to reach a position at which general subsidies would be unnecessary, and some would achieve surpluses.

This new scheme was designed to be phased in gradually. Rents were to be increased in stages, and a 'transitional subsidy' was paid. Before the transition could be completed, the Conservatives lost power in 1974, and the new Labour administration suspended the operation of the Housing Finance Act. It planned, instead, a modified version of the Conservatives' scheme that did not directly interfere with the authorities' power to fix their own rents, and did not necessarily entail a gradual phasing out of general-purpose subsidies. The general approach offered a potential for manipulation in a variety of ways, determined by the ideology of the government operating it. The approach was described by HMSO (1977, p. 83):

1 The starting-point of the calculation of subsidy would be an authority's entitlement to subsidy in the previous year.
2 Each year, a basis for calculation of the extra expenditure admissible for subsidy – including extra costs of management and maintenance assessed by an appropriate formula – would be settled for the coming year in consultation with local authorities.
3 Each year, an appropriate level of increase in the 'local contribution' to costs, from rent and rates, would be determined for the coming year, also in consultation with local authorities.
4 If the extra admissible expenditure of an authority exceeded the increase in the 'local contribution', subsidy entitlement would be increased. If, on the other

hand, the extra local contribution exceeded this extra expenditure subsidy, entitlement would be correspondingly reduced.

The Labour government fell in 1979 before it could enact this system, but the Conservatives' Housing Act of 1980 essentially took it over. Then, what became crucial (since the new government was committed to reducing as far as possible the central government subsidy to council house rents) was the annual assumptions made, under point (3) above, about appropriate levels of rent increases. This was used, particularly after the Local Government and Housing Act of 1989, to drive up rents through reduction of subsidy.

Thus, during the 1980s and 1990s, large numbers of local authorities ceased to be entitled to a subsidy from central government, other than contributions to pay the cost of rent rebates (later called housing benefit). In England in 2001–2 the subsidy to local authorities, excluding support for housing benefit, was about £996 million (Department for Transport, Local Government and the Regions, 2002, p. 2). It had been falling steadily until the government decided to enhance support for public housing a little in 2001–2.

Under the arrangements described above, rents could still be subsidized from local resources (at that time, the 'rate fund'). What in fact happened, in the early 1980s, was that there was an increased divergence between authorities. The sharp withdrawal of the central subsidy meant that, in aggregate, local subsidies to rents exceeded national subsidies by 1983. However, it was only in a small number of authorities, mostly in London, that such contributions were of any significant size (Malpass, 1990, p. 168). In around half of all authorities, no contributions were made at all. At the other extreme, an increasing number of authorities were making contributions to the rate fund from rents; that is, council tenants not on housing benefit were subsidizing rate-payers!

Legislation in 1989 forced local authorities to phase out these exchanges between housing accounts and their general accounts. This measure was widely described as 'ring-fencing' the housing-revenue accounts. Local authorities were forced to raise rents to replace local contributions. A further complication was that, in determining the rules for these accounts, the government started taking into account a notional income from housing-benefit subsidy. What this implies is that authorities may find that they are, in effect, required to subsidize the housing benefit to low-income tenants partly from the rents of other tenants. The actual situation depends on the government's application to each authority of the formula described above.

As suggested already, as the general subsidy has disappeared and general rents have increased, so housing benefit has tended to become the dominant form of subsidy going to local authority tenants. This is paid not by the DLR, but by the Department for Work and Pensions. Housing-benefit support of local authority sector rents in England cost about £3,350 million in 2001-2 (Department for Transport, Local Government and the Regions, 2002, p. 2).

The determination of capital expenditure – that is, primarily, the building of new houses – is also based on a system devised in the late 1970s by the Labour government. Before 1977, local councils determined their house-building programmes without consultation with central government. However, to implement those programmes, they had to secure central acceptance, to enable them both to undertake such extensive investment and to obtain subsidies (inasmuch as subsidies were linked to specific building projects). Local government proposed, and central government would dispose. The whole system was fairly haphazard, since central government tried to link its decisions to national and relatively local priorities, but was dependent on local initiatives, and did not necessarily have an overall view of national housing needs. Under the system established in 1977, local authorities are required to submit for annual central scrutiny their 'Housing Investment Programmes'. These include not only their plans for the provision of new local authority housing, but also their plans to make loans for house purchase, to give grants for housing improvements, to improve their own stock, to clear unfit houses, to purchase houses and to assist housing associations. Statistical returns from the authorities are required on their own current and future activities, and on their intelligence on local housing needs and problems of private sector building. On the basis of these submissions, the English local authorities then, after a process of negotiation through the regional offices of the DLR (there are similar procedures in Scotland and Wales), receive annual expenditure allocations, not in the form of specific permission for particular projects, but in the form of a broad block.

The impact of the Conservative governments between 1979 and 1997 on this system was simply to limit expenditure, particularly on new building. In the late 1970s, local authorities in the UK built a little over 100,000 dwellings each year. In the early 1980s, it was down to a little over 30,000 a year and, in the 1990s, it has dropped to a very low figure indeed. In 1998, only about 300 public sector houses were completed in England and since then the new Labour government has done little to reverse the trend. There were 700 houses completed in 2000–1. That figure (under 0.5 per cent of total completions) was dwarfed by the number of completions for housing associations (17,000, or 13 per cent of the total) (ibid., 2002, p. 4).

The changes in public housing policy in the 1980s, towards the reduction of subsidies and the restriction of new building, need to be seen together with the government's stimulation of the sale of council houses. This involved, first, sale of houses to their occupiers (see pp. 240–1), and then, later, measures to try to shift ownership of estates from local authorities to either private or housing association landlords. Initially these measures had limited success, the idea that tenants might want to choose alternative landlords proved to be wrong. A limited number of smaller local authorities transferred their stock to housing associations. However, the strict controls over local rent setting and the continuation of limitations on the availability of capital for new building by local authorities have had two effects. One has been the growth of the hitherto small housing association sector, because it has had relatively greater freedom to raise loans for building and rehabilitation work than local government. The other has been the exploration by local authorities of the case for voluntary transfer of their stock to a housing association so as to achieve greater managerial freedom, in particular the freedom to raise money for building and repairs. This latter development involves not only housing stock transfers to existing housing associations, but also the setting-up of new associations, often formed from the staff of the local authority housing departments. Interestingly, Wilcox (1998) comments on this issue, comparing Conservative and Labour policies, but coming to what may seem an unexpected conclusion (pp. 12–13):

> The whole tenor of the CSR [the comprehensive spending review initiated by the new government] has none of the last government's heavy-handed political drive towards stock transfers. . . . Nonetheless, for many councils the current capital and revenue financial regimes mean that stock transfers will remain compellingly financially attractive. Stock transfer enables councils to escape from the strongly redistributive net of the council capital finance and subsidy systems to use rental income to fund investment rather than cross-subsidize the cost of housing benefit.

Housing associations were important in the nineteenth century, as voluntary charitable bodies, but declined in relative importance with the growth of the public sector in the first half of the twentieth century. Over the last thirty years, though, housing association growth has begun to be given increasing government encouragement, being seen as an alternative form of social housing to the large, bureaucratic local authority sector. Housing associations in England may receive grants and subsidies from the government through the Housing Corporation. There is a similar, separate body in Wales. In Scotland, Scottish Homes functions both as a lender of government money and as a direct housing provider. In Northern Ireland (where, incidentally, local authority housing functions have been transferred to a single Housing Executive directly responsible to the government), there is no intermediary body for housing associations.

Since the 1980s governments, both Conservative and Labour, have made more money available to housing associations than to local government. Nevertheless, inhibitions on public capital projects have led to curbs on the resources going through the Housing Corporation and related bodies. As suggested above, however, housing associations, unlike local authorities, can raise money on the open market without government permission. Loans from central government have to some extent been replaced in this way, but with inevitable consequences for the rents charged to tenants. The legislation on rents allows new housing association tenants to be charged what are described as 'affordable rents'. What constitutes an 'affordable rent' is not clearly defined by the government, but 'was interpreted by the National Federation of Housing Associations as a rent approximately equal to 20 per cent of the tenant's average net income' (Balchin, 1995, pp. 195–6). Housing benefit is available to low-income tenants, making a formula like this somewhat hypothetical in many cases.

Housing associations vary widely in size, scope and character. Some differ little in their characteristics from private companies; these have grown in size recently, absorbing some smaller associations along the way. Others have distinct charitable aims and objects, and many are specifically local in their coverage. A small number are co-operatives.

Despite the encouragement of housing associations, social housing provision in general has diminished. The fall in the number of local authority properties has not been counterbalanced by a growth in housing association ones. In England local authority properties constituted 29 per cent of the total housing stock of 17.7 million in 1979 and only 13 per cent of the stock of 21.1 million in 2001. At the same time housing association properties had increased from 2 per cent to 7 per cent of the stock (Department for Transport, Local Government and the Regions, 2002, p. 3). In other words despite an increase in properties by 3.4 million there was a decrease in social housing accommodation of about 1.3 million. This change has been a product of both council house and housing association sales to tenants (the 'right to buy' legislation extends to housing associations) and the small amounts of new building.

The new Labour government might have been expected to be interested in reversing the trend away from social housing. However, the first new minister responsible for housing, Hilary Armstrong (1998), had this to say in a presentation of the principles that were to govern the new housing policy:

> I am agnostic about the ownership of housing – local authorities or housing associations; public or private sector – and want to move away from the

ideological baggage that comes with that issue. What is important is not, primarily, who delivers. It is what works that counts.

The policy evolution described above, ending with that statement from Hilary Armstrong, leads to a situation which Liddiard (1998, p. 121) justifiably describes as one in which 'housing is one of the UK's least contested areas of social policy'. Liddiard goes on to say:

> the apparent consensus . . . seems incomprehensible given the real problems facing housing in the UK. As we enter the new millennium, one and a half million homes are unfit for human habitation and three and a half million are in urgent need of repair while there is a widely accepted need for some 100–120,000 new social homes a year.

We will return to these issues, but first we need to look at what is happening in the other two sectors.

Owner-occupation

It has already been suggested that the examination of housing policy raises difficulties for any distinction between social policy and other areas of public policy. It might be imagined that the private market for owner-occupied houses had very little to do with social policy or indeed with government interventions in society. However, such an impression can be readily corrected by examining the attention that housing has been given in the policies of the major parties in the years since World War II. A central issue in the general elections of 1950 and 1951 was the performance of the Labour government in 'building' houses, and the claim of the Conservative opposition to be able to 'build' more houses. The argument was about the building of houses in general, not just building by public authorities. The Conservatives came to power in 1951 committed to 'building' 300,000 houses a year, but many of these were to be built by private enterprise for owner-occupation. Indeed, the Conservatives increasingly encouraged the development of this sector during the 1950s. Since then, both parties have been concerned to assist the development of owner-occupation.

How, then, do public policies influence the owner-occupied housing sector? What used to be of central importance was the large public subsidy that was given to owner-occupiers through the fact that interest payments on mortgage loans attracted relief from the income tax system. This was phased out by April 2000, but had by then played a crucial role in stimulating the very high levels of owner-occupation we have in the UK.

But it has not been only through tax relief that the government has influenced opportunities for individuals to secure owner-occupied housing. In the period immediately after World War II, the government maintained a tight control over building through control over access to building supplies. As it relaxed these controls, it stimulated private building. Then, in the 1950s, as it began to reduce the amount of local authority building, it thereby encouraged a shift of resources into building for sale. During that period of management of a full-employment economy along Keynesian lines, the government came to realize that one of the ways in which it could most easily influence the economic climate was by influencing the demand for new building. While the direct controls of the immediate post-war period have long since gone, there remain a series of factors that influence the scale of building of houses for sale: the extent to which alternative – particularly public sector – opportunities exist for the building industry; the availability of credit – particularly cheap credit – for building enterprises and land speculators; the availability of mortgage funds for home-buyers; and the availability of land.

Until the 1980s, the main suppliers of finance for house purchase were the building societies. These were comparatively cautious financial institutions, whose activities had grown slowly. Their origins lay in nineteenth-century self-help and charitable ventures. They depended for their operation on being able to attract money from small investors, influenced by the general range of opportunities open to savers, to lend to house-buyers.

Once the proportion of the population with their own houses was high enough, government encouragement of home ownership naturally entailed a concern to open opportunities for borrowing money to those who were regarded by the building societies as 'bad risks'. Hence, there was governmental pressure on these 'private' organizations to lend to more 'marginal' people or for more 'marginal' properties.

During the 1980s, the government deregulated the financial market. Restrictions on building societies' activities were removed, and other lenders, including banks, discovered opportunities to move into the domestic mortgage business. Developments occurred that today make building societies and banks more or less indistinguishable.

In the late 1980s there was a boom period when lenders saw the housing market as an ideal source of profits. Mortgages were sold aggressively, and the customary caution about the creditworthiness of borrowers was abandoned. This further fuelled the boom to which it was a response: owner-occupation expanded, and house prices rose rapidly. This boom, pushing house prices well beyond the overall rate of inflation, eventually collapsed in the recession at the end of the decade. House prices started to fall; the housing market became exceptionally static; and, with rising unemployment, many recent borrowers were soon in difficulties with their mortgage repayments.

During the 1990s the housing market recovered a little. The effect of the phasing out of mortgage tax relief and caution about the events of the late 1980s seemed for a while to have inhibited the development of another boom. Then at the beginning of this century another worrying housing boom started. An additional feature of the current boom has been new investments in housing to let, stimulated by cheap money for those who want to borrow and the low (or negative) returns on money invested elsewhere. Clearly it could be followed by a downturn with a similar impact to the last one.

Both the new Labour government and its immediate predecessor have seen control over inflation as a key policy to prevent a housing boom. They have also encouraged lenders to develop codes of practice and insurance policies that would prevent the rapid dispossession of people who became unemployed. Until the slump in the late 1980s, housing was a source of widespread capital gains. That issue is emerging again, in a context of low growth of other forms of investments. This means that very large amounts of the housing assets of the nation are held by those fortunate enough to have got onto the owner-ccupation ladder at the time when this form of housing was growing very rapidly in the second half of the twentieth century. These capital gains may of course remain locked up in property until deaths lead to their transfer to the next generation. In considering this issue as a whole, there is a connection to be made here with the discussion of the care costs of elderly people (pp. 189–90), since capital assets are taken into account in the means-testing process.

The continuing upward trend in house prices in many areas, and particularly in London, is making it increasingly difficult for people want-ing to occupy property for the first time to become owner-occupiers. This has occurred in a context in which, as shown above, the supply of social housing has fallen. People who would, in the second half of the twentieth century, have expected to buy houses relatively early in their 'housing careers' – police, teachers, civil servants etc. – are finding it difficult to do so, particularly in the London area. A measure of this problem is supplied by data on house prices. In 2000 the price of the average home in England and Wales was about £110,221, in south-east England it was £147,271 and in London £117,949 (National Statistics, 2002b, p. 175). Of course, an average can be a very misleading statistic, and the key issue here is about new entry to owner-occupation. However, the corresponding vari-ation in the average for terraced houses (generally the cheapest kinds of houses) was also very considerable: £81,148 in England and Wales, £104,242 in the south-east, and £194,967 in London. When the author first entered the housing market the conventional wisdom was that it was undesirable to purchase a house costing more than three times one's gross income. While clearly many today are much more heavily committed, that yardstick (or, at most, four times gross income) offers a basis for assessing the implications of these prices. An alternative yardstick involves looking at the size of a mortgage commitment (comparing that, for example, with the estimate of an affordable rent set out on p. 231). But then a great deal will depend upon interest rates. Currently these are low, a rise could have a disastrous impact upon new house-buyers, as of course could a fall in income.

Meanwhile house prices are rising dramatically, by 14.7 per cent in England between 2000 and 2001 (Department for Transport, Local Government and the Regions, 2002, p. 5). The continuation of a growth pattern of that kind, which must be compared with a rate of inflation of little more than 3 per cent at that time, has two implications. One is that it will obviously increase the difficulties of those trying to enter the housing market. The other is that it will yield a high long-term reward to those who manage to buy. However, unless they are able to trade down later in life those rewards may not be realized in their lifetime. The problem is that those on the house price 'escalator' have an interest in its maintenance and certainly in the avoidance of the 'negative equity' situation that was described above as temporarily arising at the end of the 1980s. Yet to have house prices rising faster than either prices or wages further distorts the housing market. Furthermore, there are questions that need attention, but are beyond the scope of this book, about the long-term dangers in having an economy in which investment in housing is seen as much safer than any other form of investment.

At the same time as there is this potentially unstable boom in London and the south east, there are other parts of the country where low demand is leading to falls in prices, in relative and sometimes actual terms. The problems that follow from this include a danger that people find it hard to move in search of work, the neglect of housing maintenance and, at worst, the abandonment of houses. Such trends then have effects upon the way an area is perceived, adding an additional twist to the downward spiral, particularly in areas where the stock is a mixture of owned and rented houses (Bright, 2001; Martin, 2002).

So we see here another challenge to the government's complacency about housing policy, attacked by Liddiard in the quotation above. One modest response to this problem is the government's 'starter home initiative'. This involves a sum of £250 million over 3 years from 2001, which the government estimates will assist around 10,000 'key workers' to buy houses (Department of the Environment, Transport and the Regions, 2000, p. 19). The discussion above suggests that a much more fundamental review of housing policy is required.

The Private Rented Sector

The private rented sector now provides about 10 per cent of the accommodation in England, and an even lower proportion in the UK as a whole. This sector has declined to that level from one in which it housed 90 per cent of the population in 1918 and still about 50 per cent in 1951.

There was a political, but now rather academic, argument about the original decline. Was it inevitable, as better outlets for investment opened up? Or was it produced by government-imposed controls? From 1916 onwards, there were rent controls of various kinds, applied with varying degrees of stringency. Controversy raged over the protection of private tenants from both eviction and high rents. Between 1965 and 1988, the fair-rent principle was adopted for most forms of private tenure. This represented a political compromise based on a comparatively nonsensical formula according to which rent officers were expected to assume that properties were let in a market in which there was no scarcity. The reality was that rents were determined by a system of comparisons at levels some way below what the market might be expected to bear. At the same time, many landlords sought to evade the rent controls altogether by legal devices such as the granting of a 'licence to occupy' rather than a tenancy. The 1988 Housing Act effectively abandoned rent control, apart from various rather complex measures of protection for tenants with agreements dating from earlier rent-control regimes. Since then there has been a very slight increase in the size of this sector.

In decontrolling private rented housing the government argued that returning it to the market-place would arrest its decline; but this depends on the alternative opportunities available to renters.

Excluding temporary residents of an area (among whom students figure as a significant group), the superior advantages of owning mean that many private tenants will tend to be low-income earners and recipients of social security benefits. To enable them to pay market rents, the government has had to allow them access to the housing benefit scheme. However, the problem with this scheme is that receipt of benefit removes any incentive to the renter to behave like a free-market participant. The cost of the rent falls on the state. To cope with this problem for the social security budget, a complex procedure has been adopted requiring rent officers to rule whether rents should be regarded as excessive for benefit purposes, and the hapless tenant (or sometimes the local authority) required to find the balance, rather than central government. In addition, the 'single room rent rule' restricts the amount of housing benefit payable to single persons under 25. In other words, a special system of benefit control has replaced rent control.

The private rented sector is unevenly distributed across the country. In some areas, particularly in the north, there are still old, poor-quality houses occupied by elderly tenants who have been in them for many years. With this property, the main public concern has been about conditions. Elsewhere, the private sector may have rather different characteristics. In London, in particular, but also in many other big cities, much of this accommodation is in the form of flats created out of large old houses. These areas tend to accommodate people whom local authorities do not see as their responsibility (or at least place very low on their scales of priorities): in particular, newcomers to the area and the young single. The decline in the rate at which social housing is provided (discussed above) intensifies the pressure on this sector. As other housing problems have been solved, the gap between the good housing conditions of the majority and the often very poor conditions experienced in this part of the private sector has become increasingly evident.

Homelessness

Homelessness has increased as a result of a combination of a decline in the supply of new accommodation, with mobility in search of work in the overcrowded south, and family breakdown. It also has causes outside the direct control of housing policy, in the unwillingness of the social security system to pay adequate benefits to some groups (in particular, the young). Finally, it must be noted that many among the homeless are in need of health and social care, to assist with problems of mental illness, alcoholism and drug abuse.

In 1977, the Housing (Homeless Persons) Act imposed a duty on local housing authorities to provide accommodation for homeless persons in certain 'priority' groups. These priority groups were, broadly, families with children or elderly or sick persons, together with those made homeless by disasters such as flood or fire. However, authorities did not have to help families who were deemed to have become homeless 'intentionally'. This controversial provision was added to the Act by an amendment, and used to justify refusal of help to someone who has been evicted for not paying rent.

The 1977 Act made it mandatory for an authority to give temporary help, and for more permanent help to be given where a homeless person had a (carefully defined) local connection. It was implicit in the Act that the homeless should be rehoused, except on a very temporary basis, in permanent homes, and not herded into inadequate accommodation. Thus they were in competition with those being rehoused by the housing departments from their waiting lists. In practice, many authorities, particularly in London, used poor-quality temporary accommodation to house homeless people for long periods of time.

The Conservative governments of the 1980s and 1990s were unwilling to pressure reluctant local authorities to fulfil their responsibilities better; and, in 1996, enacted amending legislation to limit local authority responsibility in respect of homelessness to the provision of time-limited temporary accommodation. Legislation before Parliament at the time of writing, and therefore likely to reach the statute book as the Homelessness Act 2002, largely repeals the 1996 legislation, requiring local authorities to 'adopt a strategic approach in combating homelessness' and 'removing limitations' on their obligations to the unintentionally homeless (Homelessness Bill, 2002, explanatory notes para. 4).

It must be emphasized that the policy responses described above were principally for the 'priority' groups. Local authority obligations to the younger single are simply to give advice! It is single homelessness which has grown visibly, particularly in London. It has already been suggested that the roots of this problem lie in a complex of factors, only some of which concern housing policy. Certainly, however, the hard-pressed under-resourced local authority housing departments have been unable to pay much attention to the needs of this group, particularly if the individuals need some combination of housing and social care. It has been left to other special centrally supported initiatives for 'rough sleepers' to try to respond to the problem. The Blair government quickly made this one of their special concerns, referring the issue to the newly created 'Social Exclusion Unit'. This Unit recommended the injection of new resources and the setting-up of special programmes on a nationwide basis. The result was that a Rough Sleepers Unit was set up to co-ordinate responses from local authorities and voluntary groups. A controversial aspect of this policy has been a willingness to countenance coercive measures against begging and those unwilling to avail themselves of new facilities.

In 2000–1 local authorities in England accepted responsibility for housing just over 114,000 homeless people, a small increase over the number the year before (Department for Transport, Local Government and the Regions, 2002, p. 63). There is a lack of reliable recent estimates of numbers of rough sleepers.

Housing and Social Exclusion

The government asked its Social Exclusion Unit to look at housing issues. The two specific mandates it was given were to look at problem estates and, as noted above, street homelessness. As Lee and Murie (1998) suggest in an essay on this topic, though, the issues about social exclusion are wider ranging than this. There were about a million and a half houses 'unfit for human habitation' in 1996 (Department for Transport, Local Government and the Regions, 2002, p. 5). Over half of these were owner-occupied. There were also about 300,000 unfit private rented units and a similar number of units of unfit local authority or housing association houses or flats (Wilcox, 1998, table 23b, p. 108). While these statistics are a little out of date they indicate a serious problem.

There are major concerns about some local authority owned estates. The problems of such estates are seen as involving, as well as poor housing conditions, 'crime, disorder, unemployment, community breakdown, poor health, educational underachievement and inadequate public transport and local services' (Social Exclusion Unit, 1998). The government is addressing the issues of the physical conditions of these estates by making a new 'major repairs allowance' of £1.6 billion a year available to English local authorities. At the same time it has encouraged local authorities to consider transferring their stock to housing associations, who will be less restricted by the limitations on public sector borrowing. They are also encouraging 'private finance initiatives' to raise capital for stock improvements (see discussion of this phenomenon in relation to the health service on p. 161).

A full discussion of the issues about these estates would take us far from the subject of housing. It is important to note that efforts to tackle the physical problems of such estates have often failed, in the face of the wider issues needing to be confronted (Power, 1987). However, what is relevant here is the extent to which the emergence and deterioration of these so-called problem estates has been a consequence of housing policies. This will therefore be explored here.

Allocation of social housing involves achieving a balance between what people want, what they are deemed to need, and what is available. Under conditions of housing scarcity, individuals are in a weak position to assert their wants, unless their co-operation is required with a redevelopment scheme. Housing authorities allocate on the basis of assessments of need, attempting to make the most efficient use of the housing stock. However, in the past, they often gave attention to capacity to pay rent, and many were also disposed to make judgements about potential tenants' suitability for 'good' houses.

There were efforts to move away from such discriminatory allocation of local authority housing, and as the number of families who were desperate for help declined in some areas, the balance of power between housing officers who judged needs and potential tenants who expressed their wishes inevitably shifted. In some areas, poorer houses were often only easily allocated, for example, to the homeless. Nevertheless, a reshuffling of tenants proceeds all the while, and those allocated the 'bad' houses seek transfers to better ones. Often they secure such transfers only if they have been 'good' tenants and, in particular, if they have been regular rent-payers. The only people who shift in the opposite direction are those who are punished, for rent arrears or strikingly non-conforming behaviour, by eviction from 'good' houses and allocation of 'bad' ones (see Pawson and Kintrea, 2002, for a good discussion of the complex ways in which allocation processes still influence social segregation).

Local authorities now have stocks of houses and flats of various kinds: in particular, pre-war semi-detached houses, post-war 'semis' built when standards were low, modern houses built to high standards, flats in blocks of various sizes, good old houses acquired from private owners, and patched houses with short lives pending demolition. Of course, these dwellings vary in popularity, with perhaps high-rise flats and short-life houses as the least popular. If, through allocation and transfer policies, there are various forms of segregation within an authority's housing stock, then the 'hierarchy of popularity' will have been influenced by social as well as architectural considerations. Indeed, these social factors may well complicate the hierarchy as certain estates, not necessarily characterized by severe design problems, also acquire reputations as 'rough' or 'respectable', perhaps as a result of some rather complex accidents of history. This can obviously tend to involve differentiation by income, particularly if accessibility to employment opportunities influences tenant choices. Thus the unpopular areas may contain substantial proportions of households dependent on social security benefits. Woods (1999, p. 108) also notes:

> In addition to having concentrations of low income people, local authorities have also had to contend with greater movement in and out of local authority housing. . . . A high turnover of stock makes it more difficult to develop community spirit and identity and makes it harder to achieve sustainable and supportive communities.

She goes on to paraphrase a Centre for Housing Policy report (1997), noting that:

> those moving out of the sector were generally couples aged under 45 where one or both people were working. On the other hand, those moving in to the sector were in the 16–29 age group and unemployed.

One crucial influence on this issue has been the sale of council houses, which further enhances the social divisions, since houses on popular estates and on estates in which the more prosperous tenants live will be more likely to be sold. This was a key controversial issue for housing policy in the last two decades of the twentieth century. In England nearly two million houses have been sold to their occupiers since 1980, but now the rate of sales has slowed so that in the twelve months up to June 2001 there were about 50,000 such sales. Most people likely to be able to buy council houses had done so. Transfers of local authority stock to alternative 'social landlords' has become a more important issue.

Nevertheless a brief discussion of the history and implications of the council house sales issue is appropriate. The Housing Act of 1980 provided a statutory right to most tenants to buy their own houses, at market prices less a discount based on length of tenancy ranging from 33 to 50 per cent.

The debate about the justification for selling social housing was partly a technical one about the actual effect of such sales on the housing effort as a whole and partly an ideological one about tenants' rights. There is a trade-off here between the rights of actual tenants and the interests of potential future tenants whose needs may not be met so easily because public authorities have lost control over some of their stock. The trade-off was made more evident by the refusal of the Conservative government to let all the proceeds of sales be recycled into new investment in housing.

The houses that tenants bought were principally in 'good' popular estates. The development within these estates of a mixture of owner-occupation and renting may be seen as desirable for the future of such estates, in the long run extending social mixing and social diversity to those estates. However, that development reinforced the gap between the 'good' estates and the 'bad'. In this way, it reinforced a situation in which renting of social housing is seen as a much inferior option to ownership. This development was influenced by government policies which pushed up rent levels, leaving subsidy to the benefit system, thus increasing the incentive for those required to pay full rents to seek to buy.

The provision of discounts weakened the economic arguments for sales; older houses that are, perhaps quite reasonably, sold to long-term sitting tenants at low prices still have to be replaced, if there is outstanding housing need, by new, expensive houses. Similarly, while the houses in the best state of repair were sold, local authorities were left with a stock of deteriorating houses, whose repair costs had to be met out of a falling rental income.

This issue draws our attention to a variation of the same anomaly as exists within the owner-occupied sector: there is a vast gap between the original, 'historic' costs of housing, and modern 'replacement' costs. In the owner-occupied sector, someone who bought a house, say in the 1960s, for £2,000 may today be repaying a minute (by modern standards) mortgage. If he or she dies, heirs will receive an asset worth many times the original price.

In the local authority sector, a similar house may today, assuming rents have moved in line with prices, be yielding the local authority a 'profit', which it returns to the rent pool to subsidize newer houses. What is a fair rent for such a house? And if the occupier wants to buy, what is a fair price? There are no right answers to these questions; the whole situation is riddled with anomalies. To treat such a tenant well is to give a privilege relative to those who are still seeking local authority accommodation. To treat him or her harshly is to emphasize his or her disadvantage relative to the long-term owner-occupier. However, in the long run the consequence of the processes described here has been to intensify the difficulties in providing adequate housing for those most in need.

CONCLUSIONS

The latter part of this chapter has particularly emphasized the issues that have arisen from the interaction between Britain's various housing sectors with the growth of owner-occupation and the decline of private renting. The interactions here are complex. Studies of housing have given attention to movement between the sectors, examining the filtering hypothesis which suggests that the benefits of new houses, even at the top of the owner-occupier market, filter down to contribute to the reduction of housing need. Superficially, this seems plausible. However, the 'chains' that have been traced resulting from new houses at the 'top' end of the system are often short. Typically, they extend down only to a young new entrant to owner-occupation, perhaps from that part of the private rented sector where the needs of the young mobile middle class are met, perhaps merely forming a new separate household for the first time (Murie et al., 1976; Forrest et al., 1990). The same seems to be true of purchased social housing when it is later sold by the original buyer.

At least three very different kinds of housing 'career' can be detected. One of these involves movement into or entirely within the owner-occupied sector as described above. Another involves movement, either on separation from a parental home or via the private rented sector, to social housing, but then stops there for the rest of life. A third involves difficulty in moving from the private rented sector to either of the other sectors.

These divisions may have equally serious implications for the allocation of opportunities and for territorial justice in our society. Owner-occupation conveys benefits which are passed on through inheritance, while the other sectors do not. These social divisions may be reinforced across time – this issue is attracting increasing attention; see, for example, Hamnett (1991). However, even owner-occupation is increasingly stratified in terms of the age and quality of the housing and in terms of when individuals achieved that status.

Most seriously, though, while it is accepted that the concentration of social problems in certain areas raises policy concerns far beyond those of housing policy, it is important to recognize how housing policy has been, and is, exacerbating these problems. Most fundamentally, it is disturbing that council housing, which was conceived as housing 'for the working classes', or even 'for everyone' in a brief utopian dream in the 1940s, is now increasingly seen, like the comparable sector in the USA, as welfare housing, where the 'dangerous poor' are segregated and need to be contained. It is not clear that the agnosticism of the Blair governments, as expressed in the quotation above from Hilary Armstrong, offers a solution to this problem. The concerted efforts proposed by the Social Exclusion Unit to address the constellations of problems are to be welcome, but surely the limitations of this approach are well expressed by Lee and Murie (1998, p. 37) when they say:

> If the situation where only those with no choice move into the social rented sector is to be avoided, a more radical rebuilding of that sector is required. That involves a new look at the structure of housing markets and the range of choice offered in different parts of it.

Now that issue is being joined by another issue, difficulties facing those forming new households in securing decent accommodation at costs they can afford. The decline of the social housing sector, and particularly the low rates of housing replacements in that sector, combine with rising prices in the owner-occupation sector to severely limit the opportunities open to new households. It is difficult to estimate rates of change in housing need and the relationship between that and any change in housing supply. A Joseph Rowntree Foundation report has estimated that about 210,000 new homes are needed in England each year whilst, over the past five years, only an average of 154,000 have been provided. This leads to a warning that by 2022 there will be a shortfall of 1.1 million (Joseph Rowntree Foundation, 2002).

The whole issue is complicated by population movements within the country, reducing housing pressure in some areas where jobs are scarce and increasing it elsewhere (for example, in London and south-east England). What is clear, however, is that leaving both the movement of people and the allocation of houses largely to market forces seems to be generating a new housing crisis in parts of the UK.

In the 1980s and 1990s the stance of the Conservative government was that housing should be treated as far as possible as a market commodity, it should figure as little as possible as a social policy issue (and then as mainly an issue about subsidizing low-income rent-payers through housing benefit). Since 1997 Labour has done very little to reverse that policy. Building of social housing remains at a very low level. Meanwhile, in a situation in which two-thirds of UK housing is owner-occupied, issues about the functioning of that part of the housing market (particularly for new, relatively low-income households) are throwing up a series of problems. Can the government go on treating this as not a matter for social policy?

SUGGESTIONS FOR FURTHER READING

Balchin's *Housing Policy* (1995) and Malpass and Murie's *Housing Policy and Practice* (1999) both provide good introductions to the key policy issues. Some up-to-date essays on various issues in housing policy are contained in Williams (ed.), *New Directions in Housing Policy: Towards Sustainable Housing* (1997) and in Wilcox (ed.), *Housing Finance Review* (1998). The Joseph Rowntree Foundation's report (2002) quoted in this chapter explores many of the developing issues. As that Foundation is very active in housing studies its website may also be worth consulting (www.jrf..org.uk). The website for official data on housing is, at the time of writing, www.dtlr.gov.uk, but as the department has just dropped transport from its remit the 't' may in due course be expected to disappear from that label.

Chapter 11

UK Social Policy in Comparative Perspective

- Introduction
- Comparing spending levels
- Effectiveness in social expenditure
- Classifying social policy systems: regime theory
- Conclusions
- Suggestions for further reading

Introduction

This chapter will explore ways to evaluate social policy in the UK by comparing it with that in other countries. While it has been suggested that there are ways in which policies in the various countries that constitute the UK are diverging they remain, so far, very similar – hence it is that unit rather than Britain or England that is compared with other countries. On the other side of the equation the comparison will be primarily with the other members of the European Union, though some comments will be included on other countries in the world. The choice of the EU as a comparison has been influenced by the availability of comparative data, but it is also justifiable inasmuch as it confines comparison to a group of nations without markedly divergent standards of living from those of the UK. Inevitably if one goes outside the EU one finds greater divergence, and of course very low levels of social expenditure in many nations.

Throughout the chapter, difficulties about making comparisons will be stressed. Data on social policy expenditure and on other social policy outputs is very difficult to compare when it is produced by very different policy systems. Furthermore, when the data from a number of nations are put together in the form of a table, whether it is desirable to be at the 'top' of that table is in the end a value judgement. For example, as was indicated in chapter 1, the general perspective of the author is concern about the effectiveness of public social policy. This will tend to involve a view that high levels of expenditure are necessary. But that is not a view that would go unchallenged by those who consider state intervention in the lives of citizens to be undesirable. Furthermore, even in relation to a generally pro-social-policy stance it has to be accepted that it may be important to attain levels of social and economic organization – involving high employment and coping families – in which the need for public intervention is minimized. In the comparative literature, for example, an analysis of one relatively low-spending country, Australia, will be found, in which it has been argued that egalitarian goals have been effectively pursued through the promotion of employment, with wage protection and other measures to promote the welfare of employees rather than high levels of expenditure on social benefits (Castles, 1985; Castles and Mitchell, 1992).

Comparing Spending Levels

Quite the most simple way of comparing nations in terms of their social policy is to look at their relative social protection spending levels, adjusted to take into account their relative wealth. Table 11.1 quotes European Union data for 1999 on this, listing countries from the highest relative spender to the lowest. Social protection expenditure is what was defined as social security in chapter 5. While it will be obvious that social policy expenditure involves more than this, it dominates the social policy budget.

Table 11.1 shows that the United Kingdom is well below most EU countries when looked at in this way. European social policy spending is relatively high from a wider world perspective. Countries such as the United States, Australia, Canada and Japan come out below the UK when a wider cross-section of countries is considered.

A comparison of nations in terms of overall social protection expenditure is necessarily rather crude. In the introduction it was suggested that there is a need to consider the extent to which social policy goals may be met by policies other than direct expenditure. A direct reference was made there to employment. Table 11.2 picks up that theme with reference to indices of employment and unemployment in the European Union. While the UK figures here are good, relative to those of Germany, France and Italy, the UK has not had markedly greater success than some of the very

Table 11.1   Social protection expenditure in the European Union countries, 1999

Country	Expenditure as % of the national Gross Domestic Product (GDP)
Sweden	32.9
France	30.3
Germany	29.5
Denmark	29.4
Austria	28.5
Belgium	28.2
Netherlands	28.1
Finland	26.7
Greece	25.5
Italy	25.3
Portugal	22.9
Luxemburg	21.9
United Kingdom	20.9
Spain	20.0
Ireland	14.7

Source: European Commission (2002) p. 29.

Table 11.2   Unemployment and employment rates (%) in various other EU nations

	Unemployment rate January 2001	Employment rate, 2000 15–64 year olds
Netherlands	2.7	73
Austria	3.7	68
Ireland	3.8	65
Denmark	4.6	65
United Kingdom	5.2	72
Sweden	5.4	71
Belgium	6.8	61
Germany	7.7	65
France	8.5	62
Finland	9.3	67
Italy	9.8	54
Spain	13.3	55

Sources: National Statistics (2001), table C51; European Commission (2002).

Table 11.3 Percentages (rounded-up) of population in various age groups

	Whole EU	UK	Spain	Sweden
Under 15s	17.0	19.2	15.3	18.6
15–64s	67.0	65.2	68.3	64.0
65–79s	12.4	11.7	12.8	12.5
80–	3.7	3.9	3.6	4.9

Source: European Commission (2001) p. 114.

high social protection spenders in the European Union (particularly the Netherlands and Sweden) in providing work for all who want it.

Another consideration when comparing the expenditure of nations is their demographic structure. Social policy expenditure tends to be particularly needed at the beginning and the end of the life cycle. In particular a high need for pensions and health care amongst the elderly can have a strong impact upon social policy expenditure. In this respect, however, there are no great differences between the European Union nations. Table 11.3 therefore simply highlights the overall demographic data for the EU, that for the UK and that for two nations at either extreme in terms of the percentage in the 15–64-age group. On this basis the United Kingdom's demography may seem to offer some slight reason for the UK to be a more modest spender than Sweden or Spain. But these differences are not great and a choice of other comparator nations undermines this explanation. For example, the Netherlands has only 13.5 per cent of its population over 65, compared with the UK's 15.6 per cent, and France and Germany both have very similar percentages to the UK's amongst this group.

However, all that has been said so far in this section needs to be challenged by the proposition that it is not what nations spend that is important but how they spend it. This is the subject of the next section.

Effectiveness in Social Expenditure

Any consideration of the effectiveness of social expenditure raises complicated questions about what social expenditure is trying to achieve. Many questions may be raised about this. If the well-being of the nation as a whole is what is at stake then, echoing the topics of some of the chapters of this book, there are questions about whether some nations are healthier than others, better educated, have more effective labour markets, are better housed and so on. On the other hand if social policy is seen as primarily a force towards the reduction of inequalities and poverty a rather different set of questions needs to be addressed, about variations in the extent to which policies operate redistributively. Both of these kinds of questions raise difficult methodological problems for comparative studies. It is impossible to do justice to them all in a brief chapter. However, some key observations will be reported on some issues on which some comparable outcome data are available: health differences (which may be seen to reflect the impact of a wide range of other policies as well as health care), poverty levels and the effectiveness of income-redistribution measures upon the latter.

Health differences

Two measures tend to offer good general guides to differences in health standards between nations: infant mortality rates (deaths in the first year of life per 1000 live births) and life expectancies at birth. The figures for the European Union nations are remarkably similar, so table 11.4 only highlights the best and the worst cases. They do not reflect well on the UK's record.

Statistics also show premature death rates from circulatory diseases to be particularly high in the UK relative to other EU countries, only exceeded by the rates for Finland and the Irish Republic.

Health outcomes are, as was explored in chapter 6, not necessarily reflections of health service expenditure. Nevertheless it is appropriate to explore the impact of expenditure differences. Table 11.5 takes just one of the indices looked at in table 11.4, female life expectancy, and relates it to health-expenditure data. While there are some maverick cases – Luxemburg and Denmark – there does seem to be some tendency for life

Table 11.4 Mortality indices for European Union countries, 1999

	Infant mortality rate	Male life expectancy	Female life expectancy
Sweden	3	77	82
Spain	5	75	83
Ireland	5	74	79
Portugal	5	72	79
United Kingdom	6	75	80
Greece	6	76	81
European Union	**5**	**77**	**81**

Source: European Commission (2001) p. 124.

Table 11.5 Female life expectancy and health expenditure for European Union countries, 2000

Country	Female life expectancy	Heath expenditure as % of GDP
Spain	83	7.1
France	82	9.6
Italy	82	8.4
Sweden	82	8.4
Belgium	81	8.8
Germany	81	10.6
Greece	81	8.3
Luxemburg	81	5.9
Netherlands	81	8.6
Austria	81	8.2
Finland	81	6.9
United Kingdom	80	6.7
Denmark	79	10.6
Ireland	79	6.4
Portugal	79	7.8
European Union	**81**	**8.0**

Source: Data adapted from tables in Annex 2 in European Commission (2001).

expectancy and health expenditure to be correlated. The UK is thus a low spender with a relatively low female life expectancy.

Poverty and income distribution

Evidence about poverty is clearly very important for the evaluation of the social policy performance of a nation. But there are two kinds of difficulties about this topic. One is (as has already been suggested, see chapter 5, pp. 122–3) that it should not be taken for granted that the alleviation of poverty is a central objective of social policy. That is a matter of individual value judgement, and even if it is regarded as important it should not be taken as self-evident that those who have dominated policy formation share that view.

The other difficulty is that issues about the incidence of poverty go right to the heart of the problems of what we mean by social policy, since the factors that generate any particular income distribution in society will be a consequence both of a wide range of policy interventions and of the operation of economic factors with which governments may choose not to interfere. As far as that last issue is concerned assumptions are sometimes made, particularly by advocates of the desirability of letting market forces reign, that there is some 'natural' economic order prior to government intervention. In practice, government interventions to protect some economic interests and to interfere with others have such a long history that it is impossible to identify some point at which that 'natural order' prevailed. It is not appropriate to explore that issue further here; rather, we may for the purposes of this discussion recognize the importance of a distinction between pre- and post-transfer incomes.

In chapter 5 some of the problems about providing a satisfactory measure of poverty were discussed. When we come to comparisons between nations it is inevitable that a variety of relatively unsatisfactory measures are used. Most of the more sophisticated approaches to the measurement of poverty would require at the very least a single cross-national study using the same methods in each country, and even then cultural differences might make extrapolation between societies difficult. The alternative therefore is to use measures that look at patterns of inequality within nations (coefficients, for example, that measure the ratios between high and low incomes) or to define poverty in each society in terms of proportions with incomes below some percentage of the mean or median income in that society. These measures inevitably relativize poverty since to be seriously below the average in a poor country will mean having a standard of living very much inferior to those in a similar position in a rich country. While European differences in this respect are comparatively slight from a worldwide perspective, table 11.6 provides data on median incomes alongside data for each European country, showing the percentage of persons with incomes below 60 per cent of that median. In terms of those remarks, the position in the United Kingdom, with a relatively high percentage with low incomes, may be interpreted as alternatively mitigated by a relatively high median or reflecting badly upon the failure of a comparatively rich nation to minimize poverty. The addition of worldwide data would show an even more striking contrast between a high median and high levels of low income in the United States.

The findings reported in table 11.6 are also analysed by age group. The results show that the UK had, in that year, the worst poverty rate for children under 16 (26 per cent as against an EU average of 20) and the third worst rate (after Spain and Portugal) for people over 65 (27 per cent compared with an EU average of 20).

When looking at the effectiveness of social policy interventions it is useful to consider the relationship between pre- and post-transfer income distributions. 'Transfer' here means taking account both tax deductions and social benefit additions. Marlier and Cohen-Solal (2000) have examined this. Their study suggests that amongst non-pensioner households the

Table 11.6   Low income in the European Union, 1995

Country	Households below 60% of median (%)	Median income (unit devised to reflect purchasing power parities)
Denmark	11	12,813
Luxemburg	12	18,953
Netherlands	12	11,507
Germany	16	12,813
France	16	11,958
Belgium	17	12,605
Ireland	18	8,937
Spain	18	7,585
Italy	19	8,650
United Kingdom	19	11,337
Greece	21	7,216
Portugal	22	6,300

Source: European Commission (2001) pp. 120–1.
Note: This is rather older data than some of the other material quoted in this chapter. Clearly compilation of such statistics takes time. It should also be noted that two recent additions to the EU, Sweden and Finland, are missing.

UK, along with Ireland, stands out as having higher levels of pre-redistribution poverty than elsewhere in the EU. Then, while benefits dramatically reduce poverty in Denmark and have very little impact upon poverty in Greece and Portugal, they do have some impact in the UK but insufficient to lift the country out of the lower ranks of the poverty 'league'. The UK's record in respect of the alleviation of pensioner poverty is a little better (a finding also confirmed in a study by Bradshaw and Chen, 1997). Some caution is needed in the interpretation of these findings, therefore only their key points are reported here. They are based upon an essentially simple analysis which takes a very generalized view of data, has to deal in a robust way with many methodological problems and leaves many questions unanswered. The data are rather old, and it has been noted (see Chapter 5) that the UK government has recently given rather more attention to both pensioner poverty and family poverty.

One particular problem with comparisons between pre- and post-transfer income is that they generally only take into account income, and neglect benefits in kind. An alternative methodology, which evaluates benefits but which cannot at the same time easily contrast poverty levels has been pioneered by Bradshaw, asking respondents in a sample of countries to assess the benefits accruing to typical families (see Bradshaw et al., 1993).

A particular problem about the absence of consideration of the impact of services arises from the impossibility of quantifying the comparative impact of health services in any society where these are provided directly rather than via social insurance schemes. This is of course the case with the UK. In the UK in 1996–7:

> Over half the income . . . that the poorest 10% of households receive is in the form of 'benefits-in-kind'. The poorest households received £1894 worth of services from the National Health Service, representing over a quarter of their final income.   (Gordon and Townsend, 2000, p. 14)

Of course richer households receive quite a lot of benefits from the NHS and other services, particularly free education (see Le Grand, 1982, for a discussion about the extent to which services redistribute), but the proportionate effects of these benefits upon a high income is much less than upon a low income.

Nevertheless, data on the relationship between pre- and post-transfer incomes throws an interesting light upon an important argument about social policy systems. In recent times there has been a considerable debate about the extent to which benefits are effectively targeted. *Prima facie*, it might be expected that a country like the UK that has largely turned its back upon social insurance and concentrates instead upon poverty relief through means-testing and tax credits would be more effective at reducing poverty and inequality than nations where social insurance is dominant. Yet this is not the case. How then is this explained?

The most systematic examination of this issue is an article by Korpi and Palme (1998). A crucial explanation of the 'paradox' that less well targeted systems redistribute more effectively lies in the higher levels of expenditure in those systems (as shown in much of the overall expenditure data above) and in the very low levels of benefits often provided to the poor by targeted systems. Korpi and Palme (p. 682) argue:

> Because of their low ceilings for earnings replacement, targeted programs and basic security programs stimulate program exit among the middle classes and increase the demand for private insurance.

Contrastingly:

> By providing earnings-related benefits and non-means-tested benefits, the encompassing model generates incentives to work and also avoids poverty traps. Furthermore, if citizens find that they get significant benefits in return for their taxes, their take-home pay is no longer the only basis for work incentives.   (Ibid.)

Korpi and Palme's 'encompassing model' is often described in the British literature as the 'universalist' model. The argument for universalism featured much in the arguments about UK social policy between Left and Right in the period between 1950 and 1980. Now child benefit and a social insurance pension seriously eroded in value remain the only clearly 'universalist' elements in social security. But the issues explored here remain very pertinent to arguments about the universalism of the National Health Service.

Korpi and Palme's article is one amongst a large number of efforts to classify nations in terms of the leading characteristics of their social policy systems. The way in which the United Kingdom is placed in these classifications is discussed briefly in the next section.

Classifying Social Policy Systems: Regime Theory

The main approach to the classification of welfare states is called 'regime theory'. This theory emerged from the work of various writers, of whom Gøsta Esping-Andersen (1990) is the most important. This theory identifies three regime types, whose social policies are distinguishable in terms of their contributions to social solidarity. Goodin et al. (1999, p. 39) describe the three regimes as follows:

- The *liberal welfare regime*: 'rooted in capitalist economic premises' confining the 'state to a merely residual social welfare role'.
- The *social democratic welfare regime*: 'rooted in socialist economic premises' and assigning the state 'a powerful redistributive role'.
- The *corporatist welfare regime*: 'rooted in communitarian social market economics' which 'sees the welfare regime as primarily a facilitator of group-based mutual aid and risk pooling'.

The United Kingdom is seen as a liberal regime along with Australia, the United States and New Zealand. The social democratic regimes are found in Scandinavia, while most of the continental members of the European Union are put in the corporatist category. The distinctive characteristics of the different regimes are seen as a product of political and cultural processes over a long period of time, reflecting dominant social groups and ideologies.

The approach to comparative analysis adopted by Esping-Andersen is rooted in the notion that some social policy systems may reflect and contribute to social solidarity. The concept of 'decommodification' is used by Esping-Andersen to distinguish the extent to which, in some countries, social policies provide entitlements to benefits in ways that are relatively uninfluenced by whether people are (or have been) labour-market participants. The decommodified systems of Scandinavia are contrasted with corporatist and liberal systems which more clearly reflect labour market divisions and market ideologies. These are attempts to classify national systems as a whole, with the inclusiveness of the Scandinavian systems set relative to other systems.

Esping-Andersen's initial formulation of regime theory was criticized by writers who were concerned about the lack of analysis of relationships between men and women, and of family ideologies, in his work (see, in particular, O'Connor, 1996; Sainsbury 1996; Daly, 2000). It was pointed out that while the idea of decommodification was that some welfare systems effectively reduce dependence upon the labour market, the issue for women in many societies is not dependence on the labour market but dependence upon men. In this sense the crucial distinction for women is between systems that link entitlements to 'the male breadwinner model', with women largely seen as 'dependants', and those that work with an 'individual' model (Sainsbury, 1996). Paradoxically, systems that increase the commodification of women, by expecting them to be labour-market participants, may contribute to reducing their dependence upon men. However, inasmuch as the individual character of, for example, the Swedish model of social policy rests upon an expectation that there will be a high level of labour-market participation by women, this is in some respects coerced participation, given the expectations about work imposed by the social security system. This is even more evident in nations where the rise of female labour-market participation has been recent, such as the UK. It is also often participation in the least advantaged parts of the labour market (where work is insecure and poorly paid).

The feminist work also draws attention to the importance of familist ideologies in influencing the politics of social security and determining the expectations embedded within it. Attention has been drawn to the extent to which there is a Roman Catholic and/or Southern European approach to the design of social security – alternatively to be seen either as more 'protective' of the housewife outside the labour market or as increasing her 'dependency' within the family (the source for this argument is, particularly, Ferrara, 1996).

The literature on female welfare also suggests that there is a need to consider alongside issues about the working of the income-maintenance system, issues about provision for child care and about the expectations of the roles women play (and of course men might play) in the care of sick and disabled adults (see Ungerson, 1997, 2000; and Daly and Lewis, 1998). Here are areas of social life where there are political choices being made first, about the role the state will play, and secondly about the extent such a role will involve alternatively the provision of care or the provision of cash benefits to enable people to buy care. The answers to these questions have, in practice, considerable implications for the labour-market participation of women. The high level of Scandinavian female labour-market participation has partly been generated by a willingness of the state to pay women to carry out caring tasks which elsewhere have to be carried out by (generally female) parents and relatives themselves.

What, however, is the bearing of this whole discussion about regime theory upon the way we view the UK in comparative perspective? Regime theory obviously tends to work with a very crude classification of systems. There has been no lack of theorists ready to challenge Esping-Andersen's model, either by moving the more marginal cases into alternative categories, or with new regime types such as the Southern European model mentioned above, or an East Asian regime type and/or an Antipodean one (see Esping-Andersen, 1999, for a response to these). However, the only argument that has been advanced against seeing the UK as a 'liberal' welfare state has come from those who stress the continuing universalism of the health service, rightly pointing out that like so much comparative work, Esping-Andersen's modelling has been driven by the more easily quantified social-transfer systems. The data discussed earlier in this chapter otherwise seem to offer support of various kinds for Esping-Andersen's typification of the UK.

The elements in the reservations about the way the typology handles issues about women are, however, interesting in relation to the UK case. The UK has shown signs of moving away from the 'male-breadwinner' model to the 'individual' model as female labour-market participation has increased. But the individualization of social insurance rights for women has to be seen in the context of the decline of the significance of those rights for all. At the same time social assistance (as was shown in chapter 5) has remained wedded to the 'male-breadwinner' model. When we look at the treatment of single-parent families we encounter a paradox which putting the two theoretical approaches side-by-side helps to highlight. The UK is rather exceptional in the European context in having social-assistance rules that accept that single mothers can remain out of the labour market until all their children reach school-leaving age. Until 1997 the whole thrust of government policy towards this group was to try to maximize their support by potential 'male breadwinners'. Then the Blair governments started to develop an alternative and additional approach to efforts to minimize dependence of these families upon the state, with the promotion of labour-market participation. As was shown in chapter 5, this so far does not extend to compulsion. But it is argued by the government that, in this case, this 'commodification' is in the best interests of single mothers. Well, that may be so when labour-market participation brings with it better benefit and pension entitlements, but is that the case in a 'liberal' welfare state like the UK?

Esping-Andersen defends regime theory for its capacity to sharpen awareness of the politics of welfare states. His original work looked back to the processes that created the different systems. But if his theory is to remain important it has to assist us with the analysis of where systems are going in the future. This is a project he addresses in more recent work (1996, 1999). What does being classified as a 'liberal' welfare state highlight about the UK? First, as suggested by Korpi and Palme, inasmuch as such a system is less likely to provide universal benefits it is more likely to be vulnerable to political attack. A number of writers have drawn attention to the much stronger support for the NHS than for most social benefits. Pensions stand out here as something of an exception, but it is now perhaps the case that it is getting harder and harder to mount a defence of the national insurance element in the system. Secondly, it is argued that very strongly work-related rights to welfare (as particularly entrenched in most of the corporatist/statist regimes) lead to labour-market rigidities. The liberal regimes lack these. Whether that is a good or a bad feature of such regimes was explored to some extent, with particular reference to UK labour market policy in chapter 6 (see particularly pp. 131–2). There is no doubt that this issue plays an important part in the ambivalent role of the UK government in relation to European Union social policy, where the corporatist/statist viewpoint is quite deeply embedded. Thirdly, and this point is perhaps the inverse of the first point, while liberal regimes may be more vulnerable to movements seeking social policy cuts they may equally be more open to social policy innovation inasmuch as there are no deeply embedded expectations of the system.

CONCLUSIONS

The last section concurred with the classification of the UK as a 'liberal' welfare state. Other classifications have seen the UK as a 'Beveridgean' as opposed to a 'Bismarckian' welfare state (Bonoli, 1997). The Beveridge model is seen as more universalistic and more concerned to redistribute to those in greatest need than the Bismarckian one with its relatively strict emphasis upon social insurance, with low levels of redistribution between contributors (entitlements being firmly linked to what is paid in). But there is a problem about seeing the Beveridge model as a 'universalistic' one, which is particularly brought out by the contrast between Beveridge's own country, the UK, and the Scandinavian countries which are alleged by various writers to have also rejected the Bismarckian road. In the UK case, Beveridge's scheme has proved to be peculiarly fragile, given its emphasis upon flat rate contributions and flat rate universal benefits to be underpinned by social assistance or supplemented by private benefits and savings. Efforts made in the 1960s and 1970s to move the UK scheme more in the Bismarckian direction, with graduated contributions and graduated benefits, were influenced by the recognition that such a system would have wider social support. These efforts were too little and too late. The UK now has graduated contributions, which could more honestly be described as social security tax, but flat rate benefits are steadily being eroded in value (or in some cases simply replaced by means-tested benefits. By contrast the Scandinavians have by and large achieved a compromise between Bismarckian and Beveridgean principles with benefit levels influenced by contributions but with strong redistribution towards low contributors. These issues are well explored in the article by Korpi and Palme quoted above.

The fact is that the data examined in the earlier part of this chapter show the UK to be a significantly lower spender on social welfare than most other European nations. It has much in common with Australia, New Zealand and the United States, English-speaking nations to which UK policy makers tend to turn for new social policy ideas.

It has been suggested that there are good reasons for seeing lower spending on social policy as directly correlated with a poorer record on health policy and with a high incidence of poverty. The UK has been shown to have relatively high rates of poverty (or inequality for those readers who are not happy with the rather simplistic approach to the poverty line inevitably used by poverty studies) and to have policies in respect of tax and benefits that do comparatively little to reduce poverty.

While the author has tried to set out all the evidence in neutral terms he has to acknowledge that the UK record seems a very disappointing one for the nation that saw itself in the 1940s as a social policy pioneer.

SUGGESTIONS FOR FURTHER READING

The European Commission regularly produces analyses of the 'social situation' which provide a good basis for comparing the UK with other EU countries; these analyses have been the main sources for the comparisons in this chapter. They are well worth consulting (see European Commission, 2001, 2002). See also their website (www.europa.eu.int/index_en.htm) and particularly publications from Eurostat. For UK statistical sources consult www.statistics.gov.uk.

There is now a large comparative social policy literature. Key sources drawn upon here are the books of Esping-Andersen (1990, 1996, 1999).

However, these may be regarded as too theoretical for the needs of many readers. A good up-to-date introduction to European comparisons is provided by chapter 1 of Taylor-Gooby's edited volume *Welfare States under Pressure* (2001).

Chapter 12

Social Policy, Politics and Society

- Introduction
- Social expenditure in the context of national public expenditure
- Alternative perspectives on social policy and the state
- The quest for efficient and responsive modes of social policy delivery
- Continuing social divisions of welfare
- Conclusions
- Suggestions for further reading

Introduction

This book has given attention to the major policy areas that are conventionally labelled 'social policy'. It has shown that, within these areas, the state is responsible for a wide range of activities. In the chapters on individual policies, a number of weaknesses were noted in the pattern of provision. Yet it is widely suggested today that the state takes on too much, and that the public service sector, of which the social policy areas account for a large proportion, is too large. We need therefore to look, in this final chapter, at some of the general issues regarding the role of social policy in society and at some of the attempts to make social policy, as a whole, more effective and more responsive to popular needs and attitudes. In doing so we will pay attention to 'social divsions': social policy functions very differently according to socio-economic status, gender and ethnic origin.

Social Expenditure in the Context of National Public Expenditure

About two-thirds of UK public expenditure can be described as social expenditure (as defined by the subject matter of this book). Within that two-thirds very nearly two thirds is social protection expenditure (social security, as described in chapter 5).

There was a fairly steady rise in social expenditure in real terms in the UK from the Second World War onwards. That rise continued even after the Conservatives came to power back in 1979, committed to curbing social policy expenditure. While much of the rise of this expenditure up to 1979 will be attributable to policy innovation, since then social and economic change have been important – the ageing of the population, the increase in the number of single-parent families, the lack of work and the increase of low-wage work (increasing the need for in-work benefits, including housing benefit; see Glennerster and Hills (1998) for a more detailed analysis of these issues).

Since social policy is about two-thirds of all public expenditure, any government which is concerned to keep levels of taxation and public sector debt under control will be likely to be concerned about pressures (demographic, economic or political) that tend to lead to a rise of social policy expenditure. While, as was shown in the last chapter, social expenditure levels in the UK are quite modest compared with most of the other EU nations in Northern Europe, a concern about the cost of the UK welfare state has come to dominate politics here. The various political perspectives on this issue will be explored further in the next section.

Alternative Perspectives on Social Policy and the State

The account of the development of social policy in chapter 2 showed how, between 1945 and 1979, there was a relatively high degree of consensus between the major political parties on the case for high levels of social expenditure, rising with the increase in the prosperity of the nation. Nevertheless, in the 1960s and 1970s, some of the complacency about the achievement of the UK 'welfare state' was challenged by academics and pressure groups, drawing attention to continuing problems of poverty and weaknesses in the overall policy framework.

In the early 1960s, researchers, including notably Abel-Smith and Townsend (1965), showed that extensive poverty was still present in the UK. Not only were there large numbers of people living at the subsistence level guaranteed by social assistance, but there were also many, a considerable proportion of whom were in families containing a full-time wage-earner, with incomes below or only a little above that level. Hence, it was shown that the welfare state was neither markedly redistributive nor particularly effective at eradicating poverty.

There were also elements in this developing critique of the welfare state which were critical of the institutional arrangements for policy delivery. The dominance of the medical profession in the NHS was one of the earliest causes for concern. Later, more and more attention began to be given to the notion that welfare was being delivered in a paternalistic way by professionals and bureaucrats with little attention to the interests and needs of beneficiaries; see Deakin (1994) for a good overview of these issues.

The previous three paragraphs outline what may be broadly described as the critique of the welfare state from the Left. While there were always critics of welfare from the political Right, they were relatively lonely voices until the 1970s. The Right-wing critique of social policy slowly gained sustenance from the economic problems the UK was facing. The election of the Conservative government headed by Margaret Thatcher in 1979 contributed to moving these critics much more into the political mainstream. They argued that the size of the redistributive exercise, via taxation and public expenditure, undertaken by the UK government had a disincentive impact on private initiative, and had contributed towards low productivity. They suggested that the scale and scope of the state 'bureaucracy' were such that public resources were inevitably used inefficiently. The people of the UK were alleged to be overtaxed and overgoverned (Harris and Seldon, 1979; Minford, 1984).

This Right-wing perspective sees the provision of social services as the responsibility of the individual and rejects the idea that such services should be redistributive. The role of the state is merely to alleviate the most extreme forms of hardship, but otherwise to stand back from interfering in the market. It is asserted that, instead of depending on a paternalistic state, people should be free to make choices about amounts and kinds of social benefits, just as they make choices about the purchase of ordinary consumer goods.

These advocates of less government involvement, and of the extension of the role of the market, generally have a stance on social equality too. While it could be the case that bureaucratic rigidity and lack of choice in the present social welfare system might be reduced by an extension of the free-market system, changes to such a system might well leave vulnerable low-income groups unprotected. In theory, this might be countered by government interventions to enhance the incomes of the poor and decrease inequality. Hence, the poor would gain both more income and more choice. The difficulty with such compensating changes is that they would entail extensive government intervention to equalize incomes. These would be anathema to those who expound the virtues of free enterprise. They are generally content, instead, to leave the distribution of incomes to be determined by the 'hidden hand' of the market.

In practice, the Conservative governments between 1979 and 1997 moved cautiously towards the Right-wing position (Pierson, 1994). They were eager to cut taxation and expenditure, and 'liberate' market forces, but they were also aware of public attachment to many aspects of social policy, particularly the NHS and the education system. They also, as has already been pointed out, had to face the fact that there were social and economic forces driving social expenditure upwards despite their efforts. After the middle 1980s, they came to see institutional change as important both to curb the power of the bureaucrats and professionals who were believed to be self-interestedly expanding public social services, and to increase the scope for private provision. The 'quasi-market' systems set up in the health, personal social services and education systems came to be the hallmark of the new Conservative social policy.

However, the Conservative governments of this period also countenanced changes in taxation, in the way economic opportunities were distributed and in the rules relating to social benefits which sharply increased inequality in the UK. The official statistics which highlight this most are those examining poverty, which were discussed in chapter 5 (see pp. 122–8).

This discussion has so far highlighted a critique of the UK welfare state from the Left, which has argued that too little is done (particularly for the poor), and a critique from the Right which alternatively asserts that too much is done by the government. Both positions have given some attention to institutional deficiencies, and this theme seems to have been picked up quite strongly by the Conservatives since 1979. At the same time, the Conservatives proved not surprisingly to be pragmatic politicians who moved cautiously in the direction of their Right-wing gurus. Similarly, we find that the Labour Party, out of power for a long while, sought to relocate itself in the middle ground rather than simply taking its lead from the Left-wing critique outlined above. Tony Blair and his colleagues in the new Labour government have been at pains to try to position themselves in relation to the traditional Left/Right argument in a new way. This involves endeavouring to escape from the uni-dimensional form in which that argument is typically expressed – seeing themselves as adopting a 'third' way rather than a 'middle' way. It is not helpful to discuss here the appropriateness of the imagery: whether there is one dimension, two, or more. Readers must, however, make their own judgements as to whether what they are about to read represents a radical repositioning, or as some of the government's critics have suggested, a reformulation of a centre-Right stance (new Conservative rather than new Labour). In making those

judgements, readers must bear in mind that political parties and governments are complex institutions in which there is a continuing process of
interaction between competing values. The Prime Minister, who will be
quoted here, is but the most powerful figure in debates that have been
going on within the government over its future direction.

Tony Blair set out his stance on social policy in a lecture commemorating
William Beveridge. In that lecture, he criticized the Left of the 1970s who
'trapped in a false confusion of means and ends, resisted changing the
welfare state on the grounds that to modernize . . . was to undermine it'
(Blair, 1999). On the other hand, he argued, the Right, in the 1980s and
1990s, 'were not mistaken about the importance of markets and greater
competition. But they failed to see in the modern world that it is not
enough' (ibid.).

Tony Blair went on to set out what he saw 'will be' the five necessary
characteristics of a modern welfare state. These are listed below with some
comments about them.

1　He saw the welfare state as tackling 'social exclusion', a fashionable EU notion
　mixing a relatively vague concept with the idea of focused attention on
　particular outsider groups. Tony Blair suggested some causes of social exclusion,
　such as unemployment, poor education and poor housing. There are problems
　here, discussed in the relevant chapters of this book, as to whether these are
　symptoms rather than causes of social inequalities. If they are only symptomatic
　then very specific interventions to attack them – such as special zones like
　Education Action Zones – will have severe limitations in the absence of wider
　egalitarian policies.

2　He said 'welfare will be a hand up not a hand out', offering a self-help
　perspective that was very much one of the 'Victorian values' to which Margaret
　Thatcher wanted to return. The idea of welfare as itself a 'trap' is one that has
　been widely expressed in US writings (Murray, 1984; Mead, 1986). In chapter
　6, the heavy emphasis put by the government on labour-market participation
　was fully discussed. It was argued that the success of that strategy depends not
　just on what is *done for or to* those who are expected to participate in the
　labour market but also on what is done to ensure that there are real jobs for
　them. In the absence of that, this principle may be used as an excuse for doing
　nothing for those with the greatest difficulties in making use of a 'hand up'.

3　Tony Blair then offered what may be a partial contradiction of his second point,
　saying 'where people really need security, the most help should go to those with
　the most need'. He professed an agnostic stance here, as has been the case with
　various government statements on social security, on the long-standing argu-
　ment between 'universal and targeted help'. It was suggested in chapter 5 that
　the government is nevertheless tending to opt for the targeted approach.

4　Next came a principle regularly stated by all governments: that fraud and abuse
　must be rooted out. This is not something on which there is much disagreement,
　but there is scope for a great deal of argument about the effects of rigorous

anti-fraud measures on perceptions of stigma and under-claiming of benefits and services; see the symposium on this in *Benefits* (1998).

5 Tony Blair next reiterated a Conservative stance discussed above, about the need to develop new ways of delivering welfare, including partnerships between the public and private sectors and the involvement of the voluntary sector. Earlier chapters of this book have identified this theme in various policy areas.

We see here a stance that is very like that of the former Conservative governments on self-help, targeting, the prevention of fraud and new approaches to policy delivery. The concern about social exclusion is rather different, and this was expanded by Blair elsewhere in the lecture to indicate a commitment to the eradication of poverty. Blair criticized his predecessors for the rise in poverty. There are also features of the Blair government's approach to both 'self-help' and delivery institutions that may perhaps be rather different. These will be discussed in the next section.

The Quest for Efficient and Responsive Modes of Social Policy Delivery

It has been shown above that the view that social policy interventions have not achieved the success that might have been expected from the effort put into them has now been widely accepted. It has been recognized that a complex bureaucracy has been developed to provide social services, and that efforts are therefore needed to overcome the resulting institutional problems with the system.

In the 1960s and 1970s, governments devoted a considerable amount of attention to the organization of both central and local government. There was a search for the most rational form of organization. The search was always made difficult by a wide range of political considerations: reorganization might change the balance of power, and alter the opportunities and career prospects of individuals. Moreover, established patterns of organization develop supporting sentiments and loyalties. In any case, the rationalization of government is not an easy process. There are often competing criteria for rationalization which are difficult to assess. For example, there is a conflict between the achievement of uniformity through centralization and the maximization of flexibility through decentralization. The close integration of particular services – like health and the personal social services – may weaken links between those services and other related activities (for example, the provision of housing and the achievement of high environmental standards). Rationalization seems to involve a search for the best arrangement, when perhaps, in reality, there are merely alternative arrangements, each carrying costs and benefits. These are difficult to evaluate. Finally, there are informal aspects to organizational arrangements which develop within formal structures. While, in theory, formal arrangements may be sought to maximize effective informal links, these are particularly difficult to predict. Moreover, one of the effects of a formal reorganization is to distort – and perhaps undermine – informal links operating prior to reorganization.

At central government level, there was, between the mid-1960s and the mid-1970s, a move towards super-departments embracing many different policy areas. The 1980s saw some backing away from this approach. Important here was the 'next steps' initiative whereby policy-making departments delegated their day-to-day policy-delivery tasks to executive agencies.

The 1960s and 1970s also saw a range of experiments aimed at the more effective co-ordination of public services, both at the central and the local level. At the centre, emphasis was on solving problems that cut across departmental boundaries. A small unit called the Central Policy Review Staff was set up in the early 1970s but was eventually axed by Margaret Thatcher in the 1980s. In relation to the local level, the government's concern was with the co-ordination of policy implementation, particularly in deprived areas. In the 1960s, there were Community Development Projects and Educational Priority Areas. Some of the ideas developed by these special initiatives fed into mainstream policies. In the 1980s and 1990s, initiatives like 'city challenge' required local authorities to compete for extra resources to tackle problem areas by putting together bids involving local resources of all kinds. The Blair government seems to be going back to some of the older ideas. At the central level, the Social Exclusion Unit has been developed to try to secure co-ordinated action on problems like street homelessness, deprived housing estates and truancy. At the local level, there is the idea of the development of zones in disadvantaged areas where, with help from some extra cash from the centre, policy innovation and inter-agency co-ordination may be enhanced. There is thus the setting up of Education Action Zones and Health Action Zones. 'Partnership' has become very much a 'buzz word', seen as a device to bring all interests together and solve implementation problems (see Glendinning et al., 2002). It is much too early to judge these new initiatives; however, the judgements on their predecessors do not encourage high hopes (Higgins et al., 1984; Blackstone and Plowden, 1988). The UK system remains one in which, as suggested in chapter 4, innovations in policy implementation alongside the main policy-delivery framework have considerable difficulties to overcome.

One of the most significant innovations in respect of accountability developed by the Conservatives in the 1980s and 1990s involved trying to avoid situations in which one agency was the sole provider of a publicly required service. The existence of monopoly providers was seen to contribute to inefficiency or to give too much power to key staff (particularly professional staff). In education, the Conservatives tried to increase the range of providers and to use parental choice to produce a 'quasi-market' system. In health and the personal social services, ways of splitting purchasers from providers were developed which, while they did little to empower the ultimate 'customers', seemed to offer the possibility of greater controls over providers. The Conservative hope, largely unrealized, was that competition would emerge between providers. This model also allowed for the possibility that the providers might be private bodies, even profit-making bodies. The Labour government has accepted the notion that there may be a range of providers, showing as much suspicion of local authority providers and of professional self-interest as its predecessor. However, it has, at least in respect of health care, backed away from the idea that an actual market can be created.

After the fall of Margaret Thatcher, the Conservative regime led by John Major put a strong emphasis on consumerism. Major's approach to consumerism entailed stressing the importance of information about service outputs to enable people to exercise choice, and exploring ways to provide financial compensation when services failed to deliver outputs or to deal with problems within a specific time-span. This was central to Major's 'citizens' charter'.

It is important to contrast these approaches to public policy with an alternative, which had been more popular on the Left. This was to see the key problem for public accountability as not public monopoly *per se*, but rather the absence of devices for popular participation in decision making (Donnison, 1991). The chief characteristic of this approach was that it sought to establish ways of decentralizing decision making. In the late 1970s and early 1980s, the lead in this decentralization movement was provided by Labour- (and sometimes Liberal-) controlled local authorities (Gyford, 1985, 1991). Decentralization took the form of the breakdown of some authorities into sub-areas with local offices and local committees, the development of tenants' participation in housing management, and so on.

One of the implications of the abandonment of the quasi-market idea as undesirable or impractical is that it leaves these problems about citizen-control unresolved. The idea that public services might become like high street retail shops, in which consumers might make choices between alternatives with their characteristics and their prices reasonably openly displayed, seemed to offer an approach to these issues. Its abandonment brings us back to the conflict about central control. On one side, there is the argument that centralization offers a uniform approach to standards, the equal treatment of different areas in a relatively homogeneous and compact country and the prevention of particularism and corruption at the local level. On the other side stands the view that there can only be real public accountability if the units of government are small and if local participatory devices can be developed.

It might be expected that, given the critique of the traditional methods of social policy delivery outlined above, the second side in that argument would be winning. Perhaps devolution to the much smaller Scottish, Welsh and Northern Irish societies is a step in that direction. However, as was pointed out in chapter 3, that leaves much the largest country in the UK undivided. Moreover, effective participation requires much smaller units. Yet the controls over local government are being increased, and most of the experiments in devolution within local authorities have been undermined by resource constraints.

The Blair government's position on this issue is ambivalent. Pronouncements on local government as a whole, on education and on the personal social services suggest the encouragement of experimentation at the local level, some of which may enhance local participation. On the other hand, there is a deep suspicion of local government – particularly in the light of evidence from some authorities of inefficiency and corruption in a context of long-standing one-party control and low levels of electoral participation. The government is making it very clear that local autonomy is something to be earned. The question must be asked whether independence can be enhanced by such a tutelage system and whether government ministers really want to release control over those issues most likely to be contested.

Issues about information play an important role in these struggles over control. The 'citizens' charter' ideas presuppose that making information available to citizens will increase their capacity to participate. Here again information issues sit most comfortably inside the 'high street' model of consumer accountability, helping us to choose our schools, hospitals, etc. In the absence of those choices, their function must be to enable us to participate in political decision processes. Chapter 3 explored some of the difficulties about this. The electoral-choice approach to control is a very blunt weapon. Furthermore, inasmuch as data may be used in election campaigns, there are strong temptations for politicians to manipulate it, e.g. the number of people on hospital waiting lists, indices of educational achievement, and numbers of places on employment schemes filled. Sophisticated information technology also increases the scope for the collection of data to facilitate central control over local authorities, teachers, doctors and so on.

As suggested in chapter 4 (see p. 89), where Newman's analysis (2001) of the 'new Labour' approach to these matters was discussed, contradictory threads can be seen in current policy: stressing central accountability, encouraging local democracy, indicating distrust of some of the traditional democratic models and setting up complex partnerships which may be difficult to hold to account.

Fortunately, through all this conflict over local democracy and despite the search for new methods of delivering services, mechanisms have survived that enable citizens to take action over individual grievances. In principle, the two categories into which grievance procedures fall are nearly as old as the nation-state itself: appeals to courts, and complaints to elected representatives. In practice, they take modern forms very different from these traditional grievance procedures. In centuries past, litigation *vis-à-vis* dissatisfaction with an administrative agency depended on an elaborate, costly legal procedure whereby the royal prerogative was invoked on behalf of the aggrieved citizen. It is a little easier to challenge administrative decision making now. Individuals may secure legal aid or the assistance of a voluntary organization to enable them to take grievances against public authorities to the High Court. The Human Rights Act of 1998 may well further facilitate such challenges (see Lester in Jowell and Oliver, 2000).

For everyday purposes, though, what is much more important is that a large number of lower 'courts', generally known as 'tribunals', have been set up to deal with appeals against decisions of public agencies. Furthermore, in many cases, there may be direct appeals to the courts or a supervisory tribunal, against the decisions of these bodies.

The area of social policy in which tribunals are most important is social security. Individuals may appeal against most decisions taken by social security officials. There is a two-tier appeal system for social security and housing benefits, with commissioners who operate at the top level, whose decisions are regarded as precedents for lower-tier decisions. Special systems, less detached from day-to-day decision makers, exist to deal with claimants dissatisfied with social fund decisions.

In the housing sector, tribunals deal only with a limited range of disputes, over rent levels and security of tenure in the private sector. Disputes between tenants and local authorities are not covered; these have to go to county courts.

Parents may appeal against the refusal of admission of a child to a school and against a child's exclusion from a school. A weakness of these procedures is that the appeal system is run by the very bodies whose decisions are contested. On the other hand, disputes regarding decisions about the appropriate schooling for a child with learning difficulties are heard by an independent tribunal.

The case for tribunals is that they provide for a separate (and, in the best cases, independent) review of decisions, particularly those involving official discretion. They are less important for the control of policy itself; it is comparatively rare for tribunal decisions to indicate a significant defect in policy. To aggrieved individuals, they offer not so much a chance to change policy as an opportunity to check a controversial application of policy. A Council on Tribunals oversees tribunal arrangements, and reports (if necessary, publicly) its observations to the government. There is still, nevertheless, a suspicion that some tribunals are too closely identified with the government agencies whose decisions they are expected to examine.

A number of Commissioners (popularly called 'ombudsmen') have been appointed, who are able to investigate complaints against the administration. There is a Parliamentary Commissioner who investigates individual public grievances about central government departments and agencies. There is a small team of Local Government Commissioners who investigate complaints about local government. There is also a Health Service Commissioner for the NHS. These Commissioners are concerned solely with maladministration. They do not deal with policy, so long as that policy has a clear statutory foundation. Nor do they deal with decisions that involve statutorily legitimate discretion or professional judgement. They provide, therefore, like the tribunals, only a limited protection for citizens against the worst abuses of administrative behaviour, not an opportunity to participate in policy formulation or to comment on its overall implementation. 'Below' the 'commissioners', in the sense that dissatisfied people may still go on to them, are various more local complaint-resolution systems, in particular procedures for the formal examination of health complaints.

The underlying issue throughout this section concerns the extent to which the UK has a political and administrative system which tends to exclude meaningful participation, except through representative political institutions or through very specific devices to deal with individual grievances for consumers of social services. There has been a failure to make a coherent case for quasi-market controls over social policy, except by way of the wholesale privatization favoured by some Right-wing ideologues. The case for better public control over public services is widely accepted. Inasmuch as the policies of the new Labour government have a new philosophical underpinning, it seems to come from those who see the issues about more responsive government as of central importance (Giddens, 1998). Yet, outside the devolution policies, which may of course have 'knock on' implications for other approaches to decentralization, there is little sign that a shift in this direction is occurring. In many ways, the big preoccupations of ministers are about how to extend their 'reaches' deeper into local authorities, hospitals and schools. Meanwhile, the older, more individualistic approaches to citizen control through appeals and complaints remain very important.

Continuing Social Divisions of Welfare

This chapter has looked at the general issues about social policy and society by first considering the overall picture of social policy expenditure, and then by looking at the various political perspectives on offer. It showed how the new Labour government has sought to provide a distinctively new approach, turning its back on a perspective which saw the central issue for social policy development to be to improve on the task initiated by Labour in 1945–51. In doing so, it has picked up the emphasis of the Right on self-help, targeting and the use of mixed approaches to policy delivery.

The acceptance by a Labour government of so much of the social policy agenda that was seen in the early 1980s as a new and discordant approach to social policy has reinforced the shift in the terms of the political debate. The issue now, for those with a critical perspective on social policy, is whether the more progressive elements in the Labour agenda – the concern about social exclusion, for example – can be sustained, despite a context in which so much of the social and economic *status quo* is accepted. A crucial factor is the firm adoption of a perspective which stresses labour-market participation. This involves a strong ideological emphasis on paid work, privileging it over other forms of social participation. It also involves a faith in the long-run capacity of the market to deliver acceptable jobs, and to solve the problems of poverty and social exclusion. This is linked with a view of the key role to be played by education and training, which seems alarmingly dependent on a growth of opportunities for skilled workers. This is the 'high road' to the future of work outlined by Wheelock (1999) and discussed in chapter 6. Yet, as suggested there, the evidence on the way the labour market is developing gives little scope for optimism.

Richard Titmuss (1958) argued that there are 'social divisions' in the welfare system, involving private or tax subsidies alongside state welfare, which reflect, and may reinforce, social divisions in society (see also Sinfield, 1978). A related vein of work has shown that better-off families may secure considerably more state-subsidized services than worse-off families (Le Grand, 1982; Townsend, 1979). Two crucial ingredients contributing to this are that the better off are likely to make much more use of the most expensive elements in the education system (particularly higher education) and that they are likely to make more effective demands upon a state health care system. However, the thrust of this work is a little different from that in Titmuss's and Sinfield's essays. It points to under-use, by poorer people, of universally available services, as opposed explicit subsidies for private privileges.

It is worth considering to what extent the implications of both approaches to differential experience of social policy can be generalized to explore the association between class inequalities *before* and those *after* social policy inputs. This relationship could originally be traced through a simple comparison between the welfare expectations of two broad 'classes' distinguished by work, an upper non-manual class and a lower manual one. The distinction is not so applicable today largely because of the increasing merging in the middle. It is perhaps more appropriate now to work with a 'three-class' model which recognises:

1   that the market situations and tax situations of the very well off have improved;
2   that policy developments in favour of the traditional working class have, wherever employment can be maintained, contributed to a merging of that group with the lower earners amongst non-manual workers;
3   that falling opportunities for unskilled manual work and the related high unemployment have separated this group off from the rest of the old working class.

One way of dealing with the last of these three developments has been to characterize the third group as an 'under-class' (Wilson, 1981, 1987; Dahrendorf, 1985; Field, 1989). But this usage has been linked with arguments about the behavioural characteristics of the disadvantaged, emphasizing not social but psychological processes (Murray, 1984, 1990). Mann condemns the attempt to identify the economic and social forces that create this division as 'sloppy' sociology (Mann, 1994, p. 94), encouraging a popular media usage which, in treating the underprivileged as in this sense 'outside' of society, blames the victims and derives harsh policy prescriptions from its focus on behaviour. The under-class concept implies, at best, the absence of a relationship to other classes, at worst a deliberate opting out of society. In the latter sense it is used with stigmatising intent.

Nevertheless it is fruitful to explore the extent to which 'divisions of welfare' exist in the UK, of the kind suggested by the 'three-class' model set out above. We see then clear evidence of a variety of situations in which advantaged individuals may opt out of the state social policy system, particularly in respect of health services and education, and more importantly in arrangements for most social security (particularly pensions), social care, and housing, where private arrangements are expected of them.

Then, for those who receive the benefits of state policies, there is a wide range of evidence that service standards will differ according to income levels or employment security. These differences are often perceptible in terms of differences in services between different regions or localities. The data on inequalities in health make these differences particularly evident.

In the UK the expansion of the 'welfare state' accompanied, and contributed to, the erosion of the old non-manual/manual divide but then this movement towards classlessness was undermined by two things. One of these was the massive advance of unemployment, economic insecurity and poverty. The other was the widening of the income gap through increased rewards and reduced taxation for those with the highest earnings during the 1980s. This was accompanied by deterioration of the more universal public services – health and education – increasing the incentives for the more advantaged to use private services. While unemployment now seems to be a less serious problem than it was in the 1980s and 1990s, it was suggested in chapter 6 that much employment is still insecure and poorly paid.

The retreat in the UK from the principle of universalism in social policy has undermined efforts to reduce these social divisions. As indicated in chapter 11 (pp. 253–4) universalism involves the provision of a single, relatively uniform service for all citizens, which can therefore be expected to have wide political support. If, alternatively, the state service is a second-class one, unused by the well-off and powerful, it will tend to be inferior, operating close to a minimal level of acceptability and attracting relatively poor staff.

The case for universalism is expressed very powerfully in Richard Titmuss's work, where he argues that a shared service contributes to social cohesion and solidarity, a point he made poignantly when he was dying of cancer – referring to his participation in an out-patients clinic where the only discrimination involved treating patients in the time order of their arrival (Titmuss, 1974).

However, the problem with the social inequalities argument outlined so far is that it is totally blind to issues about gender and ethnicity. We need now to add these to the analysis.

As far as gender is concerned the problem is that the development of social policy has been very much influenced by assumptions that the main and perhaps sole 'breadwinner' is male and that social benefits can be distributed to family units. When the distribution of resources within the family are unpacked, women may be found to be not only in a vulnerable position but actually deprived of opportunities to benefit from the privileges and wealth of the family unit (Walker and Parker, 1988). This becomes particularly evident when family units break down (note for example the evidence on poverty amongst the – largely female – heads of single-parent families, see p. 125).

But while there was, by the end of the twentieth century, some move-ment away from the 'male breadwinner' model as female-labour market participation increased, less progress was made in moving away from assumptions that women should be the main providers of care. Not only is it expected that women should assume caring roles with regard to children but there are also often similar expectations about the care of adults with disabilities and health problems. This has been described as 'compulsory altruism' (Land and Rose, 1985) – an expectation that caring for elderly parents (in particular), but also for other relatives will be undertaken by females without financial rewards and perhaps at the cost of abandoning opportunities to participate in the paid labour force (see also Finch and Groves, 1983). Inasmuch as governments regard social care as family care, reducing demands upon public funds, this means female care.

Similar assumptions may extend to self-care. It has been shown (Arber and Ginn, 1991) that elderly men coping on their own despite disabilities and health problems are more likely to secure statutory care services than elderly women, who are assumed to be better able to care for themselves.

Somewhat similar assumptions may be applied in relation to caring activities by voluntary organizations and even to state provision of care – that such tasks may be expected to be performed by women for little or no reward. In the case of paid work these expectations of female altruism may reinforce labour-market disadvantages (see Evers, Pijl and Ungerson, 1994). It has been pointed out that much of the growth in female labour-market participation has occurred in 'welfare state employment' – caring roles which have 'gone public' (Hernes, 1987). These tasks may be regarded, because they have come out of the family, as lower status, deserving of lower rewards and dispensable when there is a lack of public resources (see Ungerson, 2000).

Chapter 9 noted female educational advance and evidence that girls are getting better school results than boys. Yet it was noted that this has led on to an anxious official debate about male under-achievement. Moreover, the fact that female educational achievement does not seem to translate into labour-market advantage leads us to questions about whether some parents are less likely to buy expensive education for their daughters than for their sons, and whether teachers still hold unjustifiable views about the differences between the sexes in abilities and in capacity for some kinds of future employment (Spender and Sarah, 1980; Kelly, 1981). The key professions providing the social policy services are still male-dominated, and male practitioners may make sexist assumptions about the experiences and needs of women (for example, in health care – see Stacey, 1988).

If universalism is seen as potentially mitigating class divisions, what is the similar remedy as far as the inequalities between the genders are concerned? The obvious 'liberal' answer is 'equal opportunities policy'. But critiques of 'liberal feminism have indicated that equal opportunities policy on its own does not tackle the structured forms of inequality associated both with the treatment of women as a key element in the 'reserve army of labour' (socialist feminism), and with male power as exercised both in society and within the family (radical feminism). Simply requiring policies to be operated in ways which maximize female participation in economic institutions and minimize dependency assumptions (in income maintenance, for example) may disadvantage rather than advantage women if all many can achieve are inferior and poorly paid work roles from which they return in the evening to partners who expect disproportionate contributions to domestic and caring tasks.

Any discussion of racial or ethnic divisions in society starts with a definitional problem which stems from the fact that those divisions are socially and culturally determined. They may be linked with physical differences, but those differences are often exaggerated, difficult to detect at the margin and have none of the connections to abilities and attributes which earlier biological theories of racial differences suggested. Furthermore, divisions within societies may be discovered for which there are no biological cues at all but where patterns of discrimination have been developed and social barriers to contact have been set up of a very similar kind to those found in other societies where divisions are based on physical racial characteristics. This is the case where language or religion are the key criteria used by individuals to act in a discriminatory way.

In examining the implications of ethnic divisions for social policy it is important to give attention to the concept of citizenship (Marshall, 1963). This is also pertinent to the gender issues (see Lister, 1997). The feminist struggle involves a quest for full and equal citizenship for women – through political enfranchisement, the elimination of laws giving men command over the persons and property of wives and daughters, and the provision of legal guarantees of equal access to employment and social benefits. In relation to ethnic groups, issues involving the denial of citizenship in the formal sense are very salient. Systems of institutionalized and legalized discrimination deny full citizenship. It is important to recognize that this aspect of citizenship will involve political rights (the right to vote etc.), civil rights (a right to the absence of formal discrimination) and social rights (rights to social benefits).

The denial of these rights, and particularly the third, does not merely occur through formal systems of official discrimination. The rights of ethnic minorities are affected where social policies prioritize some cultural patterns relative to others, or fail to recognize the salience of some cultural characteristics and culturally determined needs. This is very fully analysed in Parekh (2000).

These denials of full citizenship tend to reinforce economic – particularly job market – disadvantages. There are, further, some particular ways in which migrants are pushed into exceptionally exploited positions. One of these is where entry to a country is only allowed if in order to perform some particularly menial and ill-rewarded task. The recruitment of domestic workers in many societies falls into this category – linking gender roles and ethnic disadvantages in a particularly exploitative way (see Brah, 2001). A perhaps even more disturbing situation arises with illegal migrants, vulnerable to exploitation and blackmail from those who purport to help them.

There was some discussion in chapter 9, with specific reference to education, about the way in which cultural differences are dealt with in the delivery of services. It was pointed out that these issues also apply to other services, such as health and social care. There is an often proffered 'liberal' approach, which is flawed (even in its own terms). This is the view that such services should be ethnicity 'blind' – people, regardless of race, creed or language, are to be treated like everyone else. That, it is argued, is what an equal-rights policy seems to require. The problems about this are as follows:

- First, it is a line of argument offered to resist scrutiny by officials who are actually discriminating. One cannot be confident about an egalitarian policy without the collecting of evidence to ensure that it is in operation (Henderson and Karn, 1987). The Parekh Report (2000) refers to a continued inadequacy in the monitoring of discriminatory behaviour.
- Secondly, to operate without regard to people's actual needs and preferences may be discriminatory. Supplying houses or income-maintenance benefits which do not enable people to meet their actual social obligations may severely disadvantage them. Supplying services which violate very deeply held beliefs and feelings – disregard of religious practices and holidays, medical services that have no regard to family cultural practices, education that imposes instruction in an alien religion – may alienate and lead to under-use of badly needed services.
- Thirdly, and more complicatedly, induction into full citizenship requires acceptance that the history, the traditions, the culture and the language of the individual has a value along with that of the dominant society. To do anything less is to send the message that many of the things that create the individual's own sense of identity are not important – an implicit way of making him or her feel a second-class citizen.

But in this context it is important to recognize the dynamic nature of culture. Individuals are not choosing between a culture from which they come and one which offers assimilation. Both are changing:

> The dynamic nature of culture lies in its capacity to link a group's history and traditions with the actual situation in the migratory process. Migrant or minority cultures are constantly recreated on the basis of the needs and experiences of the group and its interaction with the actual social environment.   (Castles and Miller, 1993, pp. 33–4)

This theme is well explored by Brah (2001), who writes:

For example, young African-Caribbean and Asian women in Britain seem to be constructing diasporic identities that simultaneously assert a sense of belonging to the locality in which they have grown up, as well as proclaiming a 'difference' that marks the specificity of the historical experience of being 'black', or 'Asian' or 'Muslim'.   (p. 228)

There is a difficult line to be drawn, in any effort to accommodate the conflicting demands of the new culture and the old one, between the extreme implied by the 'blind' approach and an opposite extreme of providing a separate socialization process for a separate people. That will be one that will reinforce separation and tend to pass on disadvantages. People will then tend to remain separate whether they like it or not.

This is an issue about which there are strong feelings. There is a view taken by radical elements within some discriminated-against groups that the prospects for the liberal model are so poor that separate institutions are preferable. Castles and Miller argue that culture is increasingly becoming politicized – exclusionary practices are based upon culture rather than overt arguments about racial superiority whilst 'the politics of minority resistance crystallise more and more around cultural symbols' (ibid., p. 35). Some fears about this as one of the directions in which UK policy is turning were highlighted in chapter 9 in the discussion of the official encouragement of new schools run by religious groups (p. 219). To respond in this way may not do justice to the complex cultural identities highlighted by Brah. We all live in a changing and heterogeneous society, conceding to demands for separate treatment for some groups will do little to help us come to terms with this. On the contrary there is a need to consider whether it is still appropriate to privilege certain indigenous cultural claims, particularly those of the Church of England, whose popular support is now much diminished.

Language differences pose particular problems inasmuch as failure to gain proficiency in a dominant language often leads on to severe economic disadvantages. Yet pressure to adopt the majority language may, if not handled properly, send discriminatory signals. Bilingualism offers a solution though dominant groups are rarely as ready to learn the less important language as subordinate groups are to learn theirs (a point that should not be lost on all those who, like the writer of this book, have the special advantage of having one of the world's dominant languages as their native tongue).

There are also some very difficult issues where cultural differences involve beliefs and practices about which there are deeply held values on either side. A central example here is family practices, involving views about appropriate relationships between men, women and children.

For many of the less successful within the UK's ethnic minorities there may be particularly strong forces which tend to ensure that they are found within the most disadvantaged sectors. Where discrimination has limited people to less well paid and less secure work, this will be reflected in minimal access to employment-related benefits. Residential segregation, whether the result of explicit discrimination or produced by a combination of low 'market power' and the selection of areas offering security and the availability of appropriate institutions (places of worship, voluntary organizations etc.) may have an impact upon choices of houses, schools and health services.

The discussion in this section can be summed up by reference to Hutton's description of the UK as a 30/30/40 society, in which 30 per cent are seriously deprived and another 30 per cent insecure (Hutton, 1995). The 'comfortable' 40 per cent are inclined to look the other way. This analysis has suggested (a) that serious inequalities in social policy are linked with this division, and (b) that there is need for particular concern about the factors that place both many women and many ethnic minority people amongst those who gain least from social policy.

Conclusions

The stance of this book has been to see social policy as a potentially progressive force for the attack on poverty, deprivation and social divisions. But it has recorded that, in various ways, the thrust of that attack, never very strong, has become seriously blunted. The feasibility of social progress, as the government is only too eager to remind us, needs to be seen in a global context. On the one hand, as was shown in chapter 11, comparisons with nations close by (in the EU) suggest that the performance of the UK welfare state could be better. On the other hand, as was suggested in chapter 6, the economic forces which make full employment difficult to sustain and low-wage sectors endemic are creating problems for even the most progressive welfare states. Economic elites – through international organizations like the Organization for Economic Cooperation and Development (OECD) and the World Bank – warn governments that high public-expenditure levels will have adverse consequences for competitiveness.

I end this edition of this book, as I ended previous editions, by stressing again that the struggle for better social policy is an increasingly difficult one. Great gains were made when humanitarian aspirations and political and economic forces were moving in the same direction. This is no longer the case. In this book, I have tried to explore what has been achieved and the complex edifice of social policy institutions which is in place and which does a great deal to advance welfare. However, I would be dishonest if I tried to end on an upbeat note. There is much still to be done, in an economic and political environment that makes social policy advance very difficult.

SUGGESTIONS FOR FURTHER READING

Hills has produced an admirable guide to the case against those who see social policy growth as impossible, in his *The Future of Welfare: A Guide to the Debate* (1997). The book by Hutton (1995) cited in the text offers progressive agendas for social and other public policy. There is a range of assessments of the social policy philosophy of the Blair governments. Texts edited by Powell (1999, 2002) were cited at the end of chapter 2. There are useful articles on this theme by Deacon (1998), F. Williams (1999) and Rake (2001).

Recommendations on the emergent literature on institutional change were included at the end of chapter 4, while Jowell and Oliver's helpful edited book on constitutional and legal change was cited at the end of chapter 3.

Fiona Williams's textbook (1989), cited at the end of chapter 1 remains the best general source on the issues about social divisions in welfare, alongside Ginsburg's (1992) comparative book on the same theme. A recent collection on some of these issues, including the essay by Brah cited in the text and another contribution from Fiona Williams, is Fink, Lewis and Clarke (2001).

References

Abel-Smith, B. 1976: *Value for Money in Health Services*. London: Heinemann.
Abel-Smith, B. and Townsend, P. 1965: *The Poor and the Poorest*. London: Bell.
Acheson, D. 1998: *Inequalities and Health*. London: HMSO.
Agulnik, P. et al. 1999: *Partnership in Pensions? Responses to the Pensions Green Paper*. Centre for Analysis of Social Exclusion Paper 24, London: London School of Economics.
Ainley, P. 2001: From a national system locally administered to a national system nationally administered: the New Leviathan in education and training in England. *Journal of Social Policy*, 30 (3), 457–76.
Alcock, P. 1997: *Understanding Poverty*, 2nd edn. Basingstoke: Macmillan.
Alcock, P. and Pearson, S. 1999: Raising the poverty plateau: the impact of means-tested rebates from local authority charges on low-income households. *Journal of Social Policy*, 27(3), 497–516.
Alcock, P., Erskine, A. and May, M. (eds) 1998: *The Student's Companion to Social Policy*. Oxford: Blackwell.
Alcock, P., Eskine, A. and May, M. 2002: *The Blackwell Dictionary of Social Policy*. Oxford: Blackwell.
Aldgate, J. and Hill, M. (eds) 1999: *Child Welfare Services*. London: Jessica Kingsley.
Arber, S. and Ginn, J. 1991: *Gender and Later Life*. London: Sage.
Armstrong, H. 1998: Principles for a new housing policy. *Housing Today*, 83.
Ashford, D. E. 1986: *The Emergence of the Welfare States*. Oxford: Blackwell.
Atkinson, A. B. 1975: Income distribution and social change revisited. *Journal of Social Policy*, (41), 57–68.
Atkinson, A. B. 1994: *State Pensions for Today and Tomorrow*. London: Welfare State Programme Discussion Paper 104.
Audit Commission 1986: *Making a Reality of Community Care*. London: HMSO.
Bachrach, P. 1969: *The Theory of Democratic Elitism*. London: University of London Press.
Balchin, N. 1995: *Housing Policy: An Introduction*. London: Routledge and Kegan Paul.
Baldwin, P. 1990: *The Politics of Social Solidarity*. Cambridge: Cambridge University Press.

Ball, S. J. 1990: *Politics and Policy Making in Education*. London: Routledge.

Barclay, P. 1982: *Social Workers: Their Roles and Tasks* (Report of a Working Party). London: Bedford Square Press.

Bardach, E. 1977: *The Implementation Game*. Cambridge, MA: MIT Press.

Barr, N. A. 1981: Empirical definitions of the poverty line. *Policy and Politics*, 1, 1–21.

Becker, S. and Silburn, R. 1990: *The New Poor Clients*. Nottingham: Benefits Research Unit.

Beer, S. H. 1965: *Modern British Politics*. London: Faber & Faber.

Benefits 1998: The politics of fraud: a symposium. *Benefits*, 21 (January), 2–19.

Bevan, A. 1952: *In Place of Fear*. London: Heinemann.

Beveridge, W. 1942: *Social Insurance and Allied Services*. Cmd 6404. London: HMSO.

Blackstone, T. and Plowden, W. 1988: *Inside the Think Tank*. London: Heinemann.

Blair, T. 1999: *Beveridge Lecture*. http://www.number10.gov.uk/public . . . s/ uktoday–right.asp?

Bonoli, G. 1997: Classifying welfare states: a two-dimensional approach. *Journal of Social Policy*, 26 (3), 351–72.

Booth, C. 1889–1903: *Life and Labour of the People in London*, 17 vols. London: Macmillan.

Bottomore, T. B. 1966: *Elites and Society*. Harmondsworth: Penguin.

Bowe, R. and Ball, S. J. 1992: *Reforming Education and Changing Schools*. London: Routledge.

Bradshaw, J. and Chen, J.-R. 1997: Poverty in the UK: a comparison with nineteen other countries. *Benefits*, 18, 13–17.

Bradshaw, J., Ditch, J., Holmes, H. and Whiteford, P. 1993: *Support for Children: A Comparison of Arrangements in Fifteen Countries*. Department of Social Security Research Report 21, London: HMSO.

Brah, A. 2001: Re-framing Europe: gendered racisms, ethnicities and nationalisms in contemporary western Europe. In J. Fink, G. Lewis and J. Clarke, (eds), *Rethinking European Welfare*, London: Sage.

Braybrooke, D. and Lindblom, C. E. 1963: *A Strategy of Decision*. New York: Free Press.

Bright, J. 2001: Wasteland. *Inside Housing* (9 February), 14–15.

Bryson, L. 1992: *Welfare and the State*. Basingstoke: Macmillan.

Budge, I., Crewe, I., McKay, D. and Newton, K. 2000: *The New British Politics*. Harlow: Longman.

Butcher, T. 2002: *Delivering Welfare*. Buckingham: Open University Press.

Butler, D., Adonis, A. and Travers, T. 1994: *Failure in British Government: The Politics of the Poll Tax*. Oxford: Oxford University Press.

Byrne, T. 2000: *Local Government in Britain*, 7th edn. Harmondsworth: Penguin.

Cahill, M. 1994: *The New Social Policy*. Oxford: Blackwell.

Cahill, M. 2002: *The Environment and Social Policy*. London: Routledge.

Cairncross, A. 1985: *Years of Recovery: British Economic Policy, 1945–51*. London: Methuen.

Campbell, C. and Wilson, G. K. 1995: *The End of Whitehall: Death of a Paradigm*. Oxford: Blackwell.

Castle, B. and Townsend, P. n.d.: *We CAN afford the Welfare State*. London.

Castles, F. 1985: *The Working Class and Welfare*. Sydney: Allen and Unwin.

Castles, F. and Mitchell, D. 1992: Identifying welfare state regimes: the links between politics, instruments and outcomes. *Governance*, 5(1), 1–26.

Castles, S. and Miller, M. J. 1993: *The Age of Migration*. Basingstoke: Macmillan.

Central Advisory Council for Education 1967: *Children and their Primary Schools* (Plowden Report). London: HMSO.

Central Statistical Office 1995: *Labour Market Trends*, Winter issue. London: HMSO.

Centre for Housing Policy 1997: *Contemporary Patterns of Residential Mobility in Relation to Social Housing in England*. York: Centre for Housing Policy.

Clarke, J. 2001: Social problems: sociological perspectives. In M. May, R. Page and E. Brunsdon (eds), *Understanding Social Problems*, Oxford: Blackwell.

Clarke, J., Cochrane, A. and McLaughlin, E. (eds) 1994: *Managing Social Policy*. London: Sage.

Cole, D. and Utting, J. 1962: *The Economic Circumstances of Old People*. London: Codicote.

Colebatch, H. K. and Larmour, P. 1993: *Market, Bureaucracy and Community: A Student's Guide to Organisation*. London: Pluto Press.

Commission of the European Communities 1993: *European Social Policy: Options for the Union*. Luxemburg: Official Publications of the European Communities.

Cousins, C. 1999: *Society, Work and Welfare in Europe*. Basingstoke: Macmillan.

Dahl, R. A. 1961: *Who Governs?* New Haven: Yale University Press.

Dahrendorf, R. 1985: *Law and Order*. London: Stevens.

Daly, M. 2000: *The Gender Division of Welfare*. Cambridge: Cambridge University Press.

Daly, M. and Lewis, J. 1998: Conceptualising social care in the context of welfare state restructuring. In J. Lewis (ed.), *Gender, Social Care and Welfare State Restructuring in Europe*, Aldershot: Ashgate.

Davies, M. (ed.) 1997: *The Blackwell Companion to Social Work*. Oxford: Blackwell.

Deacon, A. 1976: *In Search of the Scrounger*. London: Bell.

Deacon, A. 1998: The Green Paper on welfare reform: a case of enlightened self-interest? *Political Quarterly*, 69 (3), 306–11.

Deakin, N. 1994: *The Politics of Welfare: Continuities and Change*. Hemel Hempstead: Harvester Wheatsheaf.

Deakin, N. and Parry, R. 1998: The Treasury and new Labour's social policy. In E. Brunsdon, H. Dean and R. Woods (eds), *Social Policy Review 10*, London: Social Policy Association, 34–56.

Department for Education and Employment (DfEE) 1997: *Excellence in Schools*. London: HMSO.

Department for Education and Employment (DfEE) 1998: *Teachers: Meeting the Challenge of Change*. London: HMSO.

Department for Education and Employment 1999: *Sure Start: A Guide for Trailblazers*. London: HMSO.

Department for Transport, Local Government and the Regions (DTLR) 2002: *Housing Statistics Postcard*. www.housing.dtlr.gov.uk/information/keyfigures.

Department for Work and Pensions 2001: *Income Related Benefits: Estimates of Take-Up in 1999/2000*. London: Department for Work and Pensions.

Department of Education and Science 1985: *Education for All* (a brief guide by Lord Swann to the Report of the Committee of Inquiry into the Education of Children from Ethnic Minority Groups). London: HMSO.

Department of Employment 1971: *People and Jobs*. London: HMSO.

Department of Health 1995: *Child Protection: Messages from Research*. London: HMSO.

Department of Health 1997: *The New NHS*. London: HMSO.

Department of Health 1998a: *A First-Class Service: Quality in the NHS*, Consultation Document. London: HMSO.

Department of Health 1998b: *Modernising Social Services*. Cm. 4169. London: HMSO.

Department of Health 1998c: *Partnership in Action*. London: Department of Health.

Department of Health 2000: *The NHS Plan*. London: Stationery Office.

Department of Health 2001: *Modernising Social Services: The 10th Annual Report of the Chief Inspector of Social Services*. London: Department of Health.

Department of Health 2002a: www.doh.gov.uk/HPSSS

Department of Health 2002b: *Shifting the Balance of Power: The Next Steps*. www.doh.gov.uk/shiftingthebalance/nextsteps

Department of Health and Social Security (DHSS) 1976: *Priorities for Health and Personal Social Services*. London: HMSO.

Department of Social Security 1998a: *A New Contract for Welfare*. Cm 3805. London: HMSO.

Department of Social Security 1998b: *Partnership in Pensions*. London: HMSO.

Department of Social Security 2001: *Households Below Average Income, 1994/95–1999/2000*. London: Department of Social Security.

Department of the Environment, Transport and the Regions (DETR) 1998: *Modern Local Government in Touch with the People*. Cm. 4014. London: HMSO.

Dex, S. and McCulloch, A. 1995: *Flexible Employment in Britain: A Statistical Analysis*. London: Equal Opportunities Commission.

Donnison, D. 1991: *A Radical Agenda*. London: Rivers Oram.

Dorey, P. (ed.) 1999: *The Major Premiership*. Basingstoke: Macmillan.

Douglas, J. W. B. 1964: *The Home and the School*. London: Macgibbon and Kee.

Dunleavy, P. 1981: *The Politics of Mass Housing in Britain*. London: Oxford University Press.

Dunleavy, P., Gamble, A., Heffernan, R., Holliday, I. and Peele, G. (eds.) 2002: *Developments in British Politics*. New York: St Martin's Press.

Eardley, T., Bradshaw, J., Ditch, J., Gough, I. and Whiteford, P. 1996: *Social Assistance in OECD Countries: Synthesis Report*. London: HMSO.

Eckstein, H. 1960: *Pressure Group Politics*. London: Allen and Unwin.

Edgell, S. and Duke, V. 1991: *A Measure of Thatcherism*. Glasgow: HarperCollins.

Ellis, B. 1989: *Pensions in Britain, 1955–75*. London: HMSO.

Esping-Andersen, G. 1990: *The Three Worlds of Welfare Capitalism*. Cambridge: Polity Press.

Esping-Andersen, G. 1999: *Social Foundations of Post-Industrial Economies*. Oxford: Oxford University Press.

Esping-Andersen, G. (ed.) 1996: *Welfare States in Transition*. London: Sage.

Etzioni, A. 1961: *A Comparative Analysis of Complex Organisations*. New York: Free Press.

Etzioni, A. 1969: *The Semi Professions and their Organization*. New York: Free Press.

European Commission 2001: *The Social Situation in the European Union*. Luxemburg: European Commission.

European Commission 2002: *In Brief: The Social Situation in the European Union*. Luxemburg: European Commission.

Evers, A., Pijl, M. and Ungerson, C. 1994: *Payments for Care: A Comparative Overview*. Aldershot: Avebury.

Ferrara, M. 1996: The 'Southern Model' of welfare in social Europe. *Journal of European Social Policy*, 6, 17–37.

Field, F. 1989: *Losing Out: The Emergence of Britain's Underclass*. Oxford: Blackwell.

Fimister, G. 1986: *Welfare Rights in Social Services*. Basingstoke: Macmillan.

Finch, J. and Groves, D. (eds.) 1983: *A Labour of Love: Women, Work and Caring*. London: Routledge.

Finer, S. E. 1958: *Anonymous Empire*. London: Pall Mall.

Fink, J., Lewis, G. and Clarke, J. 2001: *Rethinking European Welfare*. London: Sage.

Fitzpatrick, T. 1999: *Freedom and Security: An Introduction to the Basic Income Debate*. Basingstoke: Macmillan.

Floud, J., Halsey, A. H. and Martin, F. M. 1956: *Social Class and Education Opportunity*. London: Heinemann.

Ford, J. 1969: *Social Class and the Comprehensive School*. London: Routledge and Kegan Paul.

Forrest, R., Murie, A. and Williams, P. 1990: *Home Ownership: Fragmentation and Differentiation*. London: Unwin Hyman.

Fraser, D. 2002: *The Evolution of the British Welfare State*, 3rd edn. Basingstoke: Palgrave.

Friedman, M. 1962: *Capitalism and Freedom*. Chicago: University of Chicago Press.

Friedman, M. 1977: *Inflation and Unemployment: A New Dimension of Politics*. London: Institute of Economic Affairs

Friedson, E. 1970: *Professional Dominance*. New York: Atherton.

Friend, J. K., Power, J. M. and Yewlett, C. J. L. 1974: *Public Planning: The Intercorporate Dimension*. London: Tavistock.

George, V. and Wilding, P. 1994: *Welfare and Ideology*, 2nd edn. Hemel Hempstead: Harvester Wheatsheaf.

Gewirtz, S., Ball, S.J. and Bowe, R. 1995: *Markets, Choice and Equity in Education*. Buckingham: Open University Press.

Giddens, A. 1998: *The Third Way: The Renewal of Social Democracy*. Cambridge: Polity Press.

Gilbert, B. B. 1970: *British Social Policy, 1914–39*. London: Batsford.

Gillborn, D. 1992: *Race, Ethnicity and Education*. London: Unwin Hyman.

Ginsburg, N. 1992: *Divisions of Welfare*. London: Sage.

Glendinning, C., Powell, M. and Rummery, K. (eds) 2002: *Partnership, New Labour and the Governance of Welfare*. Cambridge: Polity Press.

Glennerster, H. 1992: *Paying for Welfare*. Oxford: Blackwell.

Glennerster, H. 1995: *British Social Policy Since 1945*. Oxford: Blackwell.

Glennerster, H. 2001: Social Policy. In A. Seldon (ed.), *The Blair Effect*, London: Little Brown.

Glennerster, H. and Hills, J. (eds) 1998: *The State of Welfare*. Oxford: Oxford University Press.

Glennerster, H., Hills, J., Travers, T. and Hendry, R. 2000: *Paying for Health, Education and Housing*. Oxford: Oxford University Press.

Glennerster, H., Power, A. and Travers, T. 1991: A new era for social policy: a new enlightenment or a new Leviathan? *Journal of Social Policy*, 20(3), 389–414.

Gold, M. (ed.) 1993: *The Social Dimension*. Basingstoke: Macmillan.

Goodin, R.E., Headey, B., Muffels, R. and Dirven, H.J. 1999: *The Real Worlds of Welfare Capitalism*. Cambridge: Cambridge University Press.

Gordon, D. and Pantazis, C. 1997: *Breadline Britain in the 1990s*. Aldershot: Avebury.

Gordon, D. and Townsend, P. (eds) 2000: *Breadline Europe*. Bristol: Policy Press.

Gough, I. 1979: *The Political Economy of the Welfare State*. Basingstoke: Macmillan.

Government Press Release 2001: www.10downingstreet.gov.uk/news, 21 November.

Gregg, P. and Wadsworth, J. 1995: A short history of labour turnover, labour tenure and job security, 1975–93. *Oxford Review of Economic Policy*, 11(1), 73–90.

Gyford, J. 1985: *The Politics of Local Socialism*. London: Allen and Unwin.

Gyford, J. 1991: *Citizens, Consumers and Councils*. Basingstoke: Macmillan.

Hall, P. 1976: *Reforming the Welfare*. London: Heinemann.

Halsey, A.H. (ed.) 1972: *Educational Priority*, vol. 1. London: HMSO.

Halsey, A.H., Lauder, H., Brown, P. and Wells, A.S. 1997: *Education, Culture, Economy and Society*. Oxford: Oxford University Press.

Ham, C. 1999: *Health Policy in Britain*, Basingstoke: Macmillan.

Hamnett, C. 1991: A nation of inheritors? Housing inheritance, wealth and inequality in Britain. *Journal of Social Policy*, 20(4), 509–36.

Harris, J. 1972: *Unemployment and Politics*. London: Oxford University Press.

Harris, J. 1977: *William Beveridge: A Biography*. Oxford: Oxford University Press.

Harris, R. and Seldon, A. 1976: *Pricing or Taxing*. London: Institute of Economic Affairs.

Harris, R. and Seldon, A. 1979: *Overruled on Welfare*. London: Institute of Economic Affairs.

Harrison, S. and Pollitt, C. 1990: *Controlling Health Professionals*. Milton Keynes: Open University Press.

Heclo, H. H. 1974: *Modern Social Politics in Britain and Sweden*. New Haven: Yale University Press.

Heclo, H. H. and Wildavsky, A. 1981: *The Private Government of Public Money*. Basingstoke: Macmillan.

Henderson, J.W. and Karn, V.A. 1987: *Race, Class and State Housing*. Aldershot: Gower.

Hennessy, P. 1992: *Never Again: Britain, 1945–51*. London: Cape.

Hernes, H. 1987: *Welfare State and Women Power*. Oslo: Norwegian University Press.

Higgins, J. 1988: *The Business of Medicine: Private Health Care in Britain*. Basingstoke: Macmillan.

Higgins, J., Deakin, N., Edwards, J. and Wicks, M. 1984: *Government and Urban Poverty*. Oxford: Blackwell.

Hill, M. 1972: *The Sociology of Public Administration*. London: Weidenfeld and Nicolson.

Hill, M. 1993: *The Welfare State in Britain*. Aldershot: Edward Elgar.

Hill, M. 1996: *Social Policy: A Comparative Analysis*. Hemel Hempstead: Harvester Wheatsheaf.

Hill, M. 1997a: *The Policy Process in the Modern State*. Hemel Hempstead: Prentice Hall/Harvester Wheatsheaf.

Hill, M. (ed.) 1997b: *The Policy Process: A Reader*, 2nd edn. Hemel Hempstead: Prentice Hall/Harvester Wheatsheaf .

Hill, M. (ed.) 2000: *Local Authority Social Services*. Oxford: Blackwell.

Hill, M. and Hupe, P. 2002: *Implementing Public Policy*. London: Sage.

Hills, J. 1997: *The Future of Welfare: A Guide to the Debate*, 2nd edn. York: Joseph Rowntree Foundation.

Hirsch, F. 1976: *Social Limits to Growth*. Cambridge, MA: Harvard University Press.

HMSO 1968: *Report of the Committee on Local Authority and Allied Personal Social Services* (Seebohm Report). Cmnd 3703. London: HMSO.

HMSO 1977: *Housing Policy: A Consultative Document*. Cmnd 6851. London: HMSO.

HMSO 1989: *Caring for People: Community Care in the Next Decade and Beyond*. Cm 849. London: HMSO.

HMSO 1998: *The Government's Annual Report, 97/98*. London: HMSO.

Hood, C. 1991: A public management for all seasons. *Public Administration*, 69(1), 3–19.

House of Commons 1977: *Seventh Report from the Expenditure Committee: The Job Creation Programme*. London: HMSO.

Howard, M., Garnham, A., Fimister, G. and Veit-Wilson, J. 2001: *Poverty: The Facts*. London: Child Poverty Action Group.

Huby, M. 1998: *Social Policy and the Environment*. Buckingham: Open University Press.

Hudson, B. 1997: Michael Lipsky and street-level bureaucracy: a neglected perspective. In M. Hill (ed.), *The Policy Process: A Reader*, 2nd edn. Hemel Hempstead: Prentice Hall/Harvester Wheatsheaf, pp. 393–403.

Hudson, B. (ed.) 2000: *The Changing Role of Social Care*. London: Jessica Kingsley.

Hudson, B. and Henwood, M. 2002: The NHS and social care: the final countdown? *Policy and Politics*, 30 (2), 153–66.

Hutton, W. 1995: *The State We're In*. London: Cape.

Jackson, B. and Marsden, D. 1962: *Education and the Working Class*. London: Routledge and Kegan Paul.

Jenkins, W. I. 1978: *Policy Analysis*. London: Martin Robertson.

Jones, B., Kavanagh, D., Moran, M. and Norton, P. 2001: *Politics UK*, 4th edn. Harlow: Longman.

Jones, C. 1997: Poverty. In M. Davies (ed.), *The Blackwell Companion to Social Work*, Oxford: Blackwell, pp. 118–25.

Jordan, A. G. and Richardson, J. J. 1987: *British Politics and the Policy Process*. London: Unwin Hyman.

Joseph Rowntree Foundation 2002: *Britain's Housing in 2002*. York: Joseph Rowntree Foundation.

Jowell, J. 1973: The legal control of administrative discretion. *Public Law*, 178, 178–220.

Jowell, J. and Oliver, D. (eds) 2000: *The Changing Constitution*, 4th edn. Oxford: Oxford University Press.

Judge, K. 1987: *Rationing Social Services*. London: Heinemann.

Kelly, A. (ed.) 1981: *The Missing Half*. Manchester: Manchester University Press.

Keynes, J. M. 1936: *The General Theory of Employment, Interest and Money*. London: Macmillan.

Killeen, J., Turton, R., Diamond, W., Dosnon, O. and Wach, M. 1999: Education and the labour market: subjective aspects of human capital investment. *Journal of Education Policy*, 14 (2), 99–116.

Klein, R. 1995: *The Politics of the NHS*. London: Longman.

Kleinman, M. 2002: *A European Welfare State?* Basingstoke: Palgrave.

Knapp, M., Hardy, B. and Forder, J. 2001: Commissioning for Quality: Ten Years of Social Care Markets in England. *Journal of Social Policy*, 30 (2), 283–306.

Korpi, W. and Palme, J. 1998: The paradox of redistribution: Welfare State institutions and poverty in the Western countries. *American Sociological Review*, 63 (5), 661–87.

Labour Party 1997: *Labour Party Election Manifesto*. London: Labour Party.

Land, H. and Rose, H. 1985: Compulsory altruism for some or an altruistic society for all. In P. Bean, J. Ferris and D. Whynes (eds), *In Defence of Welfare*, London: Tavistock, pp. 74–96.

Law, I. 1996: *Racism, Ethnicity and Social Policy*. Hemel Hempstead: Prentice-Hall.

Le Grand, J. 1982: *The Strategy of Equality*. London: Allen and Unwin.

Le Grand, J. 2001: We can save the NHS – if we are ready to pay for it. *Observer*, 21 October 2001.

Le Grand, J., Mays, N. and Mulligan, J.-A. 1998: *Learning from the NHS Internal Market*. London: King's Fund.

Lee, P. and Murie, A. 1998: Social exclusion and housing. In S. Wilcox (ed.), *Housing Finance Review*, York: Joseph Rowntree Foundation, pp. 30–7.

Lester, A. 2000: Human rights and the British constitution. In J. Jowell and D. Oliver (eds), *The Changing Constitution*, 4th edn. Oxford: Oxford University Press.

Liddiard, M. 1998: Home truths. In H. Jones and S. MacGregor (eds), *Social Issues and Party Politics*, London: Routledge, pp. 132–8.

Lindblom, C. E. 1977: *Politics and Markets: The World's Political-Economic Systems*. New York: Basic Books.

Lindsey, A. 1962: *Socialised Medicine in England and Wales*. Chapel Hill: University of North Carolina Press.

Ling, T. 1994: The new managerialism and social security. In J. Clarke, A. Cochrane and E. McLaughlin (eds), *Managing Social Policy*, London: Sage, pp. 32–56.

Lipsky, M. 1980: *Street-Level Bureaucracy*. New York: Russell Sage.

Lister, R. 1997: *Citizenship: Feminist Perspectives*. Basingstoke: Macmillan.

Liu, S. 2001: *The Autonomous State of Childcare*. Aldershot: Ashgate.

Lowe, R. 1999: *The Welfare State in Britain since 1945*, 2nd edn. Basingstoke: Macmillan.

Lynes, T. 1962: *National Assistance and National Prosperity*. London: Codicote.

Lynes, T. 1997a: Supplementary pensions in Britain: is there still a role for the state? Paper given at European Institute for Social Security seminar in Dublin.

Lynes, T. 1997b: The British case. In M. Rein and E. Wadensjö (eds), *Enterprise and the Welfare State*, Cheltenham: Edward Elgar, pp. 309–51.

MacDermott, T. 1999: Poverty: Labour's inheritance. *Poverty*, 102 (Spring), 16–19.

Mack, J. and Lansley, S. 1985: *Poor Britain*. London: Allen and Unwin.

Malpass, P. 1990: *Reshaping Housing Policy*. London: Routledge.

Malpass, P. and Murie, A. 1999: *Housing Policy and Practice*, 4th edn. London: Macmillan.

Mann, K. 1994: Watching the defectives: observers of the underclass in the USA, Britain and Australia. *Critical Social Policy*, 41 (2), 79–99.

Marlier, E. and Cohen-Solal, M. 2000: Social benefits and their redistributive effect in the EU. *Statistics in Focus*. Luxemburg: Eurostat.

Marsh, D. and Rhodes, R. A. W. 1992a: *Implementing Thatcherite Policies*. Buckingham: Open University Press.

Marsh, D. and Rhodes, R. A. W. 1992b: *Policy Networks in British Government*. Oxford: Oxford University Press.

Marshall, T. H. 1963: Citizenship and social class. In *Sociology at the Crossroads*. London: Heinemann.

Martin, D. 2002: Northern Toll. *Inside Housing*, 1 February 2001, 14–15.

May, M., Page, R. and Brunsdon, E. (eds) 2001: *Understanding Social Problems*. Oxford: Blackwell.

McCarthy, M. 1986: *Campaigning for the Poor*. Beckenham: Croom Helm.

Mckay S. and Rowlingson, K. 1999: *Social Security in Britain*. Basingstoke: Macmillan.

McKeown, T. 1980: *The Role of Medicine*. Oxford: Blackwell.

Mead, L. 1986: *Beyond Entitlement: The Social Obligations of Citizenship*. New York: Free Press.

Means, R. and Smith, R. 1994: *Community Care: Policy and Practice*. Basingstoke: Macmillan.

Minford, P. 1984: State expenditure: a study in waste. *Economic Affairs* (April–June), supplement.

Moon, J. and Richardson, J. J. 1985: *Unemployment in the UK*. Aldershot: Gower.

Moran, M. and Wood, B. 1993: *States, Regulation and the Medical Profession*. Buckingham: Open University Press.

Morgan, K. O. 1984: *Labour in Power, 1945–51*. Oxford: Oxford University Press.

Murie, A., Niner, P. and Watson, C. 1976: *Housing Policy and the Housing System*. London: Allen and Unwin.

Murray, C. 1984: *Losing Ground*. New York: Basic Books.

Murray, C. 1990: *The Emerging British Underclass*. London: IEA.

National Statistics 2001: *Labour Market Trends*, 109(9). London: Stationery Office.

National Statistics 2002a: www.statistics.gov.uk.ukinfigs

National Statistics 2002b: *Social Trends*. London: Stationery Office.

Newman, J. 2001: *Modernising Governance*. London: Sage.

O'Connor, J. 1973: *The Fiscal Crisis of the State*. New York: St Martin's Press.

O'Connor, J. S. 1996: From women in the Welfare State to gendering Welfare State regimes. *Current Sociology*, 44 (2), 1–130.

Ofsted 1999: *Raising the Attainment of Minority Ethnic Pupils*. London: Ofsted.

Packman, J. 1975: *The Child's Generation*. Oxford: Blackwell.

Page, R. 2001: The exploration of social problems in the field of social policy. In M. May, R. Page and E. Brunsdon (eds), *Understanding Social Problems*, Oxford: Blackwell.

Parekh, B. 2000: *The Future of Multi-Ethnic Britain*. Report of a committee chaired by B. Parekh. London: Runnymede Trust.

Parker, H. 1989: *Instead of the Dole*. London: Routledge.

Pater, J. E. 1981: *The Making of the National Health Service*. London: King's Fund.

Pawson, H. and Kintrea, K. 2002: Part of the problem or part of the solution: social housing allocation policies and social exclusion. *Journal of Social Policy*, 31 (4).

Peters, T. and Waterman, R. 1982: *In Search of Excellence*. New York: HarperCollins.

Phillimore, P., Beattie, A. and Townsend, P. 1994: Widening inequality in health in Northern England, 1981–91. *British Medical Journal*, 308, 1125–8.

Piachaud, D. and Sutherland, H. 2001: Child poverty and the New Labour government. *Journal of Social Policy*, 30 (1), 95–118.

Pierson, P. 1994: *Dismantling the Welfare State*. Cambridge: Cambridge University Press.

Piore, M. and Sabel, C. 1984: *The Second Industrial Divide*. Oxford: Blackwell.

Pitt, G. 2000: *Employment Law*. London: Sweet and Maxwell.

Piven, F. F. and Cloward, R. A. 1972: *Regulating the Poor*. London: Tavistock.

Pollitt, C. 1990: *Managerialism and the Public Services*. Oxford: Blackwell.

Powell, M. (ed.) 1999: *New Labour: New Welfare State?* Bristol: Policy Press.

Powell, M. (ed.) 2002: *Evaluating New Labour's Welfare Reforms*. Bristol: Policy Press.

Powell, M., Exworthy, M. and Berney, L. 2001: Playing the game of partnership. In R. Sykes, C. Bochel and N. Ellison (eds), *Social Policy Review*, 13: *Developments and Debates, 2000–2001*. Bristol: Policy Press.

Power, A. 1987: *Property before People*. London: Allen and Unwin.

Rake, K. 2001: Gender and New Labour's social policies. *Journal of Social Policy*, 30 (2), 209–32.

Ranade, W. 1997: *A Future for the NHS*. Harlow: Longman.

Rao, N. 1996: *Towards Welfare Pluralism*. Aldershot: Dartmouth.

Rawnsley, A. 2001: *Servants of the People: The Inside Story of New Labour*, rev. edn. London: Penguin Books.

Roberts, D. 1960: *Victorian Origins of the British Welfare State*. New Haven, CT: Yale University Press.

Robinson, R. and Judge, K. 1987: *Public Expenditure and the NHS: Trends and Prospects*. London: King's Fund Institute.

Rose, H. 1981: Rereading Titmuss: the social division of welfare. *Journal of Social Policy*, 10 (4), 477–502.

Rowntree, B. S. 1901: *Poverty: A Study of Town Life*. London: Macmillan.

Royal Commission on Long Term Care 1999: *With Respect to Old Age*. London: HMSO.

Sainsbury, D. 1996: *Gender Equality and Welfare States*. Cambridge: Cambridge University Press.

Savage, S. P., Atkinson, R. and Robins, L. (eds) 1994: *Public Policy in Britain*. Basingstoke: Macmillan.

Savage, S. P. and Atkinson, R. (eds.) 2001: *Public Policy under Blair*. Basingstoke: Palgrave.

Schattschneider, E. E. 1960: *The Semi-Sovereign People*. New York: Holt, Rinehart and Winston.

Schumpeter, J. 1950: *Capitalism, Socialism and Democracy*. New York: Harper and Row.

Seldon, A. (ed.) 2001: *The Blair Effect*. London: Little Brown.

Semmel, B. 1961: *Imperialism and Social Reform*. London: Oxford University Press.

Sinfield, R. A. 1978: Analyses in the social division of welfare. *Journal of Social Policy*, 7 (2), 129–56.

Sinfield, R. A. 1981: *What Unemployment Means*. Oxford: Martin Robertson.

Smith, B. C. 1976: *Policy Making in British Government*. London: Martin Robertson.

Smith, M. J. 1993: *Pressure, Power and Policy*. Hemel Hempstead: Harvester Wheatsheaf.

Social Exclusion Unit 1998: *Consultation on Deprived Urban Neighbourhoods*. http://www.cabinet-office.gov.uk/seu/1998/depneigh.htm

Spender, D. and Sarah, E. 1980: *Learning to Lose: Sexism and Education*. London: The Women's Press.

Stacey, M. 1988: *The Sociology of Health and Healing*. London: Unwin Hyman.

Stanworth, P. and Giddens, A. 1974: *Elites and Power in British Society*. Cambridge: Cambridge University Press.

Taylor-Gooby, P. 1985: *Public Opinion, Ideology and State Welfare*. London: Routledge and Kegan Paul.

Taylor-Gooby, P. (ed.) 2001: *Welfare States under Pressure*. London: Sage.

Thane, P. 1996: *Foundations of the Welfare State*. London: Longman.

Timmins, N. 1996: *The Five Giants: A Biography of the Welfare State*. London: Fontana.

Titmuss, R. M. 1958: *Essays on the Welfare State*. London: Allen and Unwin.

Titmuss, R. M. 1974: *Social Policy: An Introduction*. London: Allen and Unwin.

Tomlinson, S. 2001: *Education in a Post-Welfare Society*. Buckingham: Open University Press.

Townsend, P. 1979: *Poverty in the United Kingdom*. Harmondsworth: Penguin.

Townsend, P. 1993: *The International Analysis of Poverty*. Hemel Hempstead: Harvester Wheatsheaf.

Townsend, P., Davidson, N. and Whitehead, M. (eds) 1988: *Inequalities in Health*. Harmondsworth: Penguin.

Trades Union Congress (TUC) 1999: *Labour Market Briefing*. London: TUC.

Tunstill, J. and Aldgate, J. 1999: *Children in Need: From Policy to Practice*. London: HMSO.

Ungerson, C. 1997: Social politics and the decommodification of care. *Social Politics*, 4 (3), 362–82.

Ungerson, C. 2000: Thinking about the production and consumption of long-term care in Britain: does gender still matter? *Journal of Social Policy*, 29 (4), 623–44.

Urry, J. and Wakeford, J. (eds) 1973: *Power in Britain*. London: Heinemann.

Walker, R. and Howard, M. 2000: *The Making of a Welfare Class? Benefit Receipt in Britain*. Bristol: Policy Press.

Walker, R. and Parker, G. (eds) 1988: *Money Matters: Income, Wealth and Financial Welfare*. London: Sage.

Walter, J. A. 1988: *Basic Income: Escape from the Poverty Trap*. London: Marion Boyars.

Webb, A. 1985: Alternative futures for social policy and state welfare. In R. Berthoud (ed.), *Challenges to Social Policy*, Aldershot: Gower, pp. 46–71.

Webster, C. 2002: *The National Health Service: A Political History*. Oxford: Oxford University Press.

Wheelock, J. 1999: Fear or opportunity: insecurity in employment. In J. J. Vail, J. Wheelock and M. Hill (eds), *Insecure Times*, London: Routledge, pp. 75–88.

Wheelock, J. and Vail, J. (eds) 1998: *Work and Idleness: The Political Economy of Full Employment*. Boston, MA: Kluwer.

White, M. 1991: *Against Unemployment*. London: Policy Studies Institute.

Wilcox, S. (ed.) 1998: *Housing Finance Review*. York: Joseph Rowntree Foundation.

Williams, F. 1989: *Social Policy: A Critical Introduction*. Cambridge: Polity Press.

Williams, F. 1999: Good-enough principles for welfare. *Journal of Social Policy*, 28 (4), 667–88.

Williams, F. 2001: Race/ethnicity, gender and class in welfare states: a framework for comparative analysis. In J. Fink, G. Lewis and J. Clarke (eds), *Rethinking European Welfare*, London: Sage.

Williams, P. (ed.) 1997: *New Directions in Housing Policy: Towards Sustainable Housing*. London: Chapman.

Williamson, O. E. 1975: *Markets and Hierarchies: Analysis and Antitrust Implications: A Study in the Economics of Internal Organization*. New York: Free Press.

Willis, P. 1977: *Learning to Labour*. Farnborough: Saxon House.

Wilson, W. J. 1981: Race, class and public policy. *American Sociologist*, 16 (2), 125–34.

Wilson, W. J. 1987: *The Truly Disadvantaged*. Chicago: University of Chicago Press.

Woods, R. 1999: No place like home? Insecurity in housing. In J. J. Vail, J. Wheelock and M. Hill (eds), *Insecure Times*, London: Routledge, pp. 105–18.

Wootton, G. 1970: *Interest Groups*. Englewood Cliffs, NJ: Prentice-Hall.

Index